Greek Cookbook

600 Modern & Authentic Recipes
For Amazing Greek Cooking

Maria Paulalli

Warning-Disclaimer

The purpose of this book is to educate and entertain. The author or publisher does not guarantee that anyone following the techniques, suggestions, tips, ideas, or strategies will become successful. The author and publisher shall have neither liability or responsibility to anyone with respect to any loss or damage caused, or alleged to be caused, directly or indirectly by the information contained in this book.

CONTENTS

INTRODUCTION 9

MOST POPULAR GREEK RECIPES 11

1. Horiatiki Salad (Greek Salad) 11
2. Spanakopita (Spinach & Feta Pie)...................11
3. Lamb Souvlaki 11
4. Moussaka 11
5. Greek Lemon Chicken 12
6. Keftedes (Greek Meatballs) with Tzatziki Sauce ...12
7. Greek Lemon Roasted Vegetables...................12
8. Greek Stuffed Peppers 12
9. Greek Lemon Potatoes...................................12
10. Greek Stuffed Tomatoes 13
11. Greek Lemon Rice 13
12. Fasolada (Greek Bean Soup) 13
13. Greek Baklava 13
14. Greek Meatballs...14
15. Greek Yogurt Chicken...................................14
16. Dolmades (Stuffed Grape Leaves)..................14
17. Saganaki (Fried Cheese).................................14

BREAKFAST 15

18. Bean, Ham & Sweet Potato Omelet..............15
19. Baked Shakshuka Breakfast 15
20. Easy Onion & Mushroom Omelet..................15
21. Scrambled Eggs with Cherry Tomatoes & Zucchini 15
22. Berry & Walnut Oatmeal................................16
23. Speedy Pumpkin Oatmeal..............................16
24. Wake Up Baklava French Toast 16
25. Avocado Toast with Poached Egg...................16
26. Exquisite Fruit Salad......................................17
27. Egg & Zucchini Nests....................................17
28. Almond Grits Drizzled with Honey................17
29. Orange Flavored French Toast 17
30. Egg & Vegetable S&wiches............................17
31. Pecan & Carrot Cupcakes..............................18
32. Scrambled Eggs with Smoked Salmon 18
33. Fried Eggs with Polenta & Vegetables............18
34. Zucchini & Mushroom Egg Muffins 18
35. Raspberry & Oat Pudding..............................18
36. Vegetable & Hummus Breakfast Bowl 19
37. Kale & Cheese Egg Cupcakes.........................19
38. Stuffed Tomatoes with Easy Zucchini & Egg Filling 19
39. Spinach & Artichoke Frittata.........................19
40. Cucumber & Couscous Breakfast Bowl 19
41. Baby Spinach & Anchovy S&wiches...............20
42. Basil-Tomato Eggs...20
43. Cranberry & Apple Oat Porridge....................20
44. Delicious Lentil Stuffed Pitas.........................20
45. Feta Cheese & Sweet Potato Tart 20
46. Quick Berry & Cheese Omelet 21
47. Energy Honey Breakfast Smoothie.................21
48. Strawberry-Chocolate Smoothie.....................21
49. Green Smoothie 21
50. Greek Yogurt & Raspberry Smoothie 21
51. Tomato & Cheese Omelet 21
52. Date-Apple Smoothie.....................................22
53. Peach Smoothie with Maple Syrup 22
54. Breakfast Zinger Smoothie.............................22
55. Power-Packet Juice 22
56. Morning Apple & Pumpkin Cupcakes.............22
57. Fast Blueberry Oatmeal..................................22
58. Red Bell Pepper Omelet 23
59. Green Egg Cupcakes 23
60. Fried Potatoes with Tomato Eggs 23
61. Almond Oatmeal with Chia Seeds..................23
62. Old-Fashioned Oatmeal Bowls.......................23
63. Holiday Pancakes in Berry Sauce....................24
64. Herby Tomato Eggs..24
65. Dakos with Avocado & Tomatoes....................24
66. Poppy Seed Bread with Olives 24
67. Cheesy Egg Scramble 25
68. Feta Frozen Yogurt 25
69. Dill Feta & Olive Breakfast............................25
70. Feta Egg Quiche 25
71. Cilantro Scrambled Eggs with Feta Cheese 25
72. Zucchini & Cheese Tart 26
73. Pita Sandwiches with Yogurt Sauce................26
74. Plum Parfait with Nuts 26
75. Vanilla Yogurt with Walnuts 26
76. Detox Smoothie...26
77. Parsley Tomato & Spinach Egg Wraps 27
78. Buckwheat Pancakes.......................................27
79. Yogurt Parfaits 27
80. Muesli Pots with Pistachio & Pomegranate 27
81. Peach-Yogurt Smoothie..................................27
82. Almond Milk Shake 27

SALADS 28

83. Lettuce Greek Salad.......................................28
84. Authentic Greek Salad....................................28
85. Greek Tuna & Bean Salad...............................28
86. Olive & Feta Salad...28
87. Pasta Salad in Greek Way...............................28
88. Lentil Salad with Kalamata Olives...................29
89. Simple Spring Mix Salad.................................29
90. Cheesy Brown Rice Salad...............................29

91. Chickpea Salad with Greek Flavors 29
92. Cucumber & Corn Salad 29
93. Creamy Potato Salad 30
94. Spinach & Sun-Dried Tomato Farfalle Salad 30
95. Summer Party Salad 30
96. Tangy Cucumber Salad with Mustard Dressing 30
97. Rice & Collard Green Salad 30
98. Chicken & Cucumber Spelt Salad 31
99. Tomato, Bell Pepper & Egg Salad 31
100. Chicken Salad with Avocado 31
101. Lentil & Feta Green Salad 31
102. Chickpea & Bell Pepper Salad 32
103. Green Onion Potato Salad 32
104. Refreshing Yogurt & Cucumber Salad 32
105. Smoked Salmon & Curly Salad 32
106. Vibrant Tri-Color Salad 32
107. Olive & Hazelnut Fennel Salad 32
108. Mustardy Spinach & Tomato Salad with Eggs 33
109. Green & Red Bell Pepper Salad 33
110. Tuna & Chickpea Salad 33
111. Watermelon & Feta Salad with a Balsamic Glaze 33
112. Chickpea & Broccoli Salad 33
113. Bell Pepper & Spinach Salad with Citrus Dressing   33
114. Lentil Bell Pepper Salad 34
115. Shrimp & Bean Salad with Lemon Vinaigrette 34
116. Seafood Salad 34
117. Radish & Mackerel Salad 34
118. Easy Green Salad 34
119. Cabbage Salad with Parsley & Carrots 34
120. Flavorful Cucumber & Couscous Salad 35
121. Delectable Arugula & Caper Green Salad 35
122. Tomato & Carrot Salad 35
123. Asparagus Salad 35
124. Flank Steak Salad with Spinach 35

125. Fennel & Feta Cheese Salad with Pecans 35
126. Power Green Garden Salad 36
127. Parsley Anchovy Salad with Mustard & Honey Vinaigrette 36
128. Almond & Red Cabbage Coleslaw 36
129. Bean Salad with Spinach & Black Olives 36
130. Endive & Cucumber Salad with White Beans 36
131. Chickpea & Arugula Salad 36
132. Dad´s Pork Salad 37
133. Caper & Potato Salad 37
134. Corn, Carrot & Rice Salad 37
135. Anchovy, Cucumber & Tomato Salad 37
136. Walnut, Spinach & Apple Salad 37
137. Figs & Arugula Salad with Tahini Dressing 37
138. Apple, Tomato & Anchovy Salad with Walnuts 38
139. Pea & Spinach Salad with Rice 38
140. Summer Salad with Mustard Dressing 38
141. Easy Black Olive & Radish Salad 38
142. Sweet Potato & Eggplant Salad 38
143. Fennel & Zucchini Salad 38
144. Roasted Veggie & Cheese Salad 39
145. Roasted Cabbage Salad 39
146. Luscious Endive & Pear Salad 39
147. Savory Warm Kale Salad 39
148. Basic Tuna Salad 39
149. Fresh Salad with Sunflower Seeds 40
150. Baked Pork Chop & Arugula Salad 40
151. Baby Spinach & Cherry Tomato Salad 40
152. Sesame Seed & Nut Fruit Salad 40
153. Lemon Bulgur Salad 40
154. Tangy Three-Bean Salad 41
155. Minty Fruit Salad with Cheese 41
156. Palatable Greek Salad 41
157. Bell Pepper & Mushroom Salad 41
158. Shrimp & Bell Pepper Salad with Avocado 41

SOUPS & STEWS 42

159. Green Cream Soup 42
160. Spinach & Mushroom Orzo Soup 42
161. Fire-Roasted Tomato Soup with Spicy Sausage 42
162. Creamy Feta & Cannellini Bean Soup 42
163. Kolokythosoupa (Greek Zucchini Soup) 43
164. Chickpea & Spinach Soup with Savory Sausages 43
165. Greek Bean Soup 43
166. Garden Vegetable Soup 43
167. Spicy Lentil Soup 44
168. Savory Lamb & Spinach Soup 44
169. Hearty Root Veggie Soup 44
170. Roasted Vegetable Soup 44
171. Homestyle Chicken Soup with Fresh Vegetables 44
172. Rice & Green Bean Chicken Soup 45
173. Roasted Red Pepper Soup with Feta 45
174. Carrot & Lentil Soup 45
175. Fennel, Bean & Squash Soup 45
176. Avgolemono Soup (Greek Lemon Chicken Soup) 46
177. Celery Turkey Rice Soup with Fragrant Herbs 46
178. Creamy Potato & White Bean Soup 46

179. Domatosoupa (Greek Tomato Soup) 46
180. Thick & Creamy Tomato Hummus Soup 47
181. Turkey & Cabbage Comfort Soup 47
182. Fall Pork Soup 47
183. Hearty Vegetable Lentil Soup 47
184. Navy Bean Soup with Parsley & Paprika 47
185. Leek & Kale Chicken Soup with Vermicelli 48
186. Magiritsa (Greek Easter Soup with Lamb & Greens) 48
187. Toothsome Eggplant & Chicken Soup 48
188. Stelline Chicken Soup with Garlic & Celery 48
189. Revithosoupa (Greek Chickpea Soup) 48
190. Roasted Eggplant & Tomato Soup 49
191. Scrumptious Veggie Soup 49
192. Ham & Green Lentil Soup 49
193. Easy Lamb Soup 49
194. Cold Tomato Soup with Succulent Prawns 50
195. Farro & White Bean Soup 50
196. Creamy Leek Soup with Toasted Hazelnuts 50
197. Chicken & Bean Soup 50
198. Buttermilk Leek & Shrimp Soup 50

199. Tomato Soup with Fresh Cilantro 51
200. Psarosoupa (Greek Fish Soup) 51
201. Savory Pork Meatball Soup 51
202. Buckwheat Chicken Soup 51
203. Celery & Carrot Bean Soup 52
204. Kale & Cannellini Bean Stew 52
205. Vegetarian Greek Stew 52
206. Delicious Chicken Stew 52
207. Sunday Pork & Mushroom Stew 52
208. Rich Pork Stew 53
209. Hearty Beef Stew with Seasonal Veggies 53
210. Homestyle Vegetable Stew 53

211. Red Pollock & Tomato Stew 53
212. Greek-Inspired Chicken Stew 54
213. Kokkinisto (Greek Red Meat Stew) 54
214. Cheesy Beef Stew with Eggplant 54
215. Creamy Pork Stew in Milky Broth 54
216. Sumptuous Seafood Stew 54
217. Beef Stifado (Greek Beef Stew) 55
218. Arni Fricassee (Greek Lamb Fricassee) 55
219. Horta Yahni (Greek Vegetable Stew) 55
220. Chickpea & Mushroom Stew 55
221. Horta Yahni (Greek Vegetable Stew) 55

BEANS, RICE & GRAINS 56

222. Freekeh Pilaf with Cranberry & Walnuts 56
223. Green Rice Delight 56
224. One-Skillet Vegetable Quinoa & Garbanzo 56
225. Egg Noodles & Bean in Lemon Sauce 56
226. Marinara Beanballs in Tasty Sauce 57
227. Traditional Bean Stew 57
228. Sausage & Tomato Bean Casserole 57
229. Lettuce Rolls with Hummus & Beans 57
230. Spinach & Bean Stew 58
231. Rustic Two-Bean Cassoulet 58
232. Cheesy Bean Rolls 58
233. Bean Bell & Pepper Salad 58
234. Stuffed Sweet Potatoes with Beans 58
235. Lemon Cranberry Beans 59
236. Apricot-Infused Chickpeas with Couscous 59
237. Chickpeas with Lemon & Herbs 59
238. Hot Chicken Lentils 59
239. Chickpea & Black Bean Burgers 60
240. Spinach & Chickpea Bowl 60
241. Garbanzo & Fava Beans 60
242. Revithada (Greek Chickpea Stew with Tomato & Onion)60
243. Lentils & Spinach 60
244. Sautéed Chickpeas with Asparagus 61
245. Faro & Chickpea Stew 61
246. Easy Pork & Garbanzo Cassoulet 61
247. Broccoli & Spinach Rice Bowl 61
248. Green Pepper, Eggplant & Chickpea Casserole 62

249. Cinnamon-Raspberry & Nut Quinoa 62
250. Brown Rice Pilaf with Vegetables 62
251. Caper-Brown Rice Sautée 62
252. Lentil & Rice Salad with Caramelized Onions 62
253. Sun-Dried Tomato & Basil Pilaf 63
254. Cheesy Wild Rice with Mushrooms 63
255. Cherry Tomato Rice Pilaf with Nuts 63
256. Quick Instant Pot Pork with Rice 63
257. Rice & Pork 63
258. Paprika Brown Rice Bowl 64
259. Bell Peppers Filled with Rice 64
260. Simple Brown Rice 64
261. Feta Cheese & Asparagus Rice Salad 64
262. Green Onion & Mushroom Rice Pilaf 64
263. Feta-Vegetable Millet 65
264. Cheesy Lamb Pilaf 65
265. Halloumi-Roasted Pepper Brown Rice 65
266. Mushroom Millet 65
267. Bulgur Pilaf with Almonds & Mushrooms 66
268. Tuna Barley with Okra 66
269. Rosemary Barley with Walnuts 66
270. Energy-Boosting Green Barley Pilaf 66
271. Artichoke Hearts with Pearl Barley 66
272. Sage Farro 67
273. Herby Farro Pilaf 67
274. Zucchini Millet 67
275. Buckwheat with Fresh Tarragon 67

POULTRY 68

276. Baked Chicken with Fusilli 68
277. Chicken & Potato Greek Delight 68
278. Hearty Greek-Style Chicken Stew 68
279. Herb-Infused Chicken with Asparagus Sauce 68
280. Mushroom Pappardelle with Greek-Style Chicken   69
281. Syrupy Chicken with Green Peas 69
282. Creamy Green Bean & Chicken Bake 69
283. Chicken & Egg Casserole 69
284. Chicken Rice Bowls with Dried Apricots 70
285. Saucy Chicken with Grapes 70
286. Ground Chicken Balls with Yogurt-Cucumber Sauce 70
287. Chicken Breasts with Chickpeas & Olives 70
288. Chicken & Vegetable Stir-Fry 71
289. Tomato-Glazed Chicken 71

290. Chicken Loaf with Tzatziki Sauce 71
291. Nutty-Topped Chicken Breasts 71
292. Yummy Chicken with Creamy Yogurt Sauce 71
293. Wine Chicken with Green Beans 72
294. Oven Baked Chicken with Root Vegetables 72
295. Feta-Topped Chicken Breasts 72
296. Halloumi Cheese & Chicken 72
297. Almond Chicken with Eggplants 72
298. Wine-Braised Chicken Breasts with Capers 73
299. Baby Potatoes & Chicken Traybake 73
300. Sautéed Asparagus & Chicken 73
301. Chicken Souvlaki with Vegetables 73
302. Creamy Drunken Chicken with Mushrooms 73
303. Chicken & Bean Cassoulet 74

304. Mushroom & Chicken Kabobs....................74
305. Hot Chicken Sausages with Pepper Sauce.......74
306. Delectable Chicken Pot........................74
307. Mushroom Chicken Breasts......................74
308. Juicy Chicken Breasts.........................75
309. Herby Chicken Bake............................75
310. Balsamic Chicken & Spinach Dish...............75
311. Lemony Chicken Meatballs with Peach Topping...75
312. Bell Peppers & Chicken Skillet................75
313. Chicken with Spinach & Chickpeas..............76
314. Creamy Chicken Breasts with White Sauce.......76
315. Thyme Chicken Casserole.......................76
316. Oven Roasted Peppery Chicken..................76
317. Cilantro Chicken Bowl.........................76
318. Chicken White Bean Casserole..................77
319. Stir-Fried Chicken with Zucchini..............77
320. Herbed Chicken with Tomatoes.................77
321. Cheesy Chicken Breasts........................77
322. Greek-Style Chicken Wings.....................77

323. Chicken Breasts with Greek Sauce..............78
324. Zucchini & Chicken Dish.......................78
325. Potato, Carrot & Chicken Bake.................78
326. Walnut Chicken with Tomatoes..................78
327. Carrot Chicken with Farro.....................78
328. Chicken with Caper Sauce......................79
329. Orange Chicken Thighs.........................79
330. Tasty Chicken with Green Peas.................79
331. Hot Chicken Lentils with Artichokes...........79
332. Lemony Chicken Breasts........................79
333. Almond Chicken Balls..........................80
334. Traditional Chicken Souvlaki..................80
335. Peach Glazed Chicken Drumsticks...............80
336. Basil Tomato Chicken Breasts..................80
337. Roasted Artichokes & Chicken Thighs...........80
338. Easy Chicken with Olive Tapenade.............81
339. Quick One-Pan Turkey..........................81
340. Turkey Ham Stuffed Peppers....................81
341. Turkey with Green Veggies.....................81

PORK, BEEF & LAMB 82

342. Cheesy Pork Chops.............................82
343. Pork Souvlaki with Apricot Glaze..............82
344. Garlicky Pork in Spicy Sauce..................82
345. Onion & Bell Pepper Pork Chops................82
346. Cheesy Spinach-Filled Pork Loin Delight.......83
347. Almond-Smothered Cocktail Meatballs...........83
348. Pork Chops with Apricot Chutney...............83
349. Pork Loin stuffed with Vegetables.............83
350. Melt-in-your-mouth Pork Shoulder..............84
351. Savory Rosemary Pork Chops with Veggie Medley 84
352. Pork Sausage & Herby Eggs.....................84
353. One-Tray Baked Pork Chops.....................84
354. Roast Pork Loin with Green Onions.............84
355. Sweet-Mustard Pork Chops......................85
356. Creamy Pork Tenderloin with Caraway Seeds.....85
357. Bell Pepper Pork Stew.........................85
358. Skordalia Pork Shoulder.......................85
359. Pork Loin in Oregano Tomato Sauce.............85
360. Rosemary Pork Chops in Tomato Sauce...........85
361. Quick & Easy Pork Skewers.....................86
362. Tangy Mustard Pork Tenderloin.................86
363. Cilantro-Mustard-Glazed Pork Loin.............86
364. Slow Cooker Flavorful Pork Loin...............86
365. Green Vegetable Pork Chops....................86
366. Effortless Pork Stew..........................87
367. Leek Pork Butt Delight........................87
368. One-Skillet Pork Chops in Tomato-Olive Sauce..87
369. Thyme Pork Chops..............................87
370. Chestnut & Pork Millet........................87
371. Succulent Pan-Seared Pork Chops...............88
372. Fiery Pork Meatballs..........................88
373. Mushroom Mix & Beef Stew......................88
374. Wine-Infused Pork Chops.......................88
375. Flavorful Pork Stew...........................88

376. Apple-Glazed Roasted Pork Tenderloin.........89
377. No-fuss Pork Stew.............................89
378. Hearty Mushroom Pork Stew.....................89
379. Greek Pork Au Gratin..........................89
380. Luscious Pork in Cilantro Sauce...............89
381. Party Pork Chops with Squash & Zucchini.......90
382. Peppery Parsnip & Pork........................90
383. Orecchiette Pasta with Mushroom & Sausage.....90
384. Minty Fried Beef Meatballs....................90
385. Flavorful Spiced Beef Meatballs..............90
386. Beef Gyro with Veggies........................91
387. Skirt Steak with Mushroom Mustard Sauce.......91
388. Classic Greek Meatballs.......................91
389. Baked Beef Ribs...............................91
390. Tasty Slow Cooker Beef Stew...................92
391. Greek-Inspired Burgers........................92
392. Zesty & Spicy Beef Zoodles....................92
393. Fragrant Aromatic Beef Stew...................92
394. Bell Pepper & Beef Casserole..................92
395. Tender Beef Filet Mignon in Savory Mushroom Sauce 93
396. Orange Flank Steak............................93
397. Savory Spiced Beef Meatballs..................93
398. Hearty Beef Stew..............................93
399. Allspice Beef Stuffed Peppers.................94
400. Beef Steak with Kale Slaw & Bell Peppers......94
401. Hearty Beef & Vegetable Stew..................94
402. Savory Shallot & Beef Dish....................94
403. Kalogeros (Beef with Tomato Sauce)............94
404. Scallion Beef with Walnuts....................95
405. Best-Ever Rich Beef Meal......................95
406. Seared Peach Lamb.............................95
407. Traditional Greek Roasted Lamb & Potatoes.....95
408. Creamy Fig & Yogurt Lamb Stew.................95
409. Succulent Lamb Kebabs with Yogurt Sauce.......96

410. Basil Leg Lamb 96
411. Lamb with Broccoli 96
412. Festive Holiday Leg of Lamb Delight 96
413. Paprika-Spiced Lamb with Hearty Beans 96
414. Hot Lamb with Fluffy Couscous & Chickpeas 97
415. Lamb Eggplant Moussaka 97
416. Succulent Eggplant Lamb 97

FISH & SEAFOOD 98

417. Roasted Salmon with Parsley 98
418. Juicy Salmon in Thyme Tomato Sauce 98
419. Skillet Salmon with Olives & Escarole 98
420. Savory Fennel & Bell Pepper Salmon 98
421. Wholesome Cod & Potato Dish 98
422. Deliciously Seasoned Cod 99
423. Simple Salmon Parcels 99
424. Flavorful Oven-Baked Salmon 99
425. Roasted Salmon with Asparagus 99
426. Cod Poached in Oil 99
427. Creamy Fettuccine with Cod 100
428. Salmon Coated in Walnut Crust 100
429. Easy Salmon with Balsamic Haricots Vert 100
430. Cheesy Tomato Cod 100
431. Cod with Luscious Calamari Rings 100
432. Cabbage-Roasted Cod 101
433. Fiery Cod Fillets 101
434. Mushroom-Smothered Cod Fillets 101
435. Cod Skewers Bursting with Fresh Herbs 101
436. Tarragon Haddock with Capers 101
437. Hearty Herbed Cod Stew 102
438. Cod Casserole with Leeks & Olives 102
439. Cod Fillets in White Wine Sauce 102
440. Rosemary Baked Haddock 102
441. Tomato-Dill Baked Haddock 102
442. Capered Tarragon Haddock 103
443. Tilapia with Fresh Parsley & Tomato 103
444. Flavorful Tilapia Pilaf 103
445. Creamy Avocado & Onion Tilapia 103
446. Halibut with Roasted Pepper & Parsley Garnish 103
447. Zesty Flounder with Vibrant Pasta Salad 104
448. Halibut Baked with Savory Eggplant Topping 104
449. Sautéed Leeks & Halibut Confit 104
450. Golden Crispy Sole Fillets 104
451. Bean & Canned Tuna Bowl 104
452. Spicy Flounder Parcels 105
453. Creamy Potato & Halibut Chowder 105
454. Citrus-Crusted Roasted Red Snapper 105
455. Yummy Mustard Sardine Cakes 105
456. Tzatziki Tuna Gyros 106
457. Herby Sauce-Grilled Sardines 106
458. Zesty Lemon-Garlic Sea Bass 106
459. Home-Style Tuna Burgers 106
460. Tuna Medley with Pan-Fried Vegetables 106
461. Mackerel Fillets in Herby Red Sauce 107
462. Barramundi with Date & Hazelnut Crust 107
463. Thyme Potato Hake 107
464. Avocado Anchovy Dip 107
465. Flame-Grilled Fish Fillets 107
466. Basil Hake Fillet with Tomato Sauce 108
467. Spicy Garlic Baked Anchovies 108
468. Crispy Fried Pollock Fillets 108
469. Crunchy Breaded Fish Sticks 108
470. Trout with Tzatziki Sauce 108
471. Herring & Caper Deviled Eggs 109
472. Lemon Rice & Baked Cod 109
473. Traditional Garidomakaronada (Shrimp & Pasta) 109
474. Black Olive & Shrimp Quinoa Bowl 109
475. Bulgur with Shrimp & Feta 110
476. Spinach Shrimp 110
477. Celery Sticks Stuffed with Crab 110
478. Squid & Shrimp Medley 110
479. Spicy Tomato & Caper Squid Stew 111
480. Garlic-Cilantro Calamari 111
481. Mushroom Prawns 111
482. Caper Prawns 111
483. Squid Stwe with Capers 111
484. Tomato Sauce with Shrimp & Salmon 112
485. Avocado-Enhanced Salmon Tartare 112
486. Smoked Salmon & Eggplant Rolls with Dill 112
487. Delectable Salmon Stuffed Peppers 112
488. Tomato-Caper Roasted Salmon 112
489. Delicate Orange Salmon Encased in Parchment 113
490. Grecian Sauce-Topped Crispy Salmon Patties 113
491. Celery Egg Bake with Salmon 113
492. Cucumber & Salmon Rolls 113
493. Skillet Seared Scallops & Bell Peppers 113
494. Salmon Coated in Almond Crust 114
495. Citrus-Infused Trout with Roasted Beets 114
496. Trout & Farro Bowls with Creamy Avocado 114
497. Lemony Trout fillets with Horseradish Sauce 114
498. Shrimp & White Bean Pot 114
499. Roasted Vegetables with Shrimp 115
500. Gnocchi & Shrimp with Feta Cheese 115
501. Succulent Scallops with Basil & Tomato 115
502. Black Olive & Lemon Shrimp Dish 115
503. Zucchini & Squid Dish 116
504. Tangy Lime & Orange Squid Dish 116
505. Lemon-Butter Drunken Mussels 116
506. Hearty Chickpea & Clam Stew with Veggies 116
507. Mussels & Spaghetti in Sauce 116
508. Marinara-Style Mussels with Leeks & Herbs 117
509. Clams & Snow Peas with Scallions 117
510. Clams in a Fragrant Sherry & Parsley Sauce 117
511. Steamed Clams in a White Wine 117
512. Seafood & Vegetable Stew 117

MEATLESS RECIPES 118

513. Baked Eggplant Rounds.....................118
514. Halloumi & Mint Bulgur Delight.....................118
515. Chickpea Cakes with Zesty Cilantro-Yogurt Sauce 118
516. Plant-Based Lentil Burgers 118
517. Broccoli Florets with Yogurt Sauce.....................119
518. Nutty Yogurt-Drizzled Steamed Beetroots.....................119
519. Charred Eggplant "Steaks" with Sauce 119
520. Timeless Pasta with Feta Cheese.....................119
521. Fiery Grilled Eggplant Discs.....................119
522. Classic Meatless Moussaka.....................120

523. Baked Zucchini Delight with Parsley & Olives 120
524. Feta Cheese & Swiss Chard Couscous Medley..........120
525. Couscous with Kale & Feta Cheese 120
526. Tempting Stuffed Cherry Tomatoes.....................120
527. Feta-Stuffed Baked Zucchini Boats.....................121
528. Feta-Topped Baked Beetroot Fries.....................121
529. Green Bean Quinoa.....................121
530. Hot Collard Green Oats with Halloumi.....................121
531. Ridiculously Easy Bean with Olives 121

SIDES, SAUCES & SPICES 122

532. Cheesy Pepper-Stuffed Tomatoes.....................122
533. Zesty Red Pepper & Olive Spread.....................122
534. Garlicky Broccoli Stir Fry 122
535. Feta Sweet Potato Mash 122
536. Cauliflower Mash with Fragrant Cumin 122
537. Beloved Green Bean Stir-Fry 123
538. Arugula & Zucchini Stuffed Mushrooms.....................123
539. Cheesy Olive Tapenade Flatbread 123
540. Broccoli & Cheese Quiche.....................123
541. Homemade Marinara Sauce.....................124
542. Zucchini Pasta in Tomato-Mushroom Sauce.....................124
543. Herbed Garlic Butter Spread.....................124
544. Spicy Green Chili & Herb Sauce 124

545. Roasted Asparagus & Red Onion Side Dish.....................124
546. Cheesy Zucchini Strips 125
547. Vegetarian Cream Sauce 125
548. Classic Tahini Sauce 125
549. Cherry Tomato & Fennel Roast 125
550. Spinach Side with Pine Nuts & Raisins 125
551. Fresh Herb Yogurt Sauce.....................125
552. Infused Olive Oil with Rosemary & Garlic.....................126
553. Velvety Mushroom Sauce.....................126
554. Lemony Greek Olive Oil Dressing (Ladolemono) ...126
555. Refreshing Lemon Yogurt Sauce.....................126
556. Creamy Walnut-Cucumber Yogurt Sauce.....................126

SNACKS 127

557. Peinirli (Greek Pizza) 127
558. Traditional Greek Potato Skins 127
559. Creamy White Bean Dip 127
560. Greek Yogurt Dip on Grilled Pita 127
561. Greek Cucumber Yogurt Dip.....................127
562. Flavorful Greek-Style Wraps 128
563. Roasted Sweet Potatoes with Chickpeas 128
564. Savory Roasted Butternut Squash with Tahini & Feta..128
565. Crispy Sweet Potatoes Sheet Pan 128
566. Creamy Garlic-Yogurt Dip with Walnuts 128
567. Silky Trout Spread.....................129

568. Fluffy Whipped Feta Spread.....................129
569. Hummus & Tomato Filled Cucumbers 129
570. Mouthwatering Baby Artichoke Meze 129
571. Crispy Feta & Zucchini Rosti Cakes.....................129
572. Carrot Medley with Balsamic Drizzle & Feta 129
573. Skordalia Grilled Halloumi Cheese.....................130
574. Garlicky Roasted Feta Cheese.....................130
575. Feta-Topped Vegetable Gratin 130
576. Savory Zucchini Fritters with Feta Cheese.....................130
577. Tasty Cucumber Bite Canapés 130

DESSERTS 131

578. Peach & Walnut Cake with Caramel Drizzle.....................131
579. Layered Strawberry Parfait.....................131
580. Peach & Pecan Parfait.....................131
581. Chia Banana Walnut Oatmeal.....................131
582. Yogurt & Banana Dessert Cups.....................131
583. Apple Slices with Cardamom 132
584. Bulgur Bowl with Cherries & Almonds.....................132
585. Assorted Fresh Fruit Cups.....................132
586. Frozen Yogurt Cups with Raspberry & Pecan Topping ..132
587. Pecan Stuffed Apples.....................132
588. Walnut Carrot Cake.....................132
589. Pomegranate Dark Chocolate Barks 133

590. Kid-Friendly Marzipan Bites 133
591. Pear & Pecan Crisp with Cinnamon Oats 133
592. Cinnamon Spiced Hot Chocolate.....................133
593. Vanilla Labneh Fruit Skewers.....................134
594. Mixed Berry Sorbet.....................134
595. Dark Chocolate Avocado Mousse.....................134
596. Chocolate Chia Seed Pudding.....................134
597. Classic Vanilla Cheesecake Squares 134
598. Orange Muffins 135
599. Greek-Style Orange Mug Cake 135
600. No-Bake Walnut Date Oatmeal Bars 135

INTRODUCTION

Kalimera! Welcome to my Greek cookbook!

We're thrilled to share our love for Greek cooking with you. Whether you're a novice or an experienced cook, this cookbook has something for everyone. My goal is to help you create truly unique and delicious Greek dishes that will delight your taste buds.

While Greek cuisine offers complexity and textures, I have simplified the recipes to make them accessible for weeknight cooking.

Greek food is all about balance—flavor, nuance, and temperature. By using the right combination of spices, mastering techniques like roasting and toasting, and blending richness with acidity and heat with creaminess or a touch of sweetness, you can achieve magnificent results.

A Bit of History

Greek cuisine is deeply rooted in the Mediterranean culinary tradition, one of the most popular in the world. It's a diverse and varied cuisine influenced by Europe, the Americas, Africa, and Asia. Greek food holds great significance in Greek culture and history and has also formed cooking and eating habits worldwide.

The origins of Greek cuisine can be traced back to the regional cuisines of ancient Greece, which were shaped by different social classes, agricultural conditions, and culinary traditions across the country. Throughout history, Greek cuisine has been influenced by travelers to and from Greece, resulting in various ingredients we all love.

Greek flavors

To embark on your Greek culinary journey, it's important to understand the basic flavor profiles of different ingredients. Once you grasp the harmonious combination of flavors, you can create Greek recipes without strictly following a recipe.

The foundation of Greek cuisine lies in the vibrant flavors of basil, thyme, rosemary, and olive oil. These bold and aromatic flavors allow for endless creativity in the kitchen.

Greek Staples

Greek cuisine extends far beyond the iconic moussaka and souvlaki. Greek cooking offers many possibilities, from delightful seafood and succulent meats to fresh fruits, vegetables, cheeses, and nuts.

These staples will ensure you are prepped and ready to cook accessible Greek food favorites any day of the week.

Must-Have Greek pantry essentials for Greek food enthusiasts:

- Extra Virgin Olive Oil
- Greek yogurt
- Feta cheese
- Kalamata olives
- Canned beans
- Greek Oregano
- Dill
- Lemon
- Garlic
- Lemon

Greek food lovers, this Homemade Greek Seasoning is for you!

Say goodbye to store-bought Greek seasoning! Get ready to elevate your Greek dishes to new heights with this mind-blowingly delicious homemade Greek seasoning. Here's a quick recipe to make yours:

My magic ingredients for ½ cup made only in 5 minutes:

- 1 tablespoon dried Greek oregano
- 2 tablespoons dried thyme
- 2 tablespoons dried basil
- 1 tablespoon dried parsley
- 1 tablespoon dried rosemary
- 1 tablespoon dried dill
- 1 tablespoon onion powder,
- 1 teaspoon garlic powder
- Salt and black pepper to taste

In a bowl, combine all the ingredients. Store the Greek seasoning in an airtight container in a cool, dark place for up to 6 months. Greek seasoning adds flavor to grilled meats, roasted vegetables, salads, soups, and stews. It can also be a dry rub for chicken, lamb, or fish. Adjust the quantities of the ingredients according to your taste preferences.

About the Recipes

Are you craving delicious Greek flavors without spending hours in the kitchen? You've come to the right place. This cookbook is designed to provide you with easy and mouthwatering recipes. Whether you're seeking breakfast ideas, appetizers, satisfying lunches, or delectable dinners, we've got you covered.

And finally, here are some interesting facts: do you know...?

I love Greek food, and we're sure you do, too. Whether you're a huge fan of moussaka or just looking for something new to try in your favorite restaurant, there are so many reasons why it's such a fantastic cuisine.

Here are 10 interesting facts about Greek food that I think you'll love!

1. The Mediterranean Diet, which is influenced by Greek cuisine, has been recognized as one of the healthiest diets in the world. It emphasizes fresh fruits, vegetables, grains, legumes, and olive oil.

2. Greek cuisine has a long history dating back thousands of years. Some traditional Greek recipes can be traced back to ancient times, making Greek food a culinary treasure.

3. The popular Feta cheese is a protected designation of origin (PDO) product, meaning it can only be produced in specific regions of Greece using traditional methods.

4. Greece is known for its wide variety of olives. There are over 120 different varieties of olives grown in the country, ranging in size, color, and flavor.

5. Greeks are passionate about their coffee. Greek coffee is prepared in a traditional pot called a "briki" and is often enjoyed with a touch of sweetness.

6. Spanakopita, a popular Greek dish, combines spinach and feta cheese in a flaky phyllo pastry. It is said that there are over 50 different variations of spanakopita throughout Greece.

7. Greece is famous for its delicious street food. Souvlaki, a popular Greek fast food, consists of grilled skewered meat (pork or chicken) served on pita bread with tzatziki sauce and garnishes.

8. Ouzo, a traditional Greek liqueur, is often enjoyed as an aperitif or digestif. It is made from distilled grapes and flavored with anise, giving it a distinct licorice-like taste.

9. The island of Santorini is renowned for its unique cherry tomatoes, which are grown in volcanic soil and have a sweet, intense flavor. Chefs around the world highly seek after them.

10. Greek desserts are a delight for the sweet tooth. Baklava, a rich pastry made with layers of phyllo, nuts, and honey syrup, is a beloved Greek dessert enjoyed on special occasions.

I hope these fun facts have piqued your interest and added excitement to your journey through Greek cuisine. Get ready to explore the rich flavors, vibrant ingredients, and timeless traditions that make Greek food genuinely exceptional.. Opa!

MOST POPULAR GREEK RECIPES

1. Horiatiki Salad (Greek Salad)

Serves: 4 | Ready in about: 15 minutes

4 cups chopped romaine lettuce
1 cup chopped cucumber
1 cup chopped tomato
½ cup sliced red onion

½ cup crumbled feta cheese
¼ cup pitted kalamata olives
2 tbsp olive oil
2 tbsp red wine vinegar

1 tsp dried oregano
Salt and pepper to taste

In a bowl, combine the lettuce, cucumber, tomato, red onion, feta cheese, and olives. In another bowl, whisk the olive oil, red wine vinegar, oregano, salt, and pepper. Drizzle the resulting dressing over the salad and toss to combine.

2. Spanakopita (Spinach & Feta Pie)

Serves: 4 | Ready in about: 60 minutes

10 oz fresh spinach, torn
1 cup crumbled feta cheese

2 green onions, chopped
2 eggs, beaten

8 sheets phyllo dough
½ cup butter, melted

Preheat the oven to 375 F. In a bowl, mix well the spinach, feta, green onions, and eggs. Layer the first four sheets of phyllo dough in a greased baking dish, brushing each layer with butter. Evenly spread the spinach mixture over the fourth sheet. Place the remaining four sheets of phyllo dough over the spinach mixture, coating each layer with butter. Bake for 35-40 minutes or until the top is golden brown and crisp. Allow to cool for 10 minutes. Serve sliced.

3. Lamb Souvlaki

Serves: 4 | Ready in about: 40 minutes

1 lb boneless lamb, cut into 1-inch cubes
¼ cup olive oil
2 tbsp lemon juice
2 cloves garlic, minced

1 tsp dried oregano
Salt and pepper to taste
4 pita pieces of bread

½ cup tzatziki sauce

In a bowl, whisk the olive oil, lemon juice, garlic, oregano, salt, and pepper. Add in the lamb cubes and toss to coat. Cover and refrigerate for 40 minutes. Preheat the grill to medium-high heat. Thread the lamb cubes onto skewers. Grill them for 8-10 minutes, turning occasionally, until the lamb is cooked through. Put the pita bread on the grill for 1-2 minutes per side. Serve the lamb skewers with warm pita bread and tzatziki sauce.

4. Moussaka

Serves: 4 | Ready in about: 2 hours

1 lb ground beef
1 onion, chopped
2 cloves garlic, minced
¼ cup tomato paste
¼ cup red wine

1 tsp dried oregano
Salt and pepper to taste
1 eggplant, sliced into ¼-inch rounds
¼ cup olive oil
¼ cup all-purpose flour

2 cups milk
¼ tsp ground nutmeg
½ cup grated Halloumi cheese

Preheat the oven to 375 F. Warm the olive oil in a skillet over medium heat and cook the ground beef until browned. Add onion and garlic and cook for 3 more minutes or until softened. Stir in the tomato paste, red wine, oregano, salt, and pepper. Simmer for 10 minutes.

Meanwhile, brush the eggplant slices with olive oil and season with salt and pepper. Grill or broil until tender and lightly browned. In a saucepan, whisk together the flour, milk, nutmeg, salt, and pepper. Cook over medium heat, stirring constantly, until the sauce thickens. Layer the eggplant slices in the bottom of the prepared baking dish.

Top with the ground beef mixture. Pour the milk mixture over the top. Sprinkle the Halloumi cheese over the top of the moussaka. Bake for 45-50 minutes or until the top is golden brown and the filling is bubbly. Allow to cool for 10 minutes before serving.

5. Greek Lemon Chicken

Serves: 4 | Ready in about: 45 minutes

4 boneless, skinless chicken breasts
¼ cup olive oil
¼ cup lemon juice

2 cloves garlic, minced
1 tsp dried oregano
Salt and pepper to taste

1 lemon, sliced

Preheat the oven to 375 F. In a bowl, mix together the olive oil, lemon juice, garlic, oregano, salt, and pepper. Place the chicken in a greased baking dish. Pour the lemon marinade over the top. Arrange the lemon slices around the chicken. Bake for 30-35 minutes or until the chicken is cooked through. Serve hot with the lemon slices.

6. Keftedes (Greek Meatballs) with Tzatziki Sauce

Serves: 4 | Ready in about: 45 minutes

1 lb ground beef
¼ cup chopped onion
2 cloves garlic, minced
¼ cup chopped fresh parsley
¼ cup chopped fresh mint

½ cup breadcrumbs
1 egg, beaten
Salt and pepper to taste
¼ cup olive oil
½ cup Greek yogurt

½ cucumber, grated and drained
1 clove garlic, minced
1 tbsp lemon juice

In a large bowl, combine the ground beef, onion, garlic, parsley, mint, breadcrumbs, egg, salt, and pepper. Mix well. Roll the mixture into 1-inch balls. Heat the olive oil in a large skillet over medium heat. Add the meatballs and cook until browned on all sides. Meanwhile, in a small bowl, whisk together the Greek yogurt, grated cucumber, garlic, lemon juice, salt, and pepper. Serve the meatballs hot with the tzatziki sauce.

7. Greek Lemon Roasted Vegetables

Serves: 4 | Ready in about: 60 minutes

1 lb baby potatoes, halved
1 red onion, chopped
2 bell peppers, chopped

1 zucchini, sliced
¼ cup olive oil
2 tbsp lemon juice

2 cloves garlic, minced
1 tsp dried oregano
Salt and pepper to taste

Preheat the oven to 375 F. Grease a baking sheet. In a small bowl, whisk together the olive oil, lemon juice, garlic, oregano, salt, and pepper. Place the potatoes, onion, bell peppers, and zucchini on the prepared baking sheet. Drizzle the lemon marinade over the vegetables and toss to coat. Roast for 35-40 minutes or until the vegetables are tender and lightly browned. Serve hot as a side dish.

8. Greek Stuffed Peppers

Serves: 4 | Ready in about: 60 minutes

2 tsp olive oil
4 bell peppers, halved and seeded
1 lb ground beef
1 onion, chopped

2 cloves garlic, minced
¼ cup chopped fresh parsley
¼ cup chopped fresh mint
½ cup cooked rice

¼ cup tomato paste
½ cup crumbled feta cheese
Salt and pepper to taste

Preheat the oven to 375 F. Warm the olive oil in a large skillet over medium heat and cook the onion and garlic for 3 minutes or until softened. Stir in the ground beef and cook until browned. Add parsley, mint, rice, tomato paste, feta cheese, salt, and pepper. Fill each pepper half with the ground beef mixture. Arrange the stuffed peppers on a greased baking dish. Bake for 35-40 minutes or until the peppers are tender and the filling is hot and bubbly. Serve hot with your favorite side dish.

9. Greek Lemon Potatoes

Serves: 4 | Ready in about: 60 minutes

4 potatoes, peeled and cut into wedges
¼ cup olive oil

¼ cup lemon juice
2 cloves garlic, minced

1 tsp dried oregano
Salt and pepper to taste

Preheat the oven to 375 F. In a bowl, whisk together the olive oil, lemon juice, garlic, oregano, salt, and pepper. Place the potato wedges in a greased baking dish. Pour the lemon marinade over the top. Toss the potatoes to coat in the marinade. Bake for 35-40 minutes or until the potatoes are tender and lightly browned. Serve hot as a side dish.

10. Greek Stuffed Tomatoes

Serves: 4 | Ready in about: 60 minutes

4 large tomatoes, tops removed and seeded	½ cup crumbled feta cheese	¼ cup chopped onion
	¼ cup chopped fresh parsley	2 cloves garlic, minced
1 cup cooked rice	¼ cup chopped fresh mint	Salt and pepper to taste

Preheat the oven to 375 F. Grease a baking dish. In a large bowl, combine the rice, feta cheese, parsley, mint, onion, garlic, salt, and pepper. Stuff the tomato cavities with the rice mixture. Place the stuffed tomatoes in the prepared baking dish. Bake for 35-40 minutes or until the tomatoes are tender and the filling is hot and bubbly. Serve hot with your favorite side dish.

11. Greek Lemon Rice

Serves: 4 | Ready in about: 30 minutes

1 cup long-grain white rice	2 tbsp lemon juice	Salt and pepper to taste
2 cups chicken broth	2 cloves garlic, minced	
¼ cup olive oil	1 tsp dried oregano	

In a medium saucepan, combine the rice, chicken broth, olive oil, lemon juice, garlic, oregano, salt, and pepper. Bring the mixture to a boil, then reduce heat and simmer for 20-25 minutes or until the rice is tender and the liquid has been absorbed. Fluff the rice with a fork before serving.

12. Fasolada (Greek Bean Soup)

Serves: 4 | Ready in about: 30 minutes

1 cup canned white beans	2 celery stalks, chopped	2 tbsp tomato paste
1 onion, chopped	2 cloves garlic, minced	1 tsp dried oregano
2 carrots, chopped	¼ cup olive oil	Salt and pepper to taste

In a large pot, heat the olive oil over medium heat. Add the onion, carrots, celery, and garlic. Cook until softened. Add the beans, tomato paste, oregano, salt, and pepper to the pot. Cover with water. Bring the soup to a boil, then reduce the heat and simmer for 20 minutes. Serve hot with crusty bread.

13. Greek Baklava

Serves: 4 | Ready in about: 2 hours

1 lb phyllo dough	½ cup sugar	½ cup honey
1 cup unsalted butter, melted	1 tsp ground cinnamon	¼ cup water
2 cups chopped walnuts	½ tsp ground cloves	1 tbsp lemon juice

Preheat the oven to 350 F. In a bowl, combine the walnuts, sugar, cinnamon, and cloves. Place one sheet of phyllo dough on the bottom of a greased baking dish and brush it with melted butter. Repeat with seven more sheets of phyllo dough, brushing each layer with butter. Sprinkle half of the walnut mixture over the phyllo dough.

Layer 8 more sheets of phyllo dough on top of the walnut mixture, brushing each layer with butter. Sprinkle the remaining walnut mixture over the phyllo dough.

Layer the remaining sheets of phyllo dough on top of the walnut mixture, brushing each layer with butter. Use a sharp knife to cut the baklava into diamond shapes. Bake for 45-50 minutes or until the top is golden brown and crisp.

In a small saucepan, combine the honey, water, and lemon juice. Bring to a simmer and cook for 5 minutes. Pour the honey mixture over the hot baklava. Allow the baklava to cool completely before serving.

14. Greek Meatballs

Serves: 4 | Ready in about: 45 minutes

1 lb ground beef
½ cup breadcrumbs
¼ cup chopped onion

¼ cup chopped fresh parsley
2 cloves garlic, minced
1 egg, beaten

1 tsp dried oregano
Salt and pepper to taste
¼ cup olive oil

Preheat the oven to 375 F. In a bowl, combine the ground beef, breadcrumbs, onion, parsley, garlic, egg, oregano, salt, and pepper. Mix well. Roll the mixture into 1-inch balls. Warm the olive oil in a large skillet over medium heat. Add the meatballs and cook until browned on all sides. Transfer the meatballs to a greased baking sheet. Bake for 15-20 minutes or until cooked through. Serve hot with your favorite dipping sauce.

15. Greek Yogurt Chicken

Serves: 4 | Ready in about: 45 minutes

4 boneless, skinless chicken breasts
1 cup plain Greek yogurt

¼ cup chopped fresh parsley
2 cloves garlic, minced

1 tsp dried oregano
Salt and pepper to taste

Preheat the oven to 375 F. Grease a baking dish. Whisk together the Greek yogurt, parsley, garlic, oregano, salt, and pepper in a small bowl. Place the chicken breasts in the prepared baking dish. Spread the yogurt mixture over the top. Bake for 30-35 minutes or until the chicken is cooked through and no longer pink in the center. Serve hot with your favorite side dish.

16. Dolmades (Stuffed Grape Leaves)

Serves: 4 | Ready in about: 70 minutes

1 jar grape leaves
1 cup white rice
1 medium onion, chopped

2 tsp chopped dill
2 tsp chopped parsley
2 tbsp olive oil

1 tbsp lemon juice
Salt and pepper to taste
Lemon wedges for serving

Rinse grape leaves under cold water and remove any stems. Combine the rice, onion, dill, parsley, olive oil, lemon juice, salt, and pepper in a bowl. Mix well to combine. Add a spoonful of the rice mixture to the center of each grape leaf. Roll up, folding in the ends to secure. Repeat with the remaining ingredients.

In a large pot, arrange the dolmades in a single layer, seam side down. Layer them tightly, ensuring they are snugly packed to prevent them from unraveling during cooking. Add enough water to the pot to cover the dolmades. Place a heatproof plate that fits inside the pot on top of the dolmades.

Put the pot over medium heat. Bring the dolmades to a boil. Reduce the heat and cover the pot. Let the dolmades simmer for 45-60 minutes or until the rice is tender. Once cooked, remove the dolmades from the pot and let them cool slightly. Garnish with lemon wedges to add a tangy burst of flavor. Squeeze the lemon wedges over the dolmades. Enjoy!

17. Saganaki (Fried Cheese)

Serves: 4 | Ready in about: 70 minutes

8 oz Kasseri cheese
2 tablespoons all-purpose flour

1 tablespoon olive oil
1 lemon, cut into wedges

Freshly ground black pepper to taste
2 tbsp fresh parsley for garnish

Cut the cheese into thick slices, about 1/2 inch wide. Place the flour on a shallow plate. Dredge each piece of cheese in the flour, making sure to coat all sides evenly. Shake off any excess flour.

Warm the olive oil in a non-stick pan over medium heat for 2 minutes. Add the coated cheese slices to the pan, being careful not to overcrowd the pan. Fry the cheese for 2-3 minutes per side or until golden brown, soft, and melted. Remove the Saganaki from the skillet and transfer it to a serving plate.

Squeeze some fresh lemon juice over the Saganaki and scatter with freshly ground black pepper. Garnish with parsley. Serve the Saganaki immediately accompanied by crusty bread or pita if desired.

BREAKFAST

18. Bean, Ham & Sweet Potato Omelet

Serves: 4 | Ready in about: 25 minutes

2 sweet potatoes, boiled and chopped
2 tbsp olive oil
4 eggs, whisked
1 red onion, chopped

¾ cup ham, chopped
½ cup white beans, cooked
2 tbsp Greek yogurt
Salt and black pepper to taste

10 cherry tomatoes, halved
¾ cup cheddar cheese, grated

Warm the olive oil in a skillet over medium heat, and sauté the onion for 2 minutes. Stir in the sweet potatoes, ham, beans, yogurt, salt, pepper, and tomatoes, and cook for another 3 minutes. Pour in the whisked eggs and grated cheese, cover with a lid, and cook for an additional 10 minutes. Cut before serving.

19. Baked Shakshuka Breakfast

Serves: 4 | Ready in about: 25 minutes

2 tbsp extra-virgin olive oil
1 cup chopped red onion
1 chopped red bell pepper
1 cup finely diced potatoes

1 tsp garlic powder
1 (14.5-oz) can diced tomatoes
¼ tsp turmeric
¼ tsp paprika

¼ tsp dried oregano
¼ tsp ground cardamom
4 large eggs
¼ cup chopped fresh cilantro

Preheat oven to 350 F. "Warm the olive oil in a skillet over medium heat and sauté the red onion for about 3 minutes, until fragrant. Add bell peppers, potatoes, oregano, and garlic powder. Cook for 10 minutes, stirring often.

Pour in the tomatoes, turmeric, paprika, and cardamom and mix well until bubbly. Turn off the heat. With a wooden spoon, make 4 holes in the mixture and crack the eggs into each space. Put the skillet in the oven and cook for an additional 5-10 minutes until the whites are set but the yolk is still runny. Sprinkle with the cilantro and serve.

20. Easy Onion & Mushroom Omelet

Serves: 2 | Ready in about: 15 minutes

2 tsp olive oil, divided
4 eggs, beaten

1 cup mushrooms, sliced
1 garlic clove, minced

Salt and black pepper to taste
¼ cup sliced onions

Warm 1 tsp of olive oil in a frying pan over medium heat. Add the minced garlic, sliced mushrooms, and sliced onions to the pan. Cook for 6 minutes, stirring often. Season the mixture with salt and black pepper. Increase the heat and continue cooking for an additional 3 minutes. Remove the cooked vegetables from the pan and transfer them to a plate. In the same pan, add the remaining 1 teaspoon of olive oil. Pour the beaten eggs into the pan, ensuring they are evenly spread. Top the eggs with the cooked vegetables. Cook until the omelet is set, about 3-4 minutes. Slice the omelet into wedges and serve.

21. Scrambled Eggs with Cherry Tomatoes & Zucchini

Serves: 4 | Ready in about: 15 minutes

2 tbsp olive oil
6 cherry tomatoes, halved
½ cup chopped zucchini

½ chopped green bell pepper
8 eggs, beaten
1 shallot, chopped

1 tbsp chopped fresh parsley
1 tbsp chopped fresh basil
Salt and black pepper to taste

In a pan over medium heat, warm the olive oil. Add the chopped zucchini, green bell pepper, salt, black pepper, and shallot to the pan. Cook for 4-5 minutes to sweat the shallot and soften the vegetables. Stir in the halved cherry tomatoes, chopped parsley, and chopped basil. Cook for an additional minute, allowing the flavors to blend.

Top the vegetable mixture with the beaten eggs, ensuring they are evenly distributed in the pan. Reduce the heat to low and cook for 6-7 minutes or until the eggs are set but not runny, gently stirring occasionally. Once the scrambled eggs are cooked to your desired consistency, remove them from the heat. Transfer the scrambled eggs with cherry tomatoes and zucchini to a platter or serving dish. Serve hot and savor the delicious combination of flavors.

22. Berry & Walnut Oatmeal

Serves: 2 | Ready in about: 10 minutes

1 cup mixed berries
1 ½ cups rolled oats

2 tbsp walnuts, chopped
2 tsp maple syrup

Cook the rolled oats according to the package instructions. Divide the cooked oats evenly into 2 bowls. In a microwave-safe dish, combine the maple syrup and mixed berries. Microwave for 30 seconds, then stir well to coat the berries with the syrup. Pour the warmed maple syrup and berry mixture over each bowl of oats. Top each bowl with chopped walnuts.

23. Speedy Pumpkin Oatmeal

Serves: 4 | Ready in about: 15 minutes

¼ cup pumpkin seeds
½ cup milk
1 cup old-fashioned oats

1 cup pumpkin puree
2 tbsp superfine sugar
½ tsp ground cinnamon

1 ¾ cups water
¼ tsp sea salt

In a pot over medium heat, combine the milk, salt, and 1 ¾ cups of water. Bring the mixture to a boil. Add the oats to the pot and reduce the heat to simmer. Cook for 5 minutes, stirring periodically. Remove the pot from the heat and let it sit covered for an additional 5 minutes. Stir in the pumpkin puree, cinnamon, and superfine sugar until well combined. Serve the pumpkin oatmeal hot and top it with pumpkin seeds. Enjoy your speedy pumpkin oatmeal.

24. Wake Up Baklava French Toast

Serves: 2 | Ready in about: 20 minutes

2 tbsp orange juice
3 fresh eggs, beaten
1 tsp lemon zest
1/8 tsp vanilla extract
¼ cup honey

2 tbsp whole milk
¾ tsp ground cinnamon
¼ cup walnuts, crumbled
¼ cup pistachios, crumbled
1 tbsp sugar

2 tbsp white bread crumbs
4 slices bread
2 tbsp unsalted butter
1 tsp confectioners' sugar

In a bowl, combine orange juice, beaten eggs, lemon zest, vanilla extract, honey, milk, and ground cinnamon. Set the mixture aside. Use a food processor to finely crumble the walnuts and pistachios. In a small bowl, mix the crumbled walnuts, pistachios, sugar, and bread crumbs. Spread the nut mixture evenly on 2 slices of bread. Cover with the remaining 2 slices of bread to create sandwiches.

Melt unsalted butter in a skillet over medium heat. Dip the sandwiches into the egg mixture, ensuring they are fully coated. Fry the dipped sandwiches in the skillet for approximately 4 minutes on each side or until golden. Remove the French toast sandwiches from the skillet and transfer them to a plate. Cut them diagonally. Dust with confectioners' sugar. Serve immediately and enjoy the sweet and nutty flavors of our delicious French toast creation.

25. Avocado Toast with Poached Egg

Serves: 4 | Ready in about: 15 minutes

4 bread slices, toasted
4 eggs
2 avocados, chopped

¼ cup chopped fresh cilantro
3 tbsp red wine vinegar
1 lemon, juiced and zested

1 garlic clove, minced
Salt and black pepper to taste
1 tsp hot sauce

In a bowl, use a fork to mash the avocados, cilantro, lemon juice, lemon zest, garlic, 2 tbsp of red wine vinegar, salt, black pepper, and hot sauce until smooth. In a pot, bring salted water to a boil over high heat. Add the remaining tablespoon of red wine vinegar and a pinch of salt to the boiling water.

Carefully crack each egg into the boiling water, one at a time, and poach them for 2-3 minutes until the egg whites are set and the yolks are cooked to your liking. Use a perforated spoon to remove the poached eggs from the pot and transfer them to a paper towel to drain any excess water. Spread the avocado mash onto the toasted bread slices. Top each toast with a poached egg. Serve the delicious Avocado Toast with Poached Egg immediately.

26. Exquisite Fruit Salad

Serves: 6 | Ready in about: 10 minutes + cooling time

½ cup olive oil
2 cups cubed honeydew melon
2 cups cubed cantaloupe

2 cups red seedless grapes
1 lemon, juiced and zested
½ cup slivered almonds

1 cup sliced strawberries
1 cup blueberries
¼ cup honey

In a bowl, place melon, cantaloupe, grapes, strawberries, blueberries, and lemon zest. Toss to coat and set aside. Mix the honey and lemon juice in a bowl and whisk until the honey is well incorporated. Carefully pour in the olive oil and mix well. Drizzle over the fruit and toss to combine. Transfer to the fridge covered and let chill for at least 4 hours. Stir well and top with slivered almonds before serving.

27. Egg & Zucchini Nests

Serves: 4 | Ready in about: 25 minutes

2 tbsp olive oil
4 eggs

1 lb zucchini, shredded
Salt and black pepper to taste

½ red hot pepper, minced
2 tbsp parsley, chopped

Preheat the oven to 360 F. Combine zucchini, salt, pepper, and olive oil in a bowl. Form nest shapes with a spoon onto a greased baking sheet. Crack an egg into each nest and season with salt, pepper, and hot pepper. Bake for 11 minutes. Serve topped with parsley.

28. Almond Grits Drizzled with Honey

Serves: 4 | Ready in about: 15 minutes

¼ cup slivered almonds
½ cup milk
½ tsp almond extract

½ cup quick-cooking grits
½ tsp ground cinnamon
¼ cup honey

¼ tsp sea salt

Bring to a boil the milk, salt, and 1 ½ cups of water in a pot over medium heat. Gradually add in grits, stirring constantly. Lower the heat and simmer for 6 minutes until all the liquid is absorbed. Mix in almond extract and cinnamon and cook for another minute. Ladle into individual bowls, top with almonds and honey, and serve. Enjoy!

29. Orange Flavored French Toast

Serves: 4 | Ready in about: 30 minutes

1 tbsp butter
1 orange, juiced and zested
4 bread slices

1 ½ cups milk
2 eggs, beaten
1 tsp vanilla extract

1 tsp ground cinnamon
1 tbsp powdered sugar

Beat milk, eggs, vanilla, orange zest, and orange juice in a bowl. Lay the bread in a rectangular baking dish in an even layer. Cover with the egg mixture and let it stand for 10 minutes, flipping once, to absorb well. Melt the butter in a skillet over medium heat and fry the bread in batches until golden brown on both sides, about 6-8 minutes. Dust toast with powdered sugar and cinnamon. Serve.

30. Egg & Vegetable S&wiches

Serves: 2 | Ready in about: 15 minutes

1 Iceberg lettuce head, separated into leaves
1 tbsp olive oil
1 tbsp butter
2 fontina cheese slices, grated

3 eggs
4 slices multigrain bread
3 radishes, sliced

½ cucumber, sliced
2 pimiento peppers, chopped
Salt and red pepper to taste

Warm the oil in a skillet over medium heat. Crack in the eggs and cook until the whites are set. Season with salt and red pepper; remove to a plate. Brush the bread slices with butter and toast them in the same skillet for 2 minutes per side. Arrange 2 bread slices on a flat surface and put them over the eggs. Add in the remaining ingredients and top with the remaining slices. Serve immediately.

31. Pecan & Carrot Cupcakes

Serves: 6 | Ready in about: 30 minutes

2 tbsp olive oil	½ cup old-fashioned oats	2 tsp ground cinnamon
1 ½ cups grated carrots	3 tbsp light brown sugar	¼ tsp salt
¼ cup pecans, chopped	1 tsp vanilla extract	1¼ cups soy milk
1 cup oat bran	½ lemon, zested	2 tbsp honey
1 ½ cups flour	1 tsp baking powder	1 egg

Preheat oven to 350 F. Mix flour, oat bran, oats, sugar, baking powder, cinnamon, and salt in a bowl; set aside. Beat egg with soy milk, honey, vanilla, lemon zest, and olive oil in another bowl. Pour this mixture into the flour mixture and combine to blend, leaving some lumps. Stir in carrots and pecans. Spoon batter into greased muffin cups. Bake for about 20 minutes. Prick with a toothpick, and if it comes out easily, the cakes are cooked. Let cool and serve.

32. Scrambled Eggs with Smoked Salmon

Serves: 4 | Ready in about: 35 minutes

2 tbsp olive oil	8 eggs	1 scallion, chopped
4 oz smoked salmon, flaked	Salt and black pepper to taste	2 tbsp green olives, chopped
½ red onion, finely chopped	½ tsp garlic powder	

Beat eggs, garlic powder, salt, and pepper in a bowl. Warm olive oil in a skillet over medium heat. Stir in onion and sauté for 1-2 minutes. Add in olives and salmon and cook for another minute. Pour in the eggs and stir-fry for 5-6 minutes until the eggs are set. Serve topped with scallion.

33. Fried Eggs with Polenta & Vegetables

Serves: 4 | Ready in about: 35 minutes

2 tbsp butter	2 spring onions, chopped	1 ½ cups vegetable broth
½ tsp sea salt	1 bell pepper, chopped	¼ tsp hot pepper flakes, crushed
1 cup polenta	1 zucchini, chopped	2 tbsp basil leaves, chopped
4 eggs	1 tsp ginger-garlic paste	

Melt 1 tbsp of the butter in a skillet over medium heat. Place in spring onions, ginger-garlic paste, bell pepper, and zucchini and sauté for 5 minutes; set aside. Pour the broth and 1 ½ cups of water into a pot and bring to a boil. Gradually whisk in polenta to avoid chunks, lower the heat, and simmer for 4-5 minutes. Keep whisking until it begins to thicken. Cook covered for 20 minutes, stirring often. Add the zucchini mixture, hot pepper flakes, and salt and stir.

Heat the remaining butter in a skillet. Break the eggs and fry them until set and well cooked. Divide the polenta between bowls, top with fried eggs and basil, and serve.

34. Zucchini & Mushroom Egg Muffins

Serves: 4 | Ready in about: 20 minutes

2 tbsp olive oil	1 cup mushrooms, sliced	Salt and black pepper to taste
1 cup feta, grated	1 red bell pepper, chopped	8 eggs, whisked
1 onion, chopped	1 zucchini, chopped	2 tbsp chives, chopped

Preheat the oven to 360 F. Warm the olive oil in a skillet over medium heat and sauté onion, bell pepper, zucchini, mushrooms, salt, and pepper for 5 minutes until tender. Mix with eggs and season with salt and pepper. Distribute the mixture across muffin cups and top with the feta cheese. Sprinkle with chives and bake for 10 minutes. Serve.

35. Raspberry & Oat Pudding

Serves: 2 | Ready in about: 5 minutes

1 cup almond milk	1 tbsp chia seeds	1 cup raspberries, pureed
½ cup rolled oats	2 tsp honey	1 tbsp yogurt

Toss the oats, almond milk, chia seeds, honey, and raspberries in a bowl. Serve in bowls topped with yogurt.

36. Vegetable & Hummus Breakfast Bowl

Serves: 4 | Ready in about: 15 minutes

2 tbsp butter
2 tbsp olive oil
3 cups green cabbage, shredded
3 cups kale, chopped

1 lb asparagus, chopped
½ cup hummus
1 avocado, sliced
4 boiled eggs, sliced

1 tbsp balsamic vinegar
1 garlic clove, minced
2 tsp yellow mustard
Salt and black pepper to taste

Melt butter in a skillet over medium heat and sauté asparagus for 5 minutes. Mix the olive oil, balsamic vinegar, garlic, yellow mustard, salt, and pepper in a bowl. Spoon the hummus onto the center of a salad bowl and arrange in the asparagus, kale, cabbage, and avocado. Top with the egg slices. Drizzle with the dressing and serve.

37. Kale & Cheese Egg Cupcakes

Serves: 2 | Ready in about: 30 minutes

¼ cup kale, chopped
3 eggs
1 leek, sliced

4 tbsp feta, grated
2 tbsp almond milk
1 red bell pepper, chopped

Salt and black pepper to taste
1 tomato, chopped
2 tbsp halloumi, grated

Preheat the oven to 360 F. Grease a muffin tin with cooking spray. Whisk the eggs in a bowl. Add in milk, kale, leek, feta cheese, bell pepper, salt, black pepper, tomato, and halloumi cheese and stir to combine. Divide the mixture between the cases and bake for 20-25 minutes. Let cool completely on a wire rack before serving.

38. Stuffed Tomatoes with Easy Zucchini & Egg Filling

Serves: 4 | Ready in about: 40 minutes

1 tbsp olive oil
1 small zucchini, grated

8 tomatoes, insides scooped
8 eggs

Salt and black pepper to taste

Preheat the oven to 360 F. Place tomatoes on a greased baking dish. Mix the zucchini with olive oil, salt, and pepper. Divide the mixture between the tomatoes and crack an egg on each one. Bake for 20-25 minutes. Serve warm.

39. Spinach & Artichoke Frittata

Serves: 4 | Ready in about: 55 minutes

4 oz canned artichokes, chopped
2 tsp olive oil
½ cup whole milk
8 eggs

1 cup spinach, chopped
1 garlic clove, minced
½ cup feta, crumbled

1 tsp oregano, dried
1 Jalapeño pepper, minced
Salt to taste

Preheat oven to 360 F. Warm the olive oil in a skillet over medium heat and sauté garlic and spinach for 3 minutes. Beat the eggs in a bowl. Stir in artichokes, milk, feta cheese, oregano, jalapeño pepper, and salt. Add in spinach mixture and toss to combine. Transfer to a greased baking dish and bake for 20 minutes until golden and bubbling. Slice into wedges and serve.

40. Cucumber & Couscous Breakfast Bowl

Serves: 4 | Ready in about: 15 minutes

2 tbsp olive oil
¾ cup couscous
1 cup water
1 yellow onion, chopped

2 garlic cloves, minced
2 cups canned chickpeas
Salt to taste
15 oz canned tomatoes, diced

1 cucumber, cut into ribbons
½ cup black olives, chopped
1 tbsp lemon juice
1 tbsp mint leaves, chopped

Cover the couscous with salted boiling water, cover, and let it sit for about 5 minutes. Then fluff with a fork and set aside. Warm the olive oil in a skillet over medium heat and sauté onion and garlic for 3 minutes until soft. Stir in chickpeas, salt, and tomatoes for 1-2 minutes. Turn off the heat and mix in olives, couscous, and lemon juice. Transfer to a bowl and top with cucumber ribbons and mint to serve.

41. Baby Spinach & Anchovy S&wiches

Serves: 2 | Ready in about: 5 minutes

1 avocado, mashed
4 anchovies, drained

4 whole-wheat bread slices
1 cup baby spinach

1 tomato, sliced

Spread the slices of bread with avocado mash and arrange the anchovies over. Top with baby spinach and tomato slices.

42. Basil-Tomato Eggs

Serves: 2 | Ready in about: 25 minutes

2 tsp olive oil
2 eggs, whisked

2 tomatoes, cubed
1 tbsp basil, chopped

1 green onion, chopped
Salt and black pepper to taste

Warm the oil in a skillet over medium heat and sauté tomatoes, green onion, salt, and pepper for 5 minutes. Stir in eggs and cook for another 10 minutes. Serve topped with basil.

43. Cranberry & Apple Oat Porridge

Serves: 4 | Ready in about: 15 minutes

3 green apples, cored, peeled and cubed
2 cups milk
½ cup walnuts, chopped
3 tbsp maple syrup

½ cup steel-cut oats
½ tsp cinnamon powder
½ cup cranberries, dried

1 tsp vanilla extract

Warm the milk in a pot over medium heat and stir in apples, maple syrup, oats, cinnamon powder, cranberries, vanilla extract, and 1 cup water. Simmer for 10 minutes. Spoon the porridge into serving bowls, top with walnuts, and serve.

44. Delicious Lentil Stuffed Pitas

Serves: 4 | Ready in about: 20 minutes

4 pieces of bread, halved horizontally
2 tbsp olive oil
1 tomato, cubed
1 red onion, chopped

1 garlic clove, minced
¼ cup parsley, chopped
1 cup lentils, rinsed

¼ cup lemon juice
Salt and black pepper to taste

Bring a pot of salted water to a boil over high heat. Pour in the lentils and lower the heat. Cover and let it simmer for 15 minutes or until lentils are tender, adding more water if needed. Drain and set aside.

Warm the olive oil in a skillet over medium heat and cook the onion and garlic and for 3 minutes until soft and translucent. Stir in tomato, lemon juice, salt, and pepper and cook for another 10 minutes. Add the lentils and parsley to the skillet and stir to combine. Fill the pita bread with the lentil mixture. Roll up and serve immediately. Enjoy!

45. Feta Cheese & Sweet Potato Tart

Serves: 6 | Ready in about: 1 hour 20 minutes

¼ cup olive oil
2 eggs, whisked
2 lb sweet potatoes, cubed

7 oz feta cheese, crumbled
1 white onion, chopped
¼ cup milk

Salt and black pepper to taste
6 phyllo sheets

Preheat the oven to 380 F. Line a baking sheet with parchment paper. Place potatoes, half of the olive oil, salt, and pepper in a bowl and toss to combine. Arrange on the sheet and roast for 25 minutes.

In the meantime, warm half of the remaining oil in a skillet over medium heat and sauté onion for 3 minutes. Whisk eggs, milk, feta cheese, salt, pepper, onion, sweet potatoes, and remaining oil in a bowl. Place phyllo sheets in a tart dish and rub with oil. Spoon sweet potato mixture, cover with foil and bake for 20 minutes. Remove the foil and bake another for 20 minutes. Let cool for a few minutes. Serve sliced.

46. Quick Berry & Cheese Omelet

Serves: 4 | Ready in about: 10 minutes

2 tbsp olive oil
6 eggs, whisked

1 tsp cinnamon powder
1 cup ricotta cheese

4 oz berries

Whisk eggs, cinnamon powder, ricotta cheese, and berries in a bowl. Warm the olive oil in a skillet over medium heat and pour in the egg mixture. Cook for 2 minutes, turn the egg, and cook for 2 minutes more. Serve immediately.

47. Energy Honey Breakfast Smoothie

Serves: 1 | Ready in about: 10 minutes

1 tbsp olive oil
2 tbsp almond butter
1 cup almond milk

¼ cup blueberries
1 tbsp ground flaxseed
1 tsp honey

½ tsp vanilla extract
¼ tsp ground cinnamon

In a blender, mix the almond milk, blueberries, almond butter, flaxseed, olive oil, stevia vanilla, and cinnamon and pulse until smooth and creamy. Add more milk or water to achieve your desired consistency. Serve at room temperature.

48. Strawberry-Chocolate Smoothie

Serves: 2 | Ready in about: 5 minutes

1 cup buttermilk
2 cups strawberries, hulled

1 cup crushed ice
3 tbsp cocoa powder

3 tbsp honey
2 mint leaves

In a food processor, pulse buttermilk, strawberries, ice, cocoa powder, mint, and honey until smooth. Serve.

49. Green Smoothie

Serves: 1 | Ready in about: 10 minutes

1 tbsp extra-virgin olive oil
1 avocado, peeled and pitted
1 cup milk

½ cup watercress
½ cup baby spinach leaves
½ cucumber, peeled and seeded

10 mint leaves, stems removed
½ lemon, juiced

In a blender, mix avocado, milk, baby spinach, watercress, cucumber, olive oil, mint, and lemon juice and blend until smooth and creamy. Add more milk or water to achieve your desired consistency. Serve chilled or at room temperature.

50. Greek Yogurt & Raspberry Smoothie

Serves: 2 | Ready in about: 10 minutes

2 cups raspberries
1 tsp honey

1 cup Greek yogurt
½ cup milk

8 ice cubes

In a food processor, combine yogurt, raspberries, honey, and milk. Blitz until smooth. Add in ice cubes and pulse until uniform. Serve right away.

51. Tomato & Cheese Omelet

Serves: 2 | Ready in about: 20 minutes

1 tbsp olive oil
½ pint cherry tomatoes
2 garlic cloves, minced

5 large eggs, beaten
3 tbsp milk
Salt and black pepper to taste

2 tbsp fresh oregano, minced
2 tbsp fresh basil, minced
2 oz ricotta cheese, crumbled

Warm the olive oil in a skillet over medium heat. Add the cherry tomatoes. Reduce the heat, cover the pan, and let the tomatoes soften. When the tomatoes are mostly softened and broken down, remove the lid, add garlic and continue to sauté. In a bowl, combine the eggs, milk, salt, pepper, and herbs and whisk well to combine. Increase the heat to medium, pour the egg mixture over the tomatoes and garlic, and then sprinkle with ricotta cheese. Cook for 7-8 minutes, flipping once until the eggs are set. Run a spatula around the edge of the pan to make sure they won't stick. Serve warm.

52. Date-Apple Smoothie

Serves: 1 | Ready in about: 5 minutes

1 apple, peeled and chopped
½ cup milk

4 dates
1 tsp ground cinnamon

In a blender, place the milk, ½ cup of water, dates, cinnamon, and apple. Blitz until smooth. Let chill in the fridge for 30 minutes. Serve in a tall glass.

53. Peach Smoothie with Maple Syrup

Serves: 2 | Ready in about: 5 minutes

2 cups almond milk
2 cups peaches, chopped

1 cup crushed ice
½ tsp ground ginger

1 tbsp maple syrup

In a food processor, mix milk, peaches, ice, maple syrup, and ginger until smooth. Serve.

54. Breakfast Zinger Smoothie

Serves: 2 | Ready in about: 5 minutes

1 green apple, chopped
2 cups spinach

1 avocado, peeled and diced
1 tsp honey

1 kiwi, peeled
2 cups almond milk

Place spinach, apple, avocado, honey, kiwi, and almond milk in a food processor and blend until smooth. Serve chilled.

55. Power-Packet Juice

Serves: 1 | Ready in about: 5 minutes

½ grapefruit
½ lemon
3 cups cavolo nero

1 cucumber
¼ cup fresh parsley leaves
¼ pineapple, cut into wedges

½ green apple
1 tsp grated fresh ginger

In a mixer, place the cavolo nero, parsley, cucumber, pineapple, grapefruit, apple, lemon, and ginger and pulse until smooth. Serve in a tall glass.

56. Morning Apple & Pumpkin Cupcakes

Serves: 12 | Ready in about: 30 minutes

½ cup butter, melted
1 ½ cups granulated sugar
½ cup sugar
¾ cup flour

2 tsp pumpkin pie spice
1 tsp baking soda
¼ tsp salt
¼ tsp nutmeg

1 apple, grated
1 (15-oz) can pumpkin puree
½ cup full-fat yogurt
2 large egg whites

Preheat the oven to 350 F. In a bowl, mix sugars, flour, pumpkin pie spice, baking soda, salt, and nutmeg. In a separate bowl, mix apple, pumpkin puree, yogurt, and butter.

Slowly mix the wet ingredients into the dry ingredients. Using a mixer on high, whip the egg whites until stiff and fold them into the batter. Pour the batter into a greased muffin tin, filling each cup halfway. Bake for 25 minutes or until a fork inserted in the center comes out clean. Let cool.

57. Fast Blueberry Oatmeal

Serves: 2 | Ready in about: 10 minutes + chilling time

⅔ cup milk
⅓ cup quick rolled oats

¼ cup blueberries
1 tsp honey

½ tsp ground cinnamon
¼ tsp ground cloves

Layer the oats, milk, blueberries, honey, cinnamon, and cloves into 2 mason jars. Cover and store in the refrigerator overnight. Serve cold and enjoy!

58. Red Bell Pepper Omelet

Serves: 2 | Ready in about: 10 minutes

2 tbsp olive oil
2 red bell peppers, chopped

¼ tsp nutmeg
4 eggs, beaten

2 garlic cloves, crushed
1 tsp Greek seasoning

Heat the oil in a skillet over medium heat. Stir-fry the peppers for 3 minutes or until lightly charred; reserve. Add the garlic to the skillet and sauté for 1 minute. Pour the eggs over the garlic, sprinkle with Greek seasoning and nutmeg, and cook for 2-3 minutes or until set. Using a spatula, loosen the edges and gently slide onto a plate. Add charred peppers and fold over. Serve.

59. Green Egg Cupcakes

Serves: 2 | Ready in about: 40 minutes

1 whole-grain bread slice
4 large eggs, beaten
3 tbsp milk

Salt and black pepper to taste
½ tsp onion powder
¼ tsp garlic powder

¾ cup chopped kale

Heat the oven to 350 F. Break the bread into pieces and divide between 2 greased ramekins. Mix the eggs, milk, salt, onion powder, garlic powder, pepper, and kale in a medium bowl. Pour half of the egg mixture into each ramekin and bake for 25 minutes or until the eggs are set. Serve and enjoy!

60. Fried Potatoes with Tomato Eggs

Serves: 2 | Ready in about: 20 minutes

2 tbsp + ½ cup olive oil
3 medium tomatoes, puréed
1 tbsp fresh tarragon, chopped

1 garlic clove, minced
Salt and black pepper to taste
3 potatoes, cubed

4 fresh eggs
1 tsp fresh oregano, chopped

Warm 2 tbsp of olive oil in a saucepan over medium heat. Add the garlic and sauté for 1 minute. Pour in the tomatoes, tarragon, salt, and pepper. Reduce the heat and cook for 5-8 minutes or until the sauce is thickened and bubbly. Warm the remaining olive oil in a skillet over medium heat. Fry the potatoes for 5 minutes until crisp and browned on the outside, then cover and reduce heat to low. Steam potatoes until done. Carefully crack the eggs into the tomato sauce.

Cook over low heat until the eggs are set in the sauce, about 6 minutes. Remove the potatoes from the pan, drain them on paper towels, and place them in a bowl. Sprinkle with salt and pepper and top with oregano. Carefully remove the eggs with a slotted spoon and place them on a plate with the potatoes. Spoon sauce over and serve.

61. Almond Oatmeal with Chia Seeds

Serves: 2 | Ready in about: 10 minutes + chilling time

¼ tsp almond extract
½ cup milk
½ cup rolled oats

2 tbsp almonds, sliced
2 tbsp sugar
1 tsp chia seeds

¼ tsp ground cardamom
¼ tsp ground cinnamon

Combine the milk, oats, almonds, sugar, chia seeds, cardamom, almond extract, and cinnamon in a mason jar and shake well. Keep in the refrigerator for 4 hours. Serve.

62. Old-Fashioned Oatmeal Bowls

Serves: 2 | Ready in about: 45 minutes

½ cup old-fashioned oats
¾ cup almond milk
½ tsp almond extract

½ tsp vanilla
1 egg, beaten
2 tbsp maple syrup

½ cup dried cherries, chopped
2 tbsp slivered raw almonds

In a microwave-safe bowl, combine oats, almond milk, almond extract, vanilla, egg, and maple syrup and mix well. Microwave for 5-6 minutes, stirring every 2 minutes until oats are soft. Spoon the mixture into 2 bowls. Top with cherries and almonds and serve. Enjoy!

63. Holiday Pancakes in Berry Sauce

Serves: 4 | Ready in about: 20 minutes

Pancakes

6 tbsp olive oil	¼ tsp salt	½ tsp vanilla extract
1 cup flour	2 large eggs	½ tsp dark rum
1 tsp baking powder	1 lemon, zested and juiced	

Berry Sauce

1 cup mixed berries of choice	1 tbsp lemon juice
3 tbsp sugar	½ tsp vanilla extract

In a large bowl, combine the flour, baking powder, and salt and whisk to break up any clumps. Add 4 tablespoons of olive oil, eggs, lemon zest and juice, rum, and vanilla extract and whisk to combine well. Brush a frying pan with butter over medium heat and cook the pancakes for 5-7 minutes, flipping once until bubbles form.

To make the sauce, pour the mixed berries, lemon juice, vanilla, and sugar into a small saucepan over medium heat. Cook for 3-4 minutes until bubbly, adding a little water if the mixture is too thick. Mash the berries with a fork and stir until smooth. Pour over the pancakes and serve.

64. Herby Tomato Eggs

Serves: 6 | Ready in about: 25 minutes

2 tbsp olive oil	2 garlic cloves, minced	6 large eggs
1 onion, chopped	2 (14-oz) cans tomatoes, diced	½ cup fresh chives, chopped

Warm the olive oil in a large skillet over medium heat. Add the onion and garlic and cook for 3 minutes, stirring occasionally. Pour in the tomatoes with their juices o and cook for 3 minutes until bubbling.

Crack one egg into a small custard cup. With a large spoon, make six indentations in the tomato mixture. Gently pour the first cracked egg into one indentation and repeat, cracking the remaining eggs, one at a time, into the custard cup and pouring one into each indentation. Cover the skillet and cook for 6-8 minutes. Top with chives and serve.

65. Dakos with Avocado & Tomatoes

Serves: 4 | Ready in about: 5 minutes

1 tbsp olive oil	2 tbsp lemon juice	2 tbsp parsley, chopped
1 baguette, sliced	8 cherry tomatoes, chopped	4 Kalamata olives, chopped
2 sun-dried tomatoes, chopped	¼ cup red onion, chopped	Salt and black pepper to taste
1 avocado, chopped	1 tsp dried oregano	

Preheat oven to 360 F. Arrange the bread slices on a greased baking tray and drizzle with olive oil. Bake until golden, about 6-8 minutes. Mash the avocado in a bowl with lemon juice, salt, and pepper. Stir in sun-dried tomatoes, onion, oregano, parsley, and olives. Spread the avocado mixture on toasted bread slices and top with cherry tomatoes. Serve.

66. Poppy Seed Bread with Olives

Serves: 6 | Ready in about: 40 minutes + rising time

¼ cup olive oil	2 tsp dry yeast	½ cup feta cheese, crumbled
4 cups whole-wheat flour	1 cup black olives, sliced	1 tbsp poppy seeds
3 tbsp oregano, chopped	1 cup lukewarm water	1 egg, beaten

In a bowl, combine flour, water, yeast, and olive oil and knead the dough well. Transfer to a bowl and let sit covered with plastic wrap to rise until doubled in size for 60 minutes.

Remove the wrap and fold in oregano, black olives, and feta cheese. Place on a floured surface and knead again. Shape the dough into 6 balls and place them on a lined baking sheet. Cover and let rise for another 40 minutes. Preheat the oven to 390 F. Brush the balls with the egg and sprinkle with the poppy seeds. Bake for 25-30 minutes. Serve.

67. Cheesy Egg Scramble

Serves: 4 | Ready in about: 20 minutes

½ cup feta cheese, crumbled
2 tsp olive oil
1 cup bell peppers, chopped

2 garlic cloves, minced
6 large eggs, beaten

Salt to taste
2 tbsp fresh cilantro, chopped

Warm the olive oil in a large skillet over medium heat. Add the peppers and sauté for 5 minutes, stirring occasionally. Add the garlic and cook for 1 minute. Stir in the eggs and salt and cook for 2-3 minutes until the eggs begin to set on the bottom. Top with feta cheese and cook the eggs for about 2 more minutes, stirring slowly, until the eggs are soft-set and custardy. Sprinkle with cilantro and serve.

68. Feta Frozen Yogurt

Serves: 4 | Ready in about: 20 minutes + freezing time

1 tbsp honey
1 cup Greek yogurt

½ cup feta cheese, crumbled
2 tbsp mint leaves, chopped

In a food processor, blend yogurt, honey, and feta cheese until smooth. Transfer to a wide dish, cover with plastic wrap, and put in the freezer for 2 hours or until solid. When frozen, spoon into cups, sprinkle with mint and serve.

69. Dill Feta & Olive Breakfast

Serves: 4 | Ready in about: 15 minutes

¼ cup extra-virgin olive oil
4 feta cheese squares
3 cups mixed olives, drained

3 tbsp lemon juice
1 tsp lemon zest
1 tsp dried dill

Pita bread for serving

In a small bowl, whisk together the olive oil, lemon juice, lemon zest, and dill. Place the feta cheese on a serving plate and add the mixed olives. Pour the dressing all over the feta cheese. Serve with toasted pita bread.

70. Feta Egg Quiche

Serves: 6 | Ready in about: 45 minutes

1 tbsp melted butter
1 ¼ cups crumbled feta
½ cup ricotta, crumbled

2 tbsp chopped fresh mint
1 tbsp chopped fresh dill
½ tsp lemon zest

Black pepper to taste
2 large eggs, beaten

Preheat the oven to 350 F. In a medium bowl, combine the feta and ricotta cheeses and blend them well with a fork. Stir in the mint, dill, lemon zest, and black pepper. Slowly add the eggs to the cheese mixture and blend well. Pour the batter into a greased baking dish and drizzle with melted butter. Bake until lightly browned, 35-40 minutes. Serve.

71. Cilantro Scrambled Eggs with Feta Cheese

Serves: 4 | Ready in about: 25 minutes

¼ cup olive oil
2 Roma tomatoes, chopped
¼ cup minced red onion
2 garlic cloves, minced

½ tsp dried oregano
½ tsp dried thyme
8 large eggs
Salt and black pepper to taste

¾ cup feta cheese, crumbled
¼ cup fresh cilantro, chopped

Warm the olive oil in a large skillet over medium heat. Add the chopped tomatoes and red onion and sauté for 10 minutes or until the tomatoes are soft. Add the garlic, oregano, and thyme and sauté for another 1-2 minutes until the liquid reduces.

In a medium bowl, whisk together the eggs, salt, and pepper until well combined. Add the eggs to the skillet, reduce the heat to low, and scramble until set and creamy, using a spatula to move them constantly, 3-4 minutes. Remove the skillet from the heat, stir in the feta and cilantro, and serve.

72. Zucchini & Cheese Tart

Serves: 6 | Ready in about: 60 minutes

3 tbsp olive oil
5 sun-dried tomatoes, chopped
1 prepared pie crust
1 onion, chopped
2 garlic cloves, minced

2 zucchini, chopped
1 red bell pepper, chopped
6 Kalamata olives, sliced
1 tsp fresh dill, chopped
½ cup Greek yogurt

1 cup feta cheese, crumbled
4 eggs
1 ½ cups milk
Salt and black pepper to taste

Preheat the oven to 380 F. Warm the olive oil in a skillet over medium heat and sauté garlic and onion for 3 minutes. Add in bell pepper and zucchini and sauté for another 3 minutes. Stir in olives, dill, salt, and pepper for 1-2 minutes and add tomatoes and feta cheese. Mix well and turn the heat off.

Press the crust gently into a lightly greased pie dish and prick it with a fork. Bake in the oven for 10-15 minutes until pale gold. Spread the zucchini mixture over the pie crust. Whisk the eggs with salt, pepper, milk, and yogurt in a bowl, then pour over the zucchini layer. Bake for 25-30 minutes until golden brown. Let cool before serving.

73. Pita Sandwiches with Yogurt Sauce

Serves: 4 | Ready in about: 28 minutes

1 (15-oz) can chickpeas, drained and rinsed
2 tbsp olive oil
½ cup hummus
½ cup bread crumbs
1 large egg

2 tsp dried oregano
¼ tsp black pepper
1 cucumber, shredded
1 cup Greek yogurt

1 garlic clove, minced
2 pita bread, halved
4 thick tomato slices
1 lemon, zested

Mash the chickpeas with a potato masher until coarsely mashed but chunky in a large bowl. Add the hummus, bread crumbs, egg, oregano, lemon zest, and pepper. Stir to combine. Shape the mixture into 4 balls and flatten them to make 6 burgers. Heat the oil in a large skillet over medium heat. Cook the burgers for 10 minutes, turning once.

In a small bowl, stir together the shredded cucumber, yogurt, and garlic to make the tzatziki sauce. Toast the pita bread. To assemble the pita sandwiches, lay the pita halves on a work surface. Place a chickpea patty and a tomato slice into each pita, then drizzle with the tzatziki sauce and serve.

74. Plum Parfait with Nuts

Serves: 4 | Ready in about: 10 minutes

1 tbsp honey
1 cup plums, chopped
2 cups Greek yogurt

1 tsp cinnamon powder
1 tbsp almonds, chopped
1 tbsp walnuts, chopped

¼ cup pistachios, chopped

Place a skillet over medium heat and add in plums, honey, cinnamon powder, almonds, walnuts, pistachios, and ¼ cup water. Cook for 5 minutes. Share Greek yogurt into serving bowls and top with plum mixture and toss before serving.

75. Vanilla Yogurt with Walnuts

Serves: 4 | Ready in about: 10 minutes

2 cups Greek yogurt
¾ cup maple syrup

1 cup walnuts, chopped
1 tsp vanilla extract

2 tsp cinnamon powder

Combine yogurt, walnuts, vanilla, maple syrup, and cinnamon powder in a bowl. Let sit in the fridge for 10 minutes.

76. Detox Smoothie

Serves: 2 | Ready in about: 10 minutes

1 tbsp sesame seeds
1 tsp sugar
2 peaches, cored and chopped

½ cup Greek yogurt
½ ripe avocado, chopped
2 tbsp flax meal

1 tsp vanilla extract
1 tsp orange extract

Blend the sesame seeds, sugar, peaches, yogurt, avocado, flax meal, vanilla, orange extract, and honey in your food processor until smooth. Pour the mixture into 2 bowls. Serve.

77. Parsley Tomato & Spinach Egg Wraps

Serves: 2 | Ready in about: 15 minutes

1 tbsp parsley, chopped
1 tbsp olive oil
¼ onion, chopped

3 sun-dried tomatoes, chopped
3 large eggs, beaten
2 cups baby spinach, torn

1 oz feta cheese, crumbled
Salt to taste
2 whole-wheat tortillas, warm

Warm the olive oil in a pan over medium heat. Sauté the onion and tomatoes for about 3 minutes. Add the beaten eggs and stir to scramble them, about 4 minutes. Add the spinach and parsley and stir to combine. Sprinkle the feta cheese over the eggs. Season with salt to taste. Divide the mixture between the tortillas. Roll them up and serve.

78. Buckwheat Pancakes

Serves: 2 | Ready in about: 20 minutes

½ cup buckwheat flour
½ tsp cardamom
½ tsp baking powder

½ cup milk
¼ cup plain Greek yogurt
1 egg

1 tsp lemon zest
1 tbsp honey

Mix the flour, cardamom, and baking powder in a medium bowl. Whisk the milk, yogurt, egg, lemon zest, and honey in another bowl. Add the wet ingredients to the dry ingredients and stir until the batter is smooth. Spray a frying pan with cooking oil and cook the pancakes over medium heat for 3 minutes per side or until the edges begin to brown.

79. Yogurt Parfaits

Serves: 4 | Ready in about: 5 minutes + chilling time

1 (15-oz) can pumpkin puree
4 tsp honey

¼ tsp ground cinnamon
2 cups Greek yogurt

1 cup honey granola
2 tbsp pomegranate seeds

Mix the pumpkin puree, honey, pumpkin and cinnamon in a large bowl. Layer the pumpkin mix, yogurt, and granola in small glasses. Repeat the layers. Top with pomegranate seeds. Chill for at least 3 hours before serving.

80. Muesli Pots with Pistachio & Pomegranate

Serves: 2 | Ready in about: 10 minutes

½ cup old-fashioned oats
¼ cup shelled pistachios
3 tbsp sesame seeds

2 tbsp chia seeds
¾ cup milk
½ cup Greek yogurt

2 tsp honey
½ cup pomegranate seeds

Mix the oats, pistachios, sesame seeds, chia seeds, milk, yogurt, and honey in a medium bowl. Divide the mixture between two mason jars. Top with pomegranate seeds. Cover the jar with lids and place in the refrigerator. Serve.

81. Peach-Yogurt Smoothie

Serves: 2 | Ready in about: 5 minutes

6 oz Greek yogurt
2 peaches, chopped

2 tbsp milk
7-8 ice cubes

In a food processor, place the peaches, milk, yogurt, and ice cubes. Pulse until creamy and smooth. Serve right away.

82. Almond Milk Shake

Serves: 1 | Ready in about: 5 minutes

1 large peach, sliced

6 oz peach Greek yogurt

2 tbsp almond milk

Blend the peach, yogurt, almond milk, and ice cubes in your food processor until thick and creamy. Serve and enjoy!

SALADS

83. Lettuce Greek Salad

Serves: 4 | Ready in about: 10 minutes

1 green bell pepper, cut into chunks
1 head romaine lettuce, torn
½ red onion, cut into rings
2 tomatoes, cut into wedges
1 cucumber, thinly sliced

3 tbsp extra-virgin olive oil
2 tbsp lemon juice
Garlic salt and pepper to taste
¼ tsp dried Greek oregano

1 cup feta cheese, cubed
1 handful of Kalamata olives

In a salad bowl, whisk the olive oil, lemon juice, pepper, garlic salt, and oregano. Add in the lettuce, red onion, tomatoes, cucumber, and bell pepper and mix with your hands to coat. Top with feta and olives and serve immediately.

84. Authentic Greek Salad

Serves: 4 | Ready in about: 10 minutes

2 tbsp extra-virgin olive oil
2 tomatoes, chopped
½ cup grated feta cheese
1 green bell pepper, chopped

10 Kalamata olives, chopped
1 red onion, thinly sliced
1 cucumber, chopped
2 tbsp apple cider vinegar

1 tbsp dried oregano
Salt and black pepper to taste
2 tbsp fresh parsley, chopped

In a salad bowl, combine bell pepper, red onion, tomatoes, cucumber, and olives. Mix the olive oil, apple cider vinegar, oregano, salt, and pepper in another bowl. Pour the dressing over the salad and toss to combine. Top with the feta cheese and sprinkle with parsley to serve.

85. Greek Tuna & Bean Salad

Serves: 4 | Ready in about: 10 minutes

2 (5-oz) cans can tuna packed in olive oil, drained and flaked
4 cups spring mix greens
1 (15-oz) can s, rinsed
⅔ cup feta cheese, crumbled
6 sun-dried tomatoes, sliced

10 Kalamata olives, sliced
2 thinly sliced green onions
¼ medium red onion, sliced
3 tbsp extra-virgin olive oil

½ tsp dried Greek oregano
3 leaves fresh mint, chopped
1 lemon, zested and juiced
Salt and black pepper to taste

Place the greens, chickpeas, tuna, feta, tomatoes, olives, green onions, red onion, olive oil, cilantro, mint, lemon juice, and lemon zest in a large bowl. Season with salt and pepper and mix to coat. Serve and enjoy!

86. Olive & Feta Salad

Serves: 4 | Ready in about: 10 minutes

½ cup extra-virgin olive oil
1 iceberg lettuce head, torn
2 tomatoes, sliced
1 cucumber, sliced

1 red onion, thinly sliced
¼ cup lemon juice
Salt to taste
1 clove garlic, minced

1 cup Kalamata olives, pitted
6 oz feta cheese, crumbled
2 tbsp dill, chopped

Place the lettuce in a large salad bowl. Add the tomatoes, cucumber, onion, and dill. In another small bowl, whisk together the olive oil, lemon juice, salt, and garlic. Pour the dressing over the salad and gently toss to coat evenly. Sprinkle the salad with the Kalamata olives and feta cheese. Serve and enjoy!

87. Pasta Salad in Greek Way

Serves: 4 | Ready in about: 10 minutes

2 tbsp olive oil
16 oz fusilli pasta
1 yellow bell pepper, cubed
1 green bell pepper, cubed

Salt to taste
3 tomatoes, cubed
1 red onion, sliced
2 cups feta cheese, crumbled

¼ cup lemon juice
1 tbsp lemon zest, grated
1 cucumber, cubed
1 cup Kalamata olives, sliced

Cook the fusilli pasta in boiling salted water until "al dente", 8-10 minutes. Drain and set aside to cool. Whisk together olive oil, lemon zest, lemon juice, and salt in a bowl. Add in bell peppers, tomatoes, onion, feta cheese, cucumber, olives, and pasta and toss to combine. Serve.

88. Lentil Salad with Kalamata Olives

Serves: 4 | Ready in about: 25 minutes + chilling time

1 cup red lentils, rinsed
1 tsp yellow mustard
½ lemon, juiced
2 tbsp tamari sauce
2 scallion stalks, chopped

¼ cup extra-virgin olive oil
2 garlic cloves, minced
1 cup butterhead lettuce, torn
2 tbsp fresh parsley, chopped
2 tbsp fresh cilantro, chopped

1 tsp fresh basil
1 tsp fresh oregano
12 cherry tomatoes, halved
6 Kalamata olives, halved

Pour 5 cups of salted water and lentils into a large pot over high heat and bring to a boil. Reduce the heat to medium-low and simmer for 15-18 minutes until the lentils are tender. Drain and let it cool completely. Transfer them to a salad bowl and add the remaining ingredients, except for the olives; toss until well combined. Top with olives and serve.

89. Simple Spring Mix Salad

Serves: 4 | Ready in about: 5 minutes

2 tbsp olive oil
2 tomatoes, cut into wedges
2 red bell peppers, chopped

1 cucumber, chopped
1 red onion, sliced
8 Kalamata olives, sliced

½ cup feta cheese, crumbled
¼ cup lime juice
Salt and black pepper to taste

Mix tomatoes, bell peppers, cucumber, onion, olives, lime juice, olive oil, salt, and pepper in a bowl. Divide between individual bowls and top with feta cheese to serve.

90. Cheesy Brown Rice Salad

Serves: 4 | Ready in about: 10 minutes

2 tbsp olive oil
½ cup brown rice
1 lb watercress

1 Roma tomato, sliced
4 oz feta cheese, crumbled
2 tbsp fresh basil, chopped

Salt and black pepper to taste
2 tbsp lemon juice
¼ tsp lemon zest

Bring to a boil salted water in a pot over medium heat. Add in the rice and cook for 15-18 minutes. Drain and let cool completely. Whisk the olive oil, lemon zest, lemon juice, salt, and pepper in a salad bowl. Add in the watercress, cooled rice, and basil and toss to coat. Top with feta cheese and tomato. Serve immediately.

91. Chickpea Salad with Greek Flavors

Serves: 6 | Ready in about: 15 minutes

¼ cup extra-virgin olive oil
2 (15-oz) cans chickpeas
1 cucumber, sliced

2 tbsp lemon juice
Salt and black pepper to taste
2 tomatoes, chopped

1 cup baby arugula
12 Kalamata olives, chopped

Whisk the olive oil, lemon juice, salt, and pepper in a salad bowl. Add the tomatoes, cucumber, arugula, and olives and toss to combine. Serve immediately or refrigerate in an airtight glass container for up to 1 day.

92. Cucumber & Corn Salad

Serves: 4 | Ready in about: 10 minutes

3 tbsp olive oil
3 tbsp pepitas, roasted
2 tbsp cilantro, chopped
1 cup corn

1 cup radishes, sliced
2 avocados, mashed
2 cucumbers, chopped
2 tbsp Greek yogurt

1 tsp balsamic vinegar
2 tbsp lime juice
Salt and black pepper to taste

In a bowl, whisk the olive oil, avocados, salt, pepper, lime juice, yogurt, and vinegar until smooth. Combine pepitas, cilantro, corn, radishes, and cucumbers in a salad bowl. Pour the avocado dressing over the salad and toss to combine.

93. Creamy Potato Salad

Serves: 6 | Ready in about: 20 minutes

4 peeled russet potatoes, chopped
1 cup frozen mixed veggies, thawed
3 hard-boiled eggs, chopped
½ cup Greek yogurt

10 pitted black olives
½ tsp dried mustard seeds
½ tsp lemon zest
½ tbsp lemon juice

½ tsp dried dill
Salt and black pepper to taste

Put the potatoes in a pot of salted water, bring to a boil, and cook for 5-7 minutes, until just fork-tender. Drain and set aside to cool. Mix the eggs, vegetables, yogurt, olives, pepper, mustard, lemon juice, lemon zest, and dill in a large bowl. Season with salt and pepper. Mix in potatoes. Serve.

94. Spinach & Sun-Dried Tomato Farfalle Salad

Serves: 4 | Ready in about: 45 min+cooling time

1 ½ cups farfalle
1 cup baby spinach, rinsed and dried
8 sun-dried tomatoes, sliced
1 carrot, grated
2 scallions, thinly sliced

1 garlic clove, minced
1 dill pickle, diced
⅔ cup extra-virgin olive oil
1 tbsp red wine vinegar
1 tbsp lemon juice

½ cup Greek yogurt
1 tsp chopped fresh oregano
Salt and black pepper to taste
1 cup feta cheese, crumbled

Bring a large pot of salted water to a boil, add the farfalle, and cook for 7-9 minutes until al dente. Drain the pasta and set aside to cool. Combine spinach, sun-dried tomatoes, carrot, scallions, garlic, and pickle in a large bowl. Add pasta and toss to combine. Whisk olive oil, vinegar, lemon juice, yogurt, oregano, pepper, and salt in a medium bowl. Add dressing to pasta and toss to coat. Sprinkle with feta cheese and serve.

95. Summer Party Salad

Serves: 4 | Ready in about: 10 minutes

½ cup extra virgin olive oil
2 cucumbers, sliced
2 mixed bell peppers, sliced
2 tomatoes, sliced

2 green onions, thinly sliced
2 gem lettuces, sliced
1 cup arugula
2 tbsp parsley, chopped

Salt to taste
1 cup feta cheese, crumbled
3 tbsp lemon juice

In a bowl, mix the cucumbers, bell peppers, green onions, gem lettuce, and arugula. In a small bowl, whisk the olive oil, lemon juice, and salt. Pour over the salad and toss to coat. Scatter the feta over and top with tomato and parsley.

96. Tangy Cucumber Salad with Mustard Dressing

Serves: 4 | Ready in about: 15 minutes

2 tbsp extra-virgin olive oil
2 cucumbers, chopped
1 hot red pepper, sliced

2 tbsp chives, chopped
¼ cup red wine vinegar
2 garlic cloves, minced

1 tsp yellow mustard
¼ tsp honey
Salt and black pepper to taste

Combine the cucumber, hot pepper, and chives in a bowl. Mix olive oil, honey, garlic, vinegar, mustard, salt, and pepper in another bowl. Pour over the salad and toss to combine.

97. Rice & Collard Green Salad

Serves: 4 | Ready in about: 10 minutes

1 tbsp olive oil
1 cup white rice
10 oz collard greens, torn

4 tbsp walnuts, chopped
2 tbsp balsamic vinegar
4 tbsp tahini paste

Salt and black pepper to taste
2 tbsp parsley, chopped

Bring to a boil salted water over medium heat. Add in the rice and cook for 15-18 minutes. Drain and rest to cool. Whisk tahini, 4 tbsp of cold water, and vinegar in a bowl. In a separate bowl, combine cooled rice, collard greens, walnuts, salt, pepper, olive oil, and tahini dressing. Serve topped with parsley.

98. Chicken & Cucumber Spelt Salad

Serves: 4 | Ready in about: 35 minutes

4 tbsp olive oil
½ lb chicken breasts
1 tbsp dill, chopped
2 lemons, zested

Juice of 2 lemons
3 tbsp parsley, chopped
Salt and black pepper to taste
1 cup spelt grains

1 red leaf lettuce head, torn
1 red onion, sliced
10 cherry tomatoes, halved
1 cucumber, sliced

In a bowl, combine dill, lemon zest, lemon juice, 2 tbsp olive oil, parsley, salt, and pepper and mix well. Add in chicken breasts, toss to coat, cover, and refrigerate for 30 minutes. Place spelt grains in a pot and cover with water. Stir in salt and pepper. Put over medium heat and bring to a boil. Cook for 45 minutes and drain. Transfer to a bowl and let it cool.

Preheat the grill. Remove the chicken and grill for 12 minutes on all sides. Transfer to a bowl to cool before slicing. Once the spelt is cooled, add in the remaining olive oil, lettuce, onion, tomatoes, and cucumber and toss to coat. Top the salad with sliced chicken and serve.

99. Tomato, Bell Pepper & Egg Salad

Serves: 4 | Ready in about: 15 minutes + chilling time

4 tbsp olive oil
2 hard-boiled eggs, chopped
2 cups Greek yogurt
1 cup tomatoes, chopped
2 mixed bell peppers, sliced

1 yellow onion, thinly sliced
½ tsp fresh garlic, minced
10 Kalamata olives, sliced
3 sun-dried tomatoes, chopped
1 tbsp fresh lemon juice

1 tsp dill, chopped
2 tbsp fresh parsley, chopped
Salt and black pepper to taste

In a bowl, combine the bell peppers, onion, garlic, Kalamata olives, chopped tomatoes, and sun-dried tomatoes. Stir in the chopped eggs. For the dressing, combine the lemon juice, olive oil, Greek yogurt, dill, salt, and black pepper in a bowl. Pour over the salad and transfer to the fridge to chill. Serve garnished with olives and parsley.

100.   Chicken Salad with Avocado

Serves: 4 | Ready in about: 10 minutes

1 cup cooked chicken breasts, chopped
½ cup marinated artichoke hearts
2 tbsp olive oil
6 sundried tomatoes, chopped
1 cucumber, chopped
6 black olives, 6 sliced
2 cups Iceberg lettuce, torn

2 tbsp parsley, chopped
1 avocado, peeled and cubed
½ cup feta cheese, crumbled
4 tbsp red wine vinegar
2 tbsp Dijon mustard

1 tsp basil, dried
1 garlic clove, minced
2 tsp honey
Salt and black pepper to taste
3 tbsp lemon juice

Combine chicken, tomatoes, artichokes, cucumber, olives, lettuce, parsley, and avocado in a bowl. In a separate bowl, whisk vinegar, mustard, basil, garlic, honey, olive oil, salt, pepper, and lemon juice and pour over the salad. Mix well. Top with cheese and serve.

101.   Lentil & Feta Green Salad

Serves: 4 | Ready in about: 25 min+cooling time

2 tbsp olive oil
1 head broccoli, cut into florets
1 lb baby spinach
2 green onions, sliced

1 garlic clove, minced
1 cup brown lentils
Salt and black pepper to taste
½ tsp sweet paprika

½ tsp ginger, grated
¼ cup lemon juice
¾ cup feta cheese, crumbled

Blanch the broccoli in salted water in a pot over medium heat for 3-4 minutes. Drain and set aside to cool. Warm the olive oil in the pot and cook green onions and garlic for 3 minutes. Pour in lentils and cover with water. Simmer covered for 15-20 minutes. Drain and let it cool. In a bowl, whisk lemon juice, salt, pepper, sweet paprika, and ginger. Divide the baby spinach between four salad plates, top with lentils and broccoli and drizzle with the prepared dressing. Sprinkle with feta cheese and serve topped.

102.   Chickpea & Bell Pepper Salad

Serves: 4 | Ready in about: 40 minutes + chilling time

1 cup chickpeas, soaked
1 cucumber, sliced
10 cherry tomatoes, halved
1 red bell pepper, sliced
1 green bell pepper, sliced

1 tsp yellow mustard
1 tsp coriander seeds
½ hot banana pepper, minced
1 tbsp fresh lemon juice
1 tbsp balsamic vinegar

2 tbsp olive oil
Salt and black pepper to taste
2 tbsp fresh cilantro, chopped
2 tbsp capers

Cover the chickpeas with water by 2 inches in a pot over medium heat. Bring it to a boil. Turn the heat to a simmer and continue to cook for about 40 minutes or until tender. Drain, let cool and transfer to a salad bowl. Add in the remaining ingredients and toss to combine well. Serve.

103.   Green Onion Potato Salad

Serves: 4 | Ready in about: 25 minutes

2 ½ lb baby potatoes, halved
Salt and black pepper to taste

1 cup light mayonnaise
Juice of 1 lemon

2 green onions, chopped
¼ cup parsley, chopped

Place potatoes and enough water in a pot over medium heat and bring to a boil. Cook for 12 minutes and drain; set aside. In a bowl, mix mayonnaise, salt, pepper, lemon juice, and green onions. Add in the baby potatoes and toss to coat. Top with parsley and serve immediately.

104.   Refreshing Yogurt & Cucumber Salad

Serves: 4 | Ready in about: 10 minutes + chilling time

1 tbsp olive oil
2 tbsp walnuts, ground
1 cup Greek yogurt

2 garlic cloves, minced
Salt and white pepper to taste
1 tbsp wine vinegar

1 tbsp dill, chopped
3 medium cucumbers, sliced
1 tbsp chives, chopped

Combine cucumbers, walnuts, garlic, salt, pepper, vinegar, yogurt, dill, olive oil, and chives in a bowl. Let sit in the fridge for 1 hour. Serve.

105.   Smoked Salmon & Curly Salad

Serves: 4 | Ready in about: 5 minutes

4 oz smoked salmon, flaked
2 heads curly endive, torn
2 tsp yellow mustard

¼ cup lemon juice
½ cup Greek yogurt
Salt and black pepper to taste

1 cucumber, sliced
2 tbsp chives, chopped

Toss curly endive, salmon, mustard, lemon juice, yogurt, salt, pepper, cucumber, and chives in a bowl. Serve.

106.   Vibrant Tri-Color Salad

Serves: 4 | Ready in about: 5 minutes

2 tbsp olive oil
1 cucumber, sliced
1 lb tomatoes, sliced

1 red onion, chopped
Salt and black pepper to taste
4 oz feta cheese, crumbled

2 tbsp parsley, chopped

Combine tomatoes, onion, cucumber, salt, pepper, feta cheese, parsley, and olive oil in a bowl. Serve.

107.   Olive & Hazelnut Fennel Salad

Serves: 4 | Ready in about: 5 minutes

2 tbsp olive oil
8 dates, pitted and sliced
2 fennel bulbs, sliced

2 tbsp chives, chopped
½ cup hazelnuts, chopped
2 tbsp lime juice

Salt and black pepper to taste
40 green olives, chopped

Place fennel, dates, chives, hazelnuts, lime juice, olives, olive oil, salt, and pepper in a bowl and toss to combine.

108. Mustardy Spinach & Tomato Salad with Eggs

Serves: 4 | Ready in about: 10 minutes

2 tbsp olive oil
10 oz baby spinach
6 eggs, at room temperature

Juice of 1 lime
1 cup feta cheese, crumbled
Salt and black pepper to taste

2 tbsp mustard
8 sundried tomatoes, chopped
1 cup walnuts, chopped

Bring to a boil salted water in a pot over medium heat. Add in the eggs and cook for 10 minutes. Remove to a bowl with ice-cold water and let them cool; peel and chop. Put the baby spinach on a large serving plate. Place olive oil, eggs, lime juice, feta cheese, salt, pepper, mustard, sun-dried tomatoes, and walnuts and toss to combine in a bowl. Pour the mixture over the spinach. Serve and enjoy!

109. Green & Red Bell Pepper Salad

Serves: 4 | Ready in about: 10 minutes

2 green bell peppers, cut into strips
2 red bell peppers, cut into strips

2 tbsp olive oil
½ cup feta cheese, crumbled

Salt and black pepper to taste

Combine bell peppers, olive oil, feta cheese, salt, and pepper in a bowl. Serve immediately.

110. Tuna & Chickpea Salad

Serves: 4 | Ready in about: 15 minutes

1 (6-oz) can solid white albacore tuna, drained
¼ cup olive oil
¼ cup balsamic vinegar
½ tsp minced garlic
¼ tsp dried oregano

Salt and black pepper to taste
2 tbsp capers, drained
4 cups baby greens
1 cup canned chickpeas

¼ cup olives, sliced
2 Roma tomatoes, chopped
¼ cup feta cheese, crumbled

In a bowl, whisk together the olive oil, balsamic vinegar, garlic, oregano, salt, and pepper until emulsified. Stir in capers. Place the baby greens in a salad bowl and top with tuna, chickpeas, olives, and tomatoes. Drizzle the vinaigrette over all and sprinkle with feta cheese. Serve immediately.

111. Watermelon & Feta Salad with a Balsamic Glaze

Serves: 4 | Ready in about: 10 minutes

3 cups packed arugula
2 ½ cups watermelon, cubed

2 oz feta cheese, crumbled
2 tbsp balsamic glaze

1 tsp mint leaves, chopped

Place the arugula on a salad plate. Top with watermelon cubes and sprinkle with feta cheese. Drizzle the balsamic glaze all over and garnish with chopped mint leaves. Serve.

112. Chickpea & Broccoli Salad

Serves: 6 | Ready in about: 10 minutes

¼ cup extra-virgin olive oil
10 oz broccoli florets, steamed
2 (14-oz) cans chickpeas

15 cherry tomatoes, halved
½ red onion, finely chopped
2 lemons, juiced and zested

2 garlic cloves, minced
2 tsp dried oregano
Salt and black pepper to taste

Mix the chickpeas, red onion, cherry tomatoes, and broccoli in a bowl. Combine the olive oil, lemon juice, lemon zest, oregano, garlic, salt, and pepper in another bowl. Pour over the salad and toss to combine. Serve immediately.

113. Bell Pepper & Spinach Salad with Citrus Dressing

Serves: 4 | Ready in about: 10 minutes

10 oz baby spinach
1 red bell pepper, sliced

2 cups corn
1 lemon, zested and juiced

Salt and black pepper to taste

Combine bell pepper, corn, lemon juice, lemon zest, baby spinach, salt, and pepper in a bowl. Serve immediately.

114. Lentil Bell Pepper Salad

Serves: 4 | Ready in about: 10 minutes

2 tomatoes, chopped
1 green bell pepper, chopped
14 oz canned lentils, drained

2 spring onions, chopped
1 red bell pepper, chopped
2 tbsp cilantro, chopped

2 tsp balsamic vinegar

Mix lentils, spring onions, tomatoes, bell peppers, cilantro, and vinegar in a bowl. Serve immediately.

115. Shrimp & Bean Salad with Lemon Vinaigrette

Serves: 4 | Ready in about: 15 minutes

1 lb peeled shrimp, deveined
30 oz canned cannellini beans, drained
4 tbsp olive oil
10 cherry tomatoes, halved

1 tsp lemon zest
½ cup red onion, chopped
5 oz spring mix salad
Salt and black pepper to taste

2 tbsp lemon juice
2 garlic cloves, minced

Warm half of the olive oil in a skillet over medium heat and cook the shrimp, turning once until just pink and opaque, about 4 minutes. Set aside to cool. Place the salad mix on a serving plate. In a bowl, mix cooled shrimp, cannellini beans, cherry tomatoes, and onion. Pour the mixture over the salad. In another bowl, whisk the remaining olive oil, lemon juice, garlic, lemon zest, salt, and pepper. Drizzle the dressing over the salad. Serve immediately.

116. Seafood Salad

Serves: 4 | Ready in about: 50 minutes

2 tbsp olive oil
2 cups olives, sliced
1 octopus, tentacles separated
2 oz calamari rings

3 garlic cloves, minced
1 white onion, chopped
¾ cup chicken stock
2 cups watercress, sliced

1 cup parsley, chopped
Salt and black pepper to taste
1 tbsp red wine vinegar

Place octopus, stock, calamari rings, salt, and pepper in a pot over medium heat and bring to a simmer. Cook for 40 minutes. Strain seafood and let cool completely. Chop tentacles into pieces. Remove to a serving bowl along with the calamari rings. Stir in garlic, onion, watercress, olives, parsley, red wine vinegar, and olive oil and toss to coat.

117. Radish & Mackerel Salad

Serves: 4 | Ready in about: 5 minutes

3 tbsp olive oil
4 oz smoked mackerel, flaked
10 radishes, sliced

5 oz baby arugula
1 cup corn
2 tbsp lemon juice

Sea salt to taste
2 tbsp fresh parsley, chopped

Place the arugula on a serving plate. Top with corn, mackerel, and radishes. Mix olive oil, lemon juice, and salt in a bowl and pour the dressing over the salad. Top with parsley.

118. Easy Green Salad

Serves: 4 | Ready in about: 10 minutes

2 tbsp olive oil
10 cherry tomatoes, halved

2 cucumbers, sliced
1 romaine lettuce head, torn

2 tbsp parsley, chopped
1 lemon, juiced

Combine olive oil, cucumbers, lettuce, tomatoes, parsley, and lemon juice in a bowl. Serve chilled.

119. Cabbage Salad with Parsley & Carrots

Serves: 4 | Ready in about: 10 minutes

2 tbsp olive oil
1 green cabbage head, torn

1 tbsp lemon juice
1 carrot, grated

Salt and black pepper to taste
¼ cup parsley, chopped

Mix olive oil, lemon juice, carrot, parsley, salt, pepper, and cabbage in a bowl. Serve right away.

120. Flavorful Cucumber & Couscous Salad

Serves: 4 | Ready in about: 30 minutes

¼ cup olive oil
2 tbsp balsamic vinegar

1 cup couscous
1 cucumber, sliced

Salt and black pepper to taste
2 tbsp lemon juice

Place couscous in a bowl with 3 cups of hot water and let sit for 10 minutes. Fluff with a fork and remove to a bowl. Stir in cucumber, salt, pepper, lemon juice, vinegar, and olive oil. Serve immediately.

121. Delectable Arugula & Caper Green Salad

Serves: 4 | Ready in about: 10 minutes

1 tbsp olive oil
10 green olives, sliced
4 cups baby arugula

1 tbsp capers, drained
1 tbsp balsamic vinegar
1 tsp lemon zest, grated

1 tbsp lemon juice
1 tsp parsley, chopped
Salt and black pepper to taste

Mix capers, olives, vinegar, lemon zest, lemon juice, oil, parsley, salt, pepper, and arugula in a bowl. Serve.

122. Tomato & Carrot Salad

Serves: 4 | Ready in about: 10 minutes

2 tbsp olive oil
4 tomatoes, chopped
1 carrot, grated

¼ cup lime juice
1 garlic clove, minced
Salt and black pepper to taste

1 lettuce head, chopped
2 green onions, chopped
½ cup cilantro, chopped

Toss lime juice, garlic, salt, pepper, olive oil, carrot, lettuce, onions, tomatoes, and cilantro in a bowl. Serve cold.

123. Asparagus Salad

Serves: 4 | Ready in about: 10 minutes

4 tbsp olive oil
1 lb asparagus

1 garlic clove, minced
Salt and black pepper to taste

1 tbsp balsamic vinegar
1 tbsp lemon zest

Roast the asparagus in a greased skillet over medium heat for 5-6 minutes, turning once. Season to taste. Toss with garlic, olive oil, lemon zest, and vinegar. Serve.

124. Flank Steak Salad with Spinach

Serves: 4 | Ready in about: 20 minutes

1 tsp extra-virgin olive oil
1 lb flank steak
1 tbsp garlic powder
Salt and black pepper to taste

4 cups baby spinach
10 cherry tomatoes, halved
10 white mushrooms, sliced
1 small red onion, sliced

½ red bell pepper, sliced
2 tbsp parsley, chopped

Preheat oven to 390 F. Rub the flank steak with olive oil, garlic powder, salt, and pepper. Bake for 5 minutes on each side. Leave the meat to sit on a cutting board for 10 minutes. In a large bowl, combine the spinach, tomatoes, mushrooms, onion, bell pepper, and parsley and toss well. Slice the steak on the diagonal and place it on top of the salad. Serve.

125. Fennel & Feta Cheese Salad with Pecans

Serves: 2 | Ready in about: 10 minutes

1 tbsp olive oil
2 tbsp orange juice
1 tbsp cider vinegar
1 tbsp honey

Salt and black pepper to taste
2 cups packed baby kale
1 orange, cut into segments
½ small fennel bulb, sliced

3 tbsp toasted pecans, chopped
2 oz feta cheese, crumbled

Mix the orange juice, olive oil, vinegar, and honey in a small bowl. Season with salt and pepper. Divide the baby kale, orange segments, fennel, pecans, and feta cheese evenly between two plates. Drizzle the dressing over each salad.

126.   Power Green Garden Salad

Serves: 4 | Ready in about: 10 minutes

¼ cup extra-virgin olive oil	3 tbsp balsamic vinegar	1 cup watercress
2 green onions, sliced	Salt to taste	1 cup arugula
½ tsp fresh lemon zest	2 cups baby spinach	1 celery stick, sliced

In a small bowl, whisk together the lemon zest, balsamic vinegar, olive oil, and salt. Put the remaining ingredients in a large bowl. Pour the dressing over the salad and lightly toss to coat. Serve and enjoy!

127.   Parsley Anchovy Salad with Mustard & Honey Vinaigrette

Serves: 6 | Ready in about: 10 minutes

½ cup olive oil	Salt and black pepper to taste	1 red onion, thinly sliced
½ lemon, juiced	4 tomatoes, diced	2 tbsp parsley, chopped
1 tsp mustard	1 cucumber, peeled and diced	4 anchovy filets, chopped
¼ tsp honey	1 lb arugula	

In a bowl, whisk together the olive oil, lemon juice, honey, and mustard, and season with salt and pepper. Set aside. In a separate bowl, combine all the vegetables with the parsley and toss. Add the sardine fillets on top of the salad. Drizzle the dressing over the salad just before serving.

128.   Almond & Red Cabbage Coleslaw

Serves: 4 | Ready in about: 10 minutes

2 tbsp olive oil	½ cup almonds, chopped	1 tbsp white wine vinegar
1 head red cabbage, shredded	1 tomato, cubed	
2 tbsp cilantro, chopped	Salt and black pepper to taste	

Mix red cabbage, cilantro, almonds, olive oil, tomato, salt, pepper, and vinegar in a bowl. Serve cold.

129.   Bean Salad with Spinach & Black Olives

Serves: 4 | Ready in about: 10 minutes

½ cup canned cannellini beans, drained

2 tbsp olive oil	1 cup black olives, halved	1 tbsp Dijon mustard
2 cups baby spinach	2 tbsp sunflower seeds	2 tbsp balsamic vinegar

Combine beans, olive oil, spinach, olives, sunflower seeds, mustard, and vinegar in a bowl. Serve immediately.

130.   Endive & Cucumber Salad with White Beans

Serves: 4 | Ready in about: 10 minutes

15 oz canned great northern beans

2 tbsp olive oil	1 cucumber, sliced	2 tbsp balsamic vinegar
2 tomatoes, cubed	1 tbsp parsley, chopped	
2 endive heads, sliced	Salt and black pepper to taste	

Combine beans, olive oil, endive, cucumber, parsley, tomatoes, salt, pepper, and vinegar in a bowl. Serve chilled.

131.   Chickpea & Arugula Salad

Serves: 4 | Ready in about: 10 minutes

2 tbsp olive oil	1 tbsp lime juice	½ tsp hot pepper flakes
16 oz canned chickpeas	1 tsp cumin, ground	
2 cups arugula	Salt and black pepper to taste	

Combine chickpeas, arugula, lime juice, olive oil, cumin, salt, pepper, and hot pepper flakes in a bowl. Serve cold.

132. Dad's Pork Salad

Serves: 4 | Ready in about: 20 minutes

2 tbsp olive oil
1 lb pork loin, cut into strips
3 scallions, chopped
1 cucumber, sliced

1 hot red pepper, sliced
1 tbsp parsley, chopped
¼ cup pine nuts
Salt and black pepper to taste

1 lime, juiced
1 garlic clove, minced

Warm the olive oil in a skillet over medium heat and brown pork for 10 minutes on all sides. Remove to a bowl. Stir in scallions, cucumber, hot red pepper, parsley, pine nuts, salt, pepper, lime juice, and garlic. Serve immediately.

133. Caper & Potato Salad

Serves: 4 | Ready in about: 30 minutes

2 tbsp olive oil
3 potatoes, peeled and cubed

2 tbsp capers
1 red onion, chopped

1 tbsp balsamic vinegar
Salt and black pepper to taste

Place potatoes in a pot over medium heat with enough water and bring to a boil; cook for 20 minutes. Drain and remove to a bowl. Stir in red onion, olive oil, capers, vinegar, salt, and pepper. Serve chilled.

134. Corn, Carrot & Rice Salad

Serves: 4 | Ready in about: 10 minutes

2 tbsp olive oil
1 Iceberg lettuce head, torn
2 carrots, grated

1 cup brown rice, cooked
1 red onion, sliced
½ cup mint, chopped

1 lime, juiced
½ cup corn
Salt and black pepper to taste

Mix rice, olive oil, onion, lettuce, carrot, mint, lime juice, corn, salt, and pepper in a bowl. Serve right away.

135. Anchovy, Cucumber & Tomato Salad

Serves: 4 | Ready in about: 10 minutes

2 tbsp extra virgin olive oil
1 tbsp lemon juice
4 canned anchovy fillets

6 black olives
½ head Romaine lettuce, torn
Salt and black pepper to taste

1 cucumber, cubed
3 tomatoes, cubed
2 spring onions, chopped

Whisk the olive oil, lemon juice, salt, and pepper in a bowl. Add the cucumber, tomatoes, and spring onions and toss to coat. Top with anchovies and black olives and serve.

136. Walnut, Spinach & Apple Salad

Serves: 4 | Ready in about: 5 minutes

2 oz sharp white cheddar cheese, cubed
3 tbsp olive oil
8 cups baby spinach

1 Granny Smith apple, diced
1 medium red apple, diced

½ cup toasted pecans
1 tbsp apple cider vinegar

Toss the spinach, apples, pecans, and cubed cheese together. Lightly drizzle olive oil and vinegar over the top and serve.

137. Figs & Arugula Salad with Tahini Dressing

Serves: 4 | Ready in about: 5 minutes

6 figs, quartered
2 cups arugula
1 cup strawberries, halved

1 tbsp hemp seeds
1 cucumber, sliced
1 tbsp lime juice

1 tbsp tahini paste

Spread the arugula on a serving plate. Top with strawberries, figs, and cucumber. In another bowl, whisk tahini, hemp seeds, and lime juice and pour over the salad. Serve.

138.　Apple, Tomato & Anchovy Salad with Walnuts

Serves: 4 | Ready in about: 5 minutes

2 tbsp olive oil
1 apple, peeled and chopped
1 Iceberg lettuce head, torn

1 tbsp apple cider vinegar
2 tbsp walnuts, chopped
1 tomato, sliced

8 anchovy stuffed olives
Salt to taste

Combine lettuce, apple cider vinegar, salt, olive oil, apple, and walnuts in a salad bowl. Toss to coat. Top with tomato and olives and serve right away.

139.　Pea & Spinach Salad with Rice

Serves: 2 | Ready in about: 30 minutes

1 tbsp olive oil
Salt and black pepper to taste
½ cup baby spinach

½ cup green peas, blanched
1 garlic clove, minced
½ cup white rice, rinsed

6 cherry tomatoes, halved
1 tbsp parsley, chopped
2 tbsp Greek salad dressing

Bring a large pot of salted water to a boil over medium heat. Pour in the rice, cover, and simmer on low heat for 15-18 minutes or until the rice is al dente. Drain and let cool. In a bowl, whisk the olive oil, garlic, salt, and black pepper. Toss the green peas, baby spinach, and rice together. Pour the dressing all over and gently stir to combine. Decorate with cherry tomatoes and parsley. Serve and enjoy!

140.　Summer Salad with Mustard Dressing

Serves: 4 | Ready in about: 5 minutes

4 cups spring mix salad greens
¼ cup cherry tomatoes
1 tbsp fresh parsley, chopped

3 tbsp extra-virgin olive oil
1 tbsp wine vinegar
2 tbsp minced shallots

½ tsp yogurt
½ tsp mustard
Salt and black pepper to taste

Place parsley, vinegar, shallots, yogurt, mustard, salt, and pepper in a bowl and mix until smooth. Whisking constantly, slowly drizzle in oil until emulsified. In a bowl, combine the salad greens and tomatoes. Pour the dressing over and serve.

141.　Easy Black Olive & Radish Salad

Serves: 4 | Ready in about: 10 minutes

2 tbsp olive oil
1 Romaine lettuce, shredded
1 lb red radishes, sliced

1 tbsp lemon zest
Salt and black pepper to taste
2 tbsp parsley, chopped

1 small red onion, sliced
10 black olives, sliced

Mix lemon zest, salt, pepper, parsley, olive oil, radishes, onion, olives, and lettuce in a bowl. Serve right away.

142.　Sweet Potato & Eggplant Salad

Serves: 4 | Ready in about: 25 minutes

1 tbsp olive oil
4 cups arugula
2 baby eggplants, cubed

2 sweet potatoes, cubed
1 red onion, cut into wedges
1 tsp hot paprika

2 tsp cumin, ground
Salt and black pepper to taste
¼ cup lime juice

Warm the olive oil in a skillet over medium heat and cook eggplants and potatoes for 5 minutes. Stir in onion, paprika, cumin, salt, pepper, and lime juice and cook for another 10 minutes. Mix in arugula and serve.

143.　Fennel & Zucchini Salad

Serves: 4 | Ready in about: 10 minutes

2 tbsp olive oil
1 cup fennel bulb, sliced
1 red onion, sliced

2 zucchini, cut into ribbons
Salt and black pepper to taste
2 tsp white wine vinegar

1 tsp lemon juice

In a large bowl, combine fennel, zucchini, red onion, salt, pepper, olive oil, vinegar, and lemon juice and toss to coat.

144. Roasted Veggie & Cheese Salad

Serves: 4 | Ready in about: 30 minutes

3 tbsp olive oil
1 lb eggplants, sliced
2 small tomatoes, sliced
½ cup ricotta cheese, crumbled

1 cup toasted bread chunks
2 bell peppers, halved
1 red onion, quartered
½ tsp marjoram

½ lemon, juiced
1 tsp mustard
2 cloves garlic, minced
Salt and black pepper to taste

Preheat oven to 420 F. Arrange the peppers, onion, tomatoes, and eggplants on a baking pan. Sprinkle with olive oil, marjoram, black pepper, and salt. Roast for 25 minutes, shaking often until the veggies are tender.

Meanwhile, in a bowl, combine the lemon juice, Dijon mustard, and garlic. Once the veggies are ready, pour over the mustard mixture and top with ricotta cheese toasted bread chunks to serve.

145. Roasted Cabbage Salad

Serves: 4 | Ready in about: 35 minutes

1 green cabbage head, shredded
4 tbsp olive oil
1 carrot, julienned
½ red bell pepper, julienned
½ green bell pepper, julienned

1 cucumber, shredded
1 shallot, sliced
2 tbsp parsley, chopped
1 tsp Dijon mustard

1 lemon, juiced
1 tsp mayonnaise
Salt to taste

Preheat the oven to 380 F. Season the green cabbage with salt and drizzle with some olive oil. Transfer to a baking dish and roast for 20-25 minutes, stirring often. Remove to a bowl and let cool for a few minutes. Stir in carrot, bell peppers, shallot, cucumber, and parsley. In another bowl, add the remaining olive oil, lemon juice, mustard, mayonnaise, and salt and whisk until well mixed. Drizzle over the cabbage mixture and toss to coat. Serve.

146. Luscious Endive & Pear Salad

Serves: 4 | Ready in about: 5 minutes

2 tbsp olive oil
1 tbsp balsamic vinegar
2 garlic cloves, minced
1 tsp Dijon mustard

1 tbsp lemon juice
Sea salt and pepper to taste
12 black olives, chopped
1 tbsp parsley, chopped

7 cups baby spinach
2 endives, shredded
2 pears, sliced lengthwise
2 fennel bulbs, shredded

Place spinach, endives, pears, fennel, parsley, olives, salt, pepper, lemon juice, olive oil, mustard, garlic, and balsamic vinegar in a bowl and toss to combine. Serve right away.

147. Savory Warm Kale Salad

Serves: 4 | Ready in about: 15 minutes

1 tbsp olive oil
4 cups kale, torn

2 cloves garlic, minced
1 red bell pepper, diced

Salt and black pepper to taste
½ lemon, juiced

Warm the olive oil in a large skillet over medium heat and add the garlic. Cook for 1 minute, and then add the bell pepper. Cook for 4-5 minutes until the pepper is tender. Stir in the kale. Cook for 3-4 minutes or just until wilted, then remove from heat. Place pepper and kale in a bowl and season with salt and black pepper. Drizzle with lemon juice.

148. Basic Tuna Salad

Serves: 2 | Ready in about: 10 minutes

2 tbsp olive oil
½ iceberg lettuce head, torn
¼ Endive head, chopped

1 tomato, cut into wedges
5 oz canned tuna, flaked
4 black olives, sliced

1 tbsp lemon juice
Salt and black pepper to taste

In a salad bowl, mix olive oil, lemon juice, salt, and pepper. Add in lettuce, endive, and tuna and toss to coat. Top with black olives and tomato wedges and serve.

149.   Fresh Salad with Sunflower Seeds

Serves: 4 | Ready in about: 15 minutes

<u>For the Salad</u>
1 head Romaine lettuce, separated into leaves

1 cup sunflower seeds, toasted	1 tbsp cilantro, chopped	8 cherry tomatoes, halved
1 cucumber, sliced	2 tbsp black olives, pitted	

<u>For Dressing</u>

1 lemon, juiced	2 tbsp onions, chopped	½ tsp garlic, chopped
½ tsp Mediterranean herb mix	½ tsp paprika	Salt and black pepper to taste

Toss all of the salad ingredients in a bowl. Whisk all of the dressing ingredients until creamy and smooth. Dress your salad and serve.

150.   Baked Pork Chop & Arugula Salad

Serves: 4 | Ready in about: 50 minutes

1 lb pork chops	2 tsp lemon zest	1 tbsp lemon juice
2 cups feta cheese, crumbled	½ tsp thyme, chopped	
2 garlic cloves, minced	2 cups arugula	

Preheat the oven to 390 F. Rub the pork chops with garlic, lemon zest, thyme, and lemon juice and arrange them on a greased baking pan. Roast for 30 minutes. Sprinkle with feta cheese and bake for another 10 minutes. Place the arugula on a platter and top with the pork chops to serve.

151.   Baby Spinach & Cherry Tomato Salad

Serves: 4 | Ready in about: 15 minutes

¼ cup olive oil	10 cherry tomatoes, halved	¼ cup pumpkin seeds
4 cups baby spinach leaves	Salt and black pepper to taste	½ lemon, juiced

Toast the pumpkin seeds in a dry sauté pan over medium heat for 2 minutes, shaking often. Let cool. In a small jar, add the olive oil, lemon juice, salt, and pepper. Place the baby spinach on a salad platter and top with cherry tomatoes. Drizzle with the vinaigrette and sprinkle with toasted pumpkin seeds. Serve immediately.

152.   Sesame Seed & Nut Fruit Salad

Serves: 4 | Ready in about: 15 minutes

¼ cup extra-virgin olive oil	½ cup sliced strawberries	¼ cup balsamic vinegar
2 apples, peeled and sliced	½ cup shredded coleslaw mix	2 tbsp sesame seeds
1 tbsp lemon juice	½ cup walnut halves	Salt and black pepper to taste
1 orange, peeled and diced	¼ cup slivered almonds	

Place the apples and lemon juice in a bowl and toss to prevent browning. Add the orange, strawberries, coleslaw mix, walnuts, and almonds and toss well to mix. In a bowl, whisk together the balsamic vinegar and olive oil and season with salt and pepper. Pour the dressing over the salad and toss to coat. Top with sesame seeds and serve.

153.   Lemon Bulgur Salad

Serves: 4 | Ready in about: 20 min+cooling time

½ cup olive oil	½ cup bulgur	1 tbsp lemon juice
2 cups fresh parsley, chopped	4 tomatoes, chopped	Salt and black pepper to taste
¼ cup mint leaves, chopped	4 spring onions, chopped	

Place 1 cup of water in a pot over medium heat and bring to a boil. Add in the bulgur and cook for 10-12 minutes. Let chill in a bowl. When cooled, stir in tomatoes, spring onions, black pepper, and salt. Drizzle with lemon juice and olive oil and toss to coat. Top with mint and parsley to serve.

154.   Tangy Three-Bean Salad

Serves: 6 | Ready in about: 20 minutes

2 tbsp olive oil
½ cup white beans, cooked
½ cup fava beans, cooked
½ cup lima beans, cooked

1 red bell pepper, diced
2 tbsp parsley, chopped
1 tsp ground cumin
1 celery stalk, finely chopped

1 lemon, juiced
Salt and black pepper to taste

Place the olive oil, beans, bell pepper, parsley, cumin, lemon juice, celery, salt, and pepper in a large bowl and mix well. Season to taste. Allow to sit for 5 minutes, so the flavors can come together before serving.

155.   Minty Fruit Salad with Cheese

Serves: 6 | Ready in about: 10 minutes

1 cantaloupe, quartered and seeded
2 tbsp extra-virgin olive oil
½ small seedless watermelon
1 cup grape tomatoes

2 cups feta cheese, crumbled
⅓ cup mint leaves, torn into small pieces

1 tbsp balsamic vinegar
Salt and black pepper to taste

Scoop balls out of the cantaloupe melon using a melon-baller. Put the balls in a shallow bowl. Repeat the process with the watermelon. Add the watermelon balls to the cantaloupe bowl. Add the tomatoes, feta cheese, mint, olive oil, vinegar, pepper, and salt, and gently mix until everything is incorporated. Serve and enjoy!

156.   Palatable Greek Salad

Serves: 4 | Ready in about: 15 minutes

2 pieces of pita bread, broken into pieces
3 tbsp olive oil
2 tbsp butter
3 medium tomatoes, chopped
1 cucumber, sliced

1 cup baby spinach
5 green bell peppers, chopped
5 radishes, sliced
1 lime, juiced

Salt and black pepper to taste
½ tsp cinnamon powder
¼ tsp allspice, ground

Warm the butter in a skillet over medium heat and cook the pita for 5 minutes. Remove and season with salt and pepper. Combine cooked pita, cucumber, spinach, tomatoes, bell pepper, and radishes in a bowl. Mix olive oil, lime juice, salt, pepper, cinnamon powder, and allspice in another bowl and pour over the salad. Toss to coat. Serve.

157.   Bell Pepper & Mushroom Salad

Serves: 4 | Ready in about: 15 minutes

2 tbsp olive oil
½ lb mushrooms, sliced
3 garlic cloves, minced

Salt and black pepper to taste
1 tomato, diced
1 red bell pepper, sliced

3 tbsp lime juice
½ cup chicken stock
2 tbsp cilantro, chopped

Warm the olive oil in a skillet over medium heat and sauté mushrooms for 4 minutes. Stir in garlic, salt, pepper, tomato, bell pepper, lime juice, and chicken stock and sauté for another 4 minutes. Top with cilantro and serve.

158.   Shrimp & Bell Pepper Salad with Avocado

Serves: 4 | Ready in about: 10 min+cooling time

1 lb shrimp, peeled and deveined
2 tbsp olive oil
1 tbsp lemon juice

1 yellow bell pepper, sliced
1 Romano lettuce, torn
1 avocado, chopped

Salt to taste
12 cherry tomatoes, halved

Preheat a grill pan over high heat. Drizzle the shrimp with some olive oil and arrange them on the preheated grill pan. Sear for 5 minutes on both sides until pink and cooked through. Let cool completely. On a serving plate, arrange the lettuce. Top with bell pepper, shrimp, avocado, and cherry tomatoes. In a bowl, add the lemon juice, salt, and olive oil and whisk to combine. Drizzle the dressing over the salad and serve immediately.

SOUPS & STEWS

159. Green Cream Soup

Serves: 4 | Ready in about: 20 minutes

1 tbsp olive oil
1 white onion, chopped
½ cup Greek yogurt

1 celery stalk, chopped
4 cups vegetable stock
2 cups green peas

2 tbsp mint leaves, chopped
1 cup spinach
Salt and black pepper to taste

Warm the olive oil in a pot over medium heat and cook the onion and celery for 4 minutes. Add in stock, green peas, spinach, salt, and pepper and bring to a boil. Simmer for 4 minutes. Take off the heat and let cool the soup for a few minutes. Blend the soup with an immersion blender until smooth. Apportion the soup among bowls and garnish with a swirl of Greek yogurt. Sprinkle with chopped mint and serve.

160. Spinach & Mushroom Orzo Soup

Serves: 4 | Ready in about: 20 minutes

2 tbsp butter
3 cups spinach
½ cup orzo
4 cups chicken broth

1 cup feta cheese, crumbled
Salt and black pepper to taste
½ tsp dried oregano
1 onion, chopped

2 garlic cloves, minced
1 cup mushrooms, sliced

Melt butter in a pot over medium heat and sauté onion, garlic, and mushrooms for 5 minutes until tender. Add in chicken broth, orzo, salt, pepper, and oregano. Bring to a boil and reduce the heat to a low. Continue simmering for 10 minutes, partially covered. Stir in spinach and continue to cook until the spinach wilts, about 3-4 minutes. Ladle into individual bowls and serve garnished with feta cheese.

161. Fire-Roasted Tomato Soup with Spicy Sausage

Serves: 4 | Ready in about: 25 minutes

28 oz fire-roasted diced tomatoes
1 tbsp olive oil
2 shallots, chopped
3 cloves garlic, minced

Salt and black pepper to taste
4 cups beef broth
½ cup fresh ripe tomatoes

1 tbsp red wine vinegar
3 smoked sausage, chopped
½ cup thinly chopped basil

Warm the olive oil in a large pot or saucepan over medium heat. Cook the smoked sausage until crispy, stirring occasionally, approximately 5 minutes. Remove to a plate. In the same pot, add the garlic and shallots, and sauté for about 3 minutes until they become soft. Season with salt and pepper.

Stir in the red wine vinegar, broth, diced tomatoes, and ripe tomatoes. Bring the mixture to a simmer. Cover the pot and let it cook for 4 minutes on medium heat. Pour the soup into a blender and process until smooth. Divide the soup into bowls, and top with the sausage. Finish by garnishing with basil. Serve the soup hot and enjoy its delightful flavors.

162. Creamy Feta & Cannellini Bean Soup

Serves: 4 | Ready in about: 30 minutes

2 tbsp olive oil
4 oz feta cheese, crumbled
1 cup collard greens, torn
2 cups canned cannellini beans
1 fennel bulb, chopped

1 carrot, chopped
½ cup spring onions, chopped
½ tsp dried rosemary
½ tsp dried basil
1 garlic clove, minced

4 cups vegetable broth
2 tbsp tomato paste
Salt and black pepper to taste

In a pot over medium heat, warm the olive oil. Add in fennel, garlic, carrot, and spring onions and sauté until tender, about 2-3 minutes. Stir in tomato paste, rosemary, and basil and cook for 2 more minutes. Pour in vegetable broth and cannellini beans. Bring to a boil, then lower the heat and simmer for 15 minutes. Add in collard greens and cook for another 2-3 minutes until wilted. Adjust the seasoning with salt and pepper. Top with feta cheese and serve.

163.   Kolokythosoupa (Greek Zucchini Soup)

Serves: 4 | Ready in about: 30 minutes

1 ¼ lb green beans, cut into chunks	2 garlic cloves, minced	½ tsp cayenne pepper
2 tbsp olive oil	1 zucchini, chopped	1 tsp oregano
1 onion, chopped	5 cups vegetable broth	½ tsp dried dill
1 celery with leaves, chopped	2 tomatoes, chopped	½ cup black olives, sliced
1 carrot, chopped	Salt and black pepper to taste	

Warm the olive in a pot over medium heat. Sauté the onion, celery, and carrot for about 4 minutes or until the vegetables are just tender. Add in the garlic and zucchini and continue to sauté for 1 minute or until aromatic. Pour in the broth, green beans, tomatoes, salt, black pepper, cayenne pepper, oregano, and dried dill; bring to a boil. Reduce the heat to a simmer and let it cook for about 15 minutes. Serve in individual bowls with sliced olives.

164.   Chickpea & Spinach Soup with Savory Sausages

Serves: 4 | Ready in about: 35 minutes

2 tbsp olive oil	1 onion, chopped	6 cups chicken broth
8 oz sausage, sliced	1 carrot, chopped	1 tsp dried oregano
1 (14-oz) can s	1 red bell pepper, chopped	Salt and black pepper to taste
4 cups chopped spinach	3 garlic cloves, minced	½ tsp red pepper flakes

Warm olive oil in a pot over medium heat. Sear the sausage for 5 minutes until browned. Set aside. Add carrot, onion, garlic, and bell pepper to the pot and sauté for 5 minutes until soft. Pour in broth, chickpeas, spinach, oregano, salt, pepper, and red flakes; let simmer for 5 minutes until the spinach softens. Bring the sausage back to the pot and cook for another minute. Serve warm.

165.   Greek Bean Soup

Serves: 4 | Ready in about: 40 minutes

1 tbsp olive oil	1 cup dried s	1 large celery stalk, chopped
1 onion, chopped	½ cup pinto beans, soaked	1 tsp dried thyme
2 cloves garlic, minced	½ cup navy beans, soaked	16 oz zucchini noodles
5 cups vegetable broth	3 carrots, chopped	Salt and black pepper to taste

Warm the olive oil in a large pot or saucepan over medium heat. Add the garlic and onion, and sauté for about 5 minutes until they turn golden brown. Mix in the pepper, broth, carrots, salt, pepper, celery, beans, chickpeas, and thyme. Bring the mixture to a boil, then reduce the heat to low and let it simmer for 15 minutes, uncovered. After 15 minutes, carefully stir in the zucchini noodles, allowing them to wilt in the hot soup. Once the zucchini noodles are tender, remove the pot from the heat. Serve the soup hot, and enjoy.

166.   Garden Vegetable Soup

Serves: 4 | Ready in about: 25 minutes

¼ green cabbage head, shredded

2 tbsp olive oil	1 potato, diced	½ red bell pepper, diced
1 cup leeks, chopped	1 celery stalk, diced	½ cup green beans
2 garlic cloves, minced	1 cup mushrooms	Salt and black pepper to taste
8 cups vegetable stock	1 cup broccoli florets	2 tbsp fresh parsley, chopped
1 carrot, diced	1 cup cauliflower florets	

Heat oil in a large pot over medium heat. Add garlic and leeks, and cook for about 6 minutes until they become slightly browned. Add stock, carrot, celery, broccoli, bell pepper, green beans, salt, cabbage, cauliflower, mushrooms, potato, and pepper to the pot. Cover the pot with a lid and let it cook over medium heat for approximately 10-15 minutes or until the vegetables are tender. Once the vegetables are cooked, stir in parsley for a fresh and aromatic touch. Serve the flavorful dish immediately, and enjoy!

167.   Spicy Lentil Soup

Serves: 4 | Ready in about: 25 minutes

2 tbsp olive oil

3 cups vegetable broth

1 cup tomato sauce

1 onion, chopped

1 cup dry red lentils

½ cup prepared salsa verde

2 garlic cloves, minced

1 tbsp smoked paprika

2 tsp ground cumin

¼ tsp cayenne pepper

Salt and black pepper to taste

Warm the olive oil in a large pot over medium heat. Stir in garlic and onion, and cook for about 5 minutes until they become golden brown. Add tomato sauce, broth, salsa verde, cumin, cayenne pepper, lentils, paprika, salt, and pepper to the pot. Cover the pot with a lid and let it simmer for approximately 20 minutes or until the lentils are tender and cooked through. Serve.

168.   Savory Lamb & Spinach Soup

Serves: 4 | Ready in about: 60 minutes

½ lb lamb shoulder, cut into bite-sized pieces

2 tbsp olive oil

1 onion, chopped

2 garlic cloves, minced

10 oz spinach, chopped

4 cups vegetable broth

Salt and black pepper to taste

Warm the olive oil in a large pot over medium heat. Add the lamb, onion, and garlic and cook for 6-8 minutes, stirring often. Pour in the broth and adjust the seasoning with salt and pepper. Cook covered for 30-40 minutes. Add the spinach. Cook for 5 more minutes. Serve.

169.   Hearty Root Veggie Soup

Serves: 4 | Ready in about: 40 minutes

3 cups chopped butternut squash

2 tbsp olive oil

1 carrot, chopped

1 leek, chopped

2 garlic cloves, minced

1 celery stalk, chopped

1 parsnip, chopped

1 potato, chopped

4 cups vegetable broth

1 tsp dried thyme

Salt and black pepper to taste

Warm olive oil in a pot over medium heat and sauté leek, garlic, parsnip, carrot, and celery for 5-6 minutes until the veggies start to brown. Throw in squash, potato, broth, thyme, salt, and pepper. Bring to a boil, then decrease the heat and simmer for 20-30 minutes until the veggies soften. Transfer to a food processor and blend until you get a smooth and homogeneous consistency.

170.   Roasted Vegetable Soup

Serves: 4 | Ready in about: 45 minutes

3 tbsp olive oil

2 carrots, sliced

3 sweet potatoes, sliced

1 celery stalk, sliced

1 tsp chopped dill

4 cups vegetable broth

Salt and black pepper to taste

1 tbsp Halloumi, grated

Preheat oven to 400 F. Mix carrots, sweet potatoes, and celery in a bowl. Drizzle with olive oil and toss. Sprinkle with dill, salt, and pepper. Arrange the vegetable on a lined with parchment paper sheet and bake for 30 minutes or until the veggies are tender and golden brown. Let cool slightly.

Place the veggies and some broth in a food processor and pulse until smooth; work in batches. Transfer to a pot over low heat and add in the remaining broth. Cook just until heated through. Serve topped with Halloumi cheese.

171.   Homestyle Chicken Soup with Fresh Vegetables

Serves: 4 | Ready in about: 35 minutes

2 tsp olive oil

1 cup mushrooms, chopped

1 large carrot, chopped

1 yellow onion, chopped

1 celery stalk, chopped

2 yellow squash, chopped

2 chicken breasts, cubed

½ cup chopped fresh parsley

4 cups chicken stock

Salt and black pepper to taste

Warm the oil in a skillet over medium heat. Place in carrot, onion, mushrooms, and celery and cook for 5 minutes. Stir in chicken and cook for 10 more minutes. Mix in squash, salt, and black pepper. Cook for 5 minutes, then lower the heat and pour in the stock. Cook covered for 10 more minutes. Divide between bowls and scatter with parsley.

172.   Rice & Green Bean Chicken Soup

Serves: 4 | Ready in about: 45 minutes

2 tbsp olive oil

4 cups chicken stock

½ lb chicken breasts strips

1 celery stalk, chopped

2 garlic cloves, minced

1 yellow onion, chopped

½ cup white rice

1 egg, whisked

½ lemon, juiced

1 cup green beans, chopped

1 cup carrots, chopped

½ cup dill, chopped

Salt and black pepper to taste

Warm the olive oil in a pot over medium heat and sauté onion, garlic, celery, carrots, and chicken for 6-7 minutes. Pour in stock and rice. Bring to a boil and simmer for 10 minutes. Stir in green beans, salt, and pepper and cook for 15 minutes. Whisk the egg and lemon juice and pour into the pot. Stir and cook for 2 minutes. Serve topped with dill.

173.   Roasted Red Pepper Soup with Feta

Serves: 6 | Ready in about: 30 minutes

8 roasted red peppers, chopped

2 roasted hot peppers, chopped

3 tbsp olive oil

2 shallots, chopped

4 garlic cloves, minced

2 tsp chopped fresh oregano

6 cups chicken broth

Salt and black pepper to taste

¼ cup heavy cream

1 lemon, juiced

½ cup feta cheese, crumbled

Puree all of the roasted peppers in your food processor until smooth. Warm the olive oil in a pot over medium heat and add the shallots and garlic. Cook until soft and translucent, about 5 minutes. Add the pepper mixture and oregano, followed by the broth. Bring to a boil on high heat and sprinkle with salt and pepper. Lower the heat to low and simmer for 15 minutes. Stir in the heavy cream and lemon juice. Ladle into individual bowls and garnish with feta.

174.   Carrot & Lentil Soup

Serves: 4 | Ready in about: 30 minutes

2 tbsp olive oil

1 cup lentils, rinsed

1 onion, chopped

2 carrots, chopped

1 potato, cubed

1 tomato, chopped

4 garlic cloves, minced

4 cups vegetable broth

½ tsp hot pepper powder

Salt and black pepper to taste

2 tbsp fresh parsley, chopped

Warm the olive oil in a pot over medium heat. Add in onion, garlic, and carrots and sauté for 5-6 minutes until tender. Mix in lentils, broth, salt, pepper, hot pepper powder, potato, and tomato. Bring to a boil, lower the heat and simmer for 15-18 minutes, stirring often. Top with parsley and serve.

175.   Fennel, Bean & Squash Soup

Serves: 4 | Ready in about: 55 minutes

2 tbsp olive oil

1 yellow onion, chopped

2 garlic cloves, minced

1 carrot, chopped

1 zucchini, chopped

1 squash, peeled and cubed

2 tbsp parsley, chopped

¼ fennel bulb, chopped

30 oz canned cannellini beans

2 cups veggie stock

¼ tsp dried thyme

Salt and black pepper to taste

1 cup green beans

¼ cup Halloumi, grated

Warm the olive oil in a pot over medium heat and cook the onion, garlic, carrot, squash, zucchini, and fennel for 5 minutes. Stir in cannellini beans, veggie stock, 4 cups of water, thyme, salt, and pepper and bring to a boil; cook for 10 minutes. Put in green beans and cook for another 10 minutes. Serve sprinkled with Halloumi cheese and parsley.

176. Avgolemono Soup (Greek Lemon Chicken Soup)

Serves: 4 | Ready in about: 40 minutes

2 tbsp olive oil
1 lb boneless chicken thighs
¼ cup pearl barley
1 red onion, chopped

2 cloves garlic, minced
4 cups chicken broth
¼ tsp oregano
½ lemon, juiced

¼ tsp parsley
¼ cup scallions, chopped
Salt and black pepper to taste

Heat the olive oil in a pot over medium heat and sweat the onion and garlic for 2-3 minutes until tender. Place in chicken thighs and cook for 5-6 minutes, stirring often. Pour in chicken broth and barley and bring to a boil. Then lower the heat and simmer for 5 minutes. Remove the chicken and shred it with two forks. Return to the pot and add in lemon, oregano, and parsley. Simmer for 20-22 more minutes. Stir in shredded chicken and adjust the seasoning. Divide between 4 bowls and top with chopped scallions.

177. Celery Turkey Rice Soup with Fragrant Herbs

Serves: 4 | Ready in about: 40 minutes

2 tbsp olive oil
1 lb turkey breasts, cubed
½ cup rice
1 onion, chopped

1 celery stalk, chopped
1 carrot, sliced
1 egg
2 tbsp yogurt

1 tsp dried tarragon
1 tsp lemon zest
2 tbsp fresh parsley, chopped
Salt and black pepper to taste

Heat olive oil in a pot over medium heat and sauté the onion, celery, turkey, and carrot for 6-7 minutes, stirring occasionally. Stir in the rice for 1-2 minutes, pour in 4 cups of water, and season with salt and pepper. Bring the soup to a boil. Lower the heat and simmer for 20 minutes.

In a bowl, beat the egg with yogurt until well combined. Remove 1 cup of the hot soup broth with a spoon and add slowly to the egg mixture, stirring constantly. Pour the whisked mixture into the pot and stir in salt, black pepper, tarragon, and lemon zest. Garnish with parsley and serve.

178. Creamy Potato & White Bean Soup

Serves: 4 | Ready in about: 50 minutes

2 tbsp olive oil
2 shallots, chopped
1 potato, chopped
5 celery sticks, chopped

1 carrot, chopped
½ tsp dried oregano
1 bay leaf
30 oz canned white beans

2 tbsp tomato paste
4 cups chicken stock

Warm the olive oil in a pot over medium heat and cook shallots, celery, carrot, bay leaf, and oregano for 5 minutes. Stir in beans, tomato paste, potato, and chicken stock and bring to a boil. Cook for 20 minutes. Remove the bay leaf.

179. Domatosoupa (Greek Tomato Soup)

Serves: 4 | Ready in about: 30 minutes

1 cup roasted bell peppers, chopped
2 tbsp olive oil
3 tomatoes, cored and halved
2 cloves garlic, minced
1 yellow onion, quartered

1 celery stalk, chopped
1 carrot, shredded
½ tsp ground cumin
½ tsp hot pepper
4 cups vegetable broth

½ tsp red pepper flakes
2 tbsp fresh basil, chopped
Salt and black pepper to taste
¼ cup crème fraîche

Heat oven to 380 F. Arrange the tomatoes and peppers on a roasting pan. Drizzle olive oil over the vegetables. Roast for 20 minutes until charred. Remove, let cool, and peel them.

Heat olive oil in a pot over medium heat and sauté onion, garlic, celery, and carrots for 3-5 minutes until tender. Stir in hot pepper and cumin for 1-2 minutes. Pour in roasted bell peppers and tomatoes, stir, then add in the vegetable broth. Season with salt and pepper. Bring to a boil and reduce the heat; simmer for 10 minutes. Using an immersion blender, purée the soup until smooth. Sprinkle with pepper flakes and basil. Serve topped with crème fraîche.

180. Thick & Creamy Tomato Hummus Soup

Serves: 4 | Ready in about: 10 minutes

1 (14-oz) can diced tomatoes	4 cups chicken stock	1 cup garlic croutons
1 cup traditional hummus	¼ cup basil leaves, sliced	

Place the tomatoes, hummus, and chicken stock in your blender and blend until smooth. Pour the mixture into a saucepan over medium heat and bring it to a boil. Pour the soup into bowls. Sprinkle with basil and serve with croutons.

181. Turkey & Cabbage Comfort Soup

Serves: 4 | Ready in about: 40 minutes

2 tbsp olive oil	2 cups green cabbage, grated	½ tsp ground nutmeg
½ lb turkey breast, cubed	4 celery sticks, chopped	Salt and black pepper to taste
2 leeks, sliced	4 cups vegetable stock	
4 spring onions, chopped	½ tsp sweet paprika	

Warm the olive oil in a pot over medium heat and brown the turkey for 4 minutes, stirring occasionally. Add in leeks, spring onions, and celery and cook for another minute. Stir in cabbage, vegetable stock, sweet paprika, nutmeg, salt, and pepper and bring to a boil. Cook for 30 minutes. Serve.

182. Fall Pork Soup

Serves: 4 | Ready in about: 40 minutes

2 tbsp olive oil	1 cup mushrooms, chopped	14 oz canned tomatoes
1 onion, chopped	1 carrot, chopped	4 cups vegetable stock
2 garlic cloves, minced	1 celery stalk, chopped	½ tsp nutmeg, ground
1 pork loin, chopped	Salt and black pepper to taste	2 tsp parsley, chopped

Warm the olive oil in a pot over medium heat and cook pork meat, onion, celery, and garlic for 5 minutes. Put in mushrooms, carrots, salt, pepper, tomatoes, vegetable stock, and nutmeg and bring to a boil. Cook for 25 minutes. Sprinkle with parsley. Serve warm.

183. Hearty Vegetable Lentil Soup

Serves: 4 | Ready in about: 55 minutes

2 tbsp olive oil	2 garlic cloves, minced	½ cup red lentils
1 yellow onion, chopped	2 tbsp ginger, grated	1 cup spinach, torn
2 celery stalks, chopped	1 tsp turmeric powder	14 oz canned tomatoes, diced
1 carrot, sliced	2 tsp sweet paprika	4 cups chicken stock
2 tbsp parsley, chopped	1 tsp cinnamon powder	Salt and black pepper to taste

Warm the olive oil in a pot over medium heat and sauté onion, ginger, garlic, celery, and carrot for 5 minutes. Stir in turmeric powder, sweet paprika, cinnamon powder, red lentils, tomatoes, chicken stock, salt, and pepper and bring to a boil. Simmer for 15 minutes. Stir in spinach for 5 minutes until the spinach is wilted. Sprinkle with parsley and serve.

184. Navy Bean Soup with Parsley & Paprika

Serves: 4 | Ready in about: 50 minutes

2 tbsp olive oil	1 yellow onion, chopped	½ tsp paprika
6 cups veggie stock	2 garlic cloves, minced	1 tsp thyme
1 cup celery, chopped	½ cup navy beans, soaked	Salt and black pepper to taste
1 cup carrots, chopped	2 tbsp chopped parsley	

Warm olive oil in a saucepan and sauté onion, garlic, carrots, and celery for 5 minutes, stirring occasionally. Stir in paprika, thyme, salt, and pepper for 1 minute. Pour in broth and navy beans. Bring to a boil, then reduce the heat and simmer for 40 minutes. Sprinkle with parsley and serve.

185. Leek & Kale Chicken Soup with Vermicelli

Serves: 4 | Ready in about: 25 minutes

2 tbsp olive oil
1 carrot, chopped
1 leek, chopped
½ cup vermicelli

4 cups chicken stock
2 cups kale, chopped
2 chicken breasts, cubed
1 cup orzo

¼ cup lemon juice
2 tbsp parsley, chopped
Salt and black pepper to taste

Warm the olive oil in a pot over medium heat and sauté leek and chicken for 6 minutes. Stir in carrot and chicken stock and bring to a boil. Cook for 10 minutes. Add vermicelli, kale, orzo, and lemon juice and continue cooking for another 5 minutes. Adjust the seasoning with salt and pepper and sprinkle with parsley. Ladle into soup bowls. Serve.

186. Magiritsa (Greek Easter Soup with Lamb & Greens)

Serves: 4 | Ready in about: 50 minutes

2 tbsp olive oil
½ lb lamb meat, cubed
3 eggs, whisked

4 cups beef broth
5 spring onions, chopped
2 tbsp mint, chopped

2 lemons, juiced
Salt and black pepper to taste
1 cup baby spinach

Warm the olive oil in a pot over medium heat and cook the lamb for 10 minutes, stirring occasionally. Add in spring onions and cook for another 3 minutes. Pour beef broth, salt, and pepper and simmer for 30 minutes. Whisk eggs with lemon juice and some soup, pour into the pot, and spinach and cook for 5 minutes. Sprinkle with mint and serve.

187. Toothsome Eggplant & Chicken Soup

Serves: 4 | Ready in about: 40 minutes

2 tbsp butter
¼ tsp celery seeds
2 cups eggplants, cubed
Salt and black pepper to taste
1 red onion, chopped

2 garlic cloves, minced
1 red bell pepper, chopped
1 red hot pepper
2 tbsp parsley, chopped
2 tbsp oregano, chopped

4 cups chicken stock
1 lb chicken breasts, cubed
1 cup half and half
1 egg yolk

Melt butter in a pot over medium heat and sauté chicken, garlic, and onion for 10 minutes. Put in bell pepper, eggplant, salt, pepper, red hot pepper, celery seeds, oregano, and chicken stock and bring to a simmer. Cook for 20 minutes. Whisk egg yolk, half and half, and 1 cup of the soup in a bowl and pour gradually into the pot. Sprinkle with parsley.

188. Stelline Chicken Soup with Garlic & Celery

Serves: 4 | Ready in about: 40 minutes

2 tbsp olive oil
1 onion, chopped
2 garlic cloves, minced
1 celery stalk, chopped

1 carrot, chopped
4 cups chicken stock
Salt and black pepper to taste
¼ cup lemon juice

1 chicken breast, cubed
½ cup stelline pasta
6 mint leaves, chopped

Warm the olive oil in a pot over medium heat and sauté onion, garlic, celery, and carrot for 5 minutes until tender. Add in the chicken and cook for another 4-5 minutes, stirring occasionally. Pour in chicken stock and bring to a boil; cook for 10 minutes. Add in the stelline pasta and let simmer for 10 minutes. Stir in lemon juice and adjust the seasoning with salt and pepper. Sprinkle with mint and serve immediately.

189. Revithosoupa (Greek Chickpea Soup)

Serves: 6 | Ready in about: 30 minutes

2 tbsp olive oil
1 onion, diced
3 garlic cloves, minced
1 tsp cinnamon
1 tsp ground cumin

1 tsp ground coriander
1 (14-oz) can tomatoes, diced
6 cups vegetable stock
1 ½ cups canned chickpeas
1 carrot, chopped

½ tsp dried thyme
Salt and black pepper to taste
1 tbsp fresh mint, chopped

Warm the olive oil in a large stockpot over medium heat. Sauté the onions and garlic just until tender and translucent, 3 minutes. Stir in cinnamon, cumin, ground coriander, thyme, salt, and pepper for 30 seconds. Pour in the vegetable stock and bring to a boil, stirring frequently. Add the chickpeas and carrot and simmer for 15 minutes. Spoon into individual bowls and top with fresh mint.

190.   Roasted Eggplant & Tomato Soup

Serves: 4 | Ready in about: 60 minutes

2 tbsp olive oil	2 tbsp garlic, minced	5 cups chicken broth
3 eggplants, sliced lengthwise	1 tsp dried thyme	¼ cup heavy cream
Salt to taste	Salt and black pepper to taste	2 tbsp fresh basil, chopped
1 red onion, chopped	2 ripe tomatoes, halved	

Preheat oven to 400 F. Place the eggplants on a greased sheet pan and drizzle with some olive oil. Roast for 45 minutes. Remove from oven and allow to cool. When cool, remove all of the insides, discarding the skins.

Warm the remaining olive oil in a large skillet over medium heat. Add the onions and garlic and cook for 5 minutes until soft and translucent. Add the thyme and season with salt and pepper. Put the eggplant, tomatoes, and onion in your food processor and process until smooth. Pour the chicken broth into a pot and bring to a boil. Reduce heat to a simmer and add the eggplant mixture. Stir until well combined and fold in the heavy cream. Adjust to taste. Serve topped with basil.

191.   Scrumptious Veggie Soup

Serves: 4 | Ready in about: 40 minutes

2 tbsp olive oil	½ head broccoli, chopped	½ tsp cayenne pepper
2 potatoes, peeled and cubed	1 onion, chopped	4 cups vegetable stock
1 celery stalk, chopped	1 carrot, cubed	Salt and black pepper to taste
1 zucchini, chopped	1 tsp dried rosemary	1 tbsp chives, chopped

Warm the olive oil in a pot over medium heat and sauté onion, celery, and carrot for 5 minutes. Add in rosemary, cayenne pepper, potatoes, and zucchini and sauté for 5 minutes. Pour in the vegetable stock and bring to a simmer. Cook for 20 minutes. Adjust the seasoning and add in the broccoli; cook for 5-8 minutes. Sprinkle with chives.

192.   Ham & Green Lentil Soup

Serves: 4 | Ready in about: 30 minutes

2 tbsp olive oil	3 garlic cloves, chopped	4 cups vegetable stock
½ lb ham, cubed	Salt and black pepper to taste	3 tbsp tomato paste
1 onion, chopped	1 carrot, chopped	2 tomatoes, chopped
2 tsp parsley, dried	½ tsp paprika	
1 potato, chopped	½ cup green lentils, rinsed	

Warm the olive oil in a pot over medium heat and cook ham, onion, carrot, and garlic for 4 minutes. Stir in tomato paste, paprika, and tomatoes for 2-3 minutes. Pour in lentils, vegetable stock, and potato and bring to a boil. Cook for 18-20 minutes. Adjust the seasoning with salt and pepper and sprinkle with parsley. Serve warm.

193.   Easy Lamb Soup

Serves: 4 | Ready in about: 40 minutes

2 tbsp olive oil	2 garlic cloves, minced	8 oz leftover lamb, shredded
2 carrots, chopped	1 tbsp thyme, chopped	14 oz canned chickpeas
1 red onion, chopped	4 cups vegetable stock	2 tbsp cilantro, chopped
2 celery stalks, chopped	1 cup mushrooms, sliced	

Warm the olive oil in a pot over medium heat and cook the onion, garlic, celery, mushrooms, carrots, and thyme for 5 minutes until tender. Stir in vegetable stock and lamb and bring to a boil. Reduce the heat to low and simmer for 20 minutes. Mix in chickpeas and cook for an additional 5 minutes. Ladle your soup into individual bowls. Top with cilantro.

194.   Cold Tomato Soup with Succulent Prawns

Serves: 4 | Ready in about: 15 minutes

1 lb prawns, peeled and deveined

3 tbsp olive oil	3 roasted red peppers, chopped	Salt and black pepper to taste
1 cucumber, chopped	2 tbsp balsamic vinegar	½ tsp cumin
3 cups tomato juice	1 garlic clove, minced	1 tsp thyme, chopped

In a food processor, blitz tomato juice, cucumber, red peppers, 2 tbsp of olive oil, vinegar, cumin, salt, pepper, and garlic until smooth. Remove to a bowl and transfer to the fridge for 10 minutes. Warm the remaining oil in a pot over medium heat and sauté prawns, salt, pepper, and thyme for 4 minutes on all sides. Let cool. Ladle the soup into individual bowls and serve topped with prawns.

195.   Farro & White Bean Soup

Serves: 6 | Ready in about: 2 hours 10 minutes

1 (14-oz) can diced tomatoes with juice

2 tbsp olive oil	2 garlic cloves, minced	1 cup farro
1 onion, diced	6 cups chicken broth	½ tsp rosemary
1 celery stalk, diced	1 cup white beans, soaked	Salt and black pepper to taste

Warm the olive oil in a large stockpot over medium heat. Sauté the onion, celery, and garlic cloves just until tender. Add the broth, beans, tomatoes, farro, and seasonings, and bring to a simmer. Cover and cook for 2 hours or until the beans and farro are tender. Season with salt and pepper.

196.   Creamy Leek Soup with Toasted Hazelnuts

Serves: 4 | Ready in about: 25 minutes

2 tbsp olive oil	1 onion, chopped	¼ cup heavy cream
1 tbsp ground hazelnuts	2 garlic cloves, minced	2 tbsp chopped chives
4 leeks (white part), sliced	4 cups chicken stock	

Warm the olive oil in a medium saucepan. Add the leeks, garlic, and onion and sauté over low heat until tender, 3-5 minutes. Add ½ cup of chicken stock, then puree the mixture in a blender until smooth. Return the chicken stock mixture to the saucepan. Add the remaining chicken stock and simmer for 10 minutes. Stir in the heavy cream until combined. Pour into bowls and garnish with hazelnuts and chives. Serve and enjoy!

197.   Chicken & Bean Soup

Serves: 6 | Ready in about: 40 minutes

3 tbsp olive oil	4 cups chicken stock	14 oz canned white beans
3 garlic cloves, minced	1 lb chicken breasts, cubed	1 lime, zested and juiced
1 onion, chopped	1 red hot pepper, chopped	Salt and black pepper to taste
3 tomatoes, chopped	1 tbsp fennel seeds, crushed	2 tbsp parsley, chopped

Warm the olive oil in a pot over medium heat. Cook the onion and garlic, adding a splash of water, for 10 minutes until aromatic. Add in the chicken and hot pepper and sit-fry for another 6-8 minutes. Put in tomatoes, chicken stock, beans, lime zest, lime juice, salt, pepper, and fennel seeds and bring to a boil; cook for 30 minutes. Serve topped with parsley.

198.   Buttermilk Leek & Shrimp Soup

Serves: 6 | Ready in about: 40 minutes

1 lb shrimp, peeled and deveined

3 tbsp olive oil	2 garlic cloves, minced	2 tbsp buttermilk
1 celery stalk, chopped	Salt and black pepper to taste	1 lemon, juiced
1 leek, sliced	1 tbsp coriander seeds	
1 fennel bulb, chopped	6 cups vegetable broth	

Warm the oil in a large pot oven over medium heat. Add the celery, leek, and fennel, and cook for about 5 minutes until tender. Add the garlic and season with salt and pepper. Add the coriander seeds and stir. Pour in the broth, bring to a boil, and then reduce to a simmer and cook for 20 more minutes. Add the shrimp to the soup and cook until just pink, about 3 minutes. Stir in buttermilk and lemon juice. Serve.

199. Tomato Soup with Fresh Cilantro

Serves: 6 | Ready in about: 30 minutes

2 tbsp olive oil
1 onion, chopped
3 garlic cloves, minced
8 large tomatoes, chopped

1 tsp paprika
1 tsp ground cumin
6 cups chicken broth
Salt and black pepper to taste

1 cup half-and-half
2 tbsp chopped cilantro

Warm the olive oil in a large pot over medium heat. Add the onion and garlic and cook until soft and translucent, 3 minutes. Stir in paprika, cumin, salt, and pepper for 1 minute. Pour in the tomatoes and chicken broth. Simmer for 15 minutes. Puree the soup with an immersion blender. Stir in half-and-half and serve garnished with cilantro.

200. Psarosoupa (Greek Fish Soup)

Serves: 6 | Ready in about: 35 minutes

1 lb sea bass, cubed
2 tbsp olive oil
1 cup green peas
1 onion, chopped
1 red bell pepper, chopped
1 green bell pepper, chopped

2 garlic cloves, minced
1 tsp ground turmeric
1 tsp dried thyme
2 tsp smoked paprika
½ cup instant brown rice

4 cups fish broth
1 (28-oz) can diced tomatoes
2 tbsp fresh dill, chopped

Warm the olive oil in a large stockpot over medium heat. Add the onion, red and green bell peppers, and garlic. Cook for 5 minutes, stirring occasionally. Add the turmeric, thyme, and smoked paprika, and cook for another 2 minutes. Stir in the rice, sea bass, and broth. Bring to a boil and simmer for 12-15 minutes. Stir in peas, tomatoes, and sea bass. Cook for 4-6 minutes. Sprinkle with dill and serve in individual bowls.

201. Savory Pork Meatball Soup

Serves: 4 | Ready in about: 35 minutes

2 tbsp olive oil
½ cup white rice
½ lb ground pork
Salt and black pepper to taste

2 garlic cloves, minced
1 onion, chopped
½ tsp dried thyme
4 cups beef stock

½ tsp saffron powder
14 oz canned tomatoes, diced
1 tbsp parsley, chopped

In a bowl, mix ground pork, rice, salt, and pepper with your hands. Shape the mixture into ½-inch balls; set aside. Warm the olive oil in a pot over medium heat and cook the onion and garlic for 5 minutes. Pour in beef stock, thyme, saffron powder, and tomatoes and bring to a boil. Add in the pork balls and cook for 20 minutes. Adjust the seasoning with salt and pepper. Serve sprinkled with parsley.

202. Buckwheat Chicken Soup

Serves: 6 | Ready in about: 40 minutes

1 tbsp olive oil
1 lb chicken breasts, cubed
Salt and black pepper to taste
2 celery stalks, chopped

1 carrot, chopped
1 red onion, chopped
6 cups chicken stock
½ cup parsley, chopped

½ cup buckwheat
1 tsp lime juice
1 lime, sliced

Warm the olive oil in a pot over medium heat. Season chicken breasts with salt and pepper and cook for 8 minutes. Stir in onion, carrot, and celery and sauté for another 3 minutes or until soft and aromatic. Put in chicken stock and buckwheat and bring to a boil. Reduce the heat to low. Let it simmer for about 20 minutes and add in lime juice. Sprinkle with parsley. Ladle your soup into individual bowls and serve warm with gremolata toast and lime slices. Yummy!

203. Celery & Carrot Bean Soup

Serves: 6 | Ready in about: 35 minutes

3 tbsp olive oil
1 onion, finely chopped
3 garlic cloves, minced
2 cups carrots, diced

2 cups celery, diced
1 medium potato, cubed
2 oz cubed pancetta
2 (15-oz) cans white beans, rinsed

6 cups vegetable broth
Salt and black pepper to taste

Heat the olive oil in a stockpot over medium heat. Add the pancetta, onion, and garlic and cook for 3-4 minutes, stirring often. Add the carrots and celery and cook for another 3-5 minutes until tender. Add the beans, potato, broth, salt, and pepper. Stir and simmer for about 20 minutes, stirring occasionally. Serve warm.

204. Kale & Cannellini Bean Stew

Serves: 4 | Ready in about: 45 minutes

2 tbsp olive oil
1 onion, chopped
2 cloves garlic, minced
2 carrots, peeled and chopped

1 cup celery, chopped
4 cups vegetable broth
1 cup canned cannellini beans
1 tsp dried thyme

1 tsp dried rosemary
1 bay leaf
1 cup kale, torn
Salt and black pepper to taste

Warm the olive oil in a pot over medium heat. Stir in garlic and onion, and cook for 3 minutes until tender and fragrant. Mix in celery and carrots and cook for 2-3 minutes more until they start to soften. Add broth, bay leaf, thyme, rosemary, cannellini beans, and salt. Cook covered for 30 minutes. Stir in kale and allow to sit for 2-4 minutes until the spinach wilts. Season with pepper and salt.

205. Vegetarian Greek Stew

Serves: 4 | Ready in about: 10 minutes

2 cups canned garbanzo beans
1 cucumber, thinly sliced
1 tsp garlic, minced
1 red onion, chopped

2 hot green peppers, chopped
2 tomatoes, diced
1 red bell pepper, sliced
1 fresh lemon, juiced

¼ tsp hot pepper flakes
1 cup feta cheese, crumbled
Salt and black pepper to taste
Fresh mint leaves, chopped

In a bowl, combine the garbanzo beans with cucumber, garlic, onion, hot peppers, tomatoes, bell pepper, lemon juice, hot pepper flakes, salt, and black pepper. Adjust the seasonings. Serve topped with feta and mint leaves.

206. Delicious Chicken Stew

Serves: 4 | Ready in about: 20 minutes

2 peeled fire-roasted tomatoes, chopped
2 lb chicken wings
2 potatoes, peeled and chopped
1 carrot, chopped

2 garlic cloves, chopped
2 tbsp olive oil
1 tsp smoked paprika, ground
4 cups chicken broth

2 tbsp fresh parsley, chopped
Salt and black pepper to taste
1 cup spinach, chopped

Preheat your Instant Pot to Sauté mode. Rub the chicken with salt, pepper, and paprika, and place in the pot. Stir in all remaining ingredients. Seal the lid and cook on High Pressure for 8 minutes. When ready, do a quick release.

207. Sunday Pork & Mushroom Stew

Serves: 2 | Ready in about: 50 minutes

2 pork chops, bones removed and cut into pieces
1 cup crimini mushrooms, chopped
2 large carrots, chopped
½ tsp garlic powder

Salt and black pepper to taste
2 tbsp butter
1 cup beef broth

1 tbsp apple cider vinegar
2 tbsp cornstarch

Preheat your Instant Pot to Sauté mode. Season the meat with salt and pepper. Add butter and pork chops to the pot and brown for 10 minutes, stirring occasionally. Add mushrooms and cook for 5 minutes. Add the remaining ingredients and seal the lid. Cook on High Pressure for 25 minutes. Do a quick release and serve hot.

208. Rich Pork Stew

Serves: 4 | Ready in about: 45 minutes

16 oz pork tenderloin, cut into bite-sized pieces

1 onion, peeled, chopped	½ tbsp red wine	Salt and black pepper to taste
2 tbsp vegetable oil	½ tbsp beef broth	
4 tomatoes, peeled, diced	2 tbsp fresh basil, chopped	

Preheat your Instant Pot to Sauté mode and heat the olive oil. Stir-fry the onions for 3 minutes until translucent. Add the meat, salt, pepper, wine, and basil. Cook for 10 minutes. Pour in broth, seal the lid and cook on High Pressure for 25 minutes. Do a quick release. Do a quick release. Season with salt, pepper, and red pepper flakes. Add butter and cook until the liquid evaporates – for 10 minutes on Sauté mode.

209. Hearty Beef Stew with Seasonal Veggies

Serves: 6 | Ready in about: 75 minutes

¼ cup flour	3 garlic cloves, minced	3 cups carrots, chopped
1 tsp paprika	1 cup dry red wine	3 tomatoes, chopped
1 tsp ground black pepper	2 cups beef stock	2 bell peppers, chopped
2 lb beef chuck, cubed	1 tbsp dried Greek seasoning	Salt and black pepper to taste
2 tbsp olive oil	2 tsp Worcestershire sauce	2 tbsp fresh parsley, chopped
2 tbsp butter	4 cups potatoes, diced	
1 onion, diced	2 celery stalks, chopped	

Preheat your Instant Pot to Sauté mode. In a bowl, mix black pepper, beef, flour, paprika, and salt. Toss the ingredients and ensure the beef is well-coated. Warm the butter and oil in the pot, add in the meat, and cook for 8- 10 minutes until browned. Set aside. To the same fat, add garlic, onion, and celery, bell peppers, and cook for 4-5 minutes until tender.

Deglaze with wine and scrape the bottom to get rid of any browned beef bits. Pour in beef stock, Worcestershire sauce, and Greek seasoning. Return beef to the pot; add carrots, tomatoes, and potatoes. Seal the lid, press Meat/Stew and cook on High Pressure for 35 minutes. Release Pressure naturally for 10 minutes. Taste and adjust the seasonings as necessary. Serve on plates and scatter over the parsley.

210. Homestyle Vegetable Stew

Serves: 4 | Ready in about: 55 minutes

1 lb potatoes, peeled, cut into bite-sized pieces

2 carrots, peeled, chopped	½ cup celery leaves, chopped	1 tbsp paprika
3 celery stalks, chopped	2 tbsp butter, unsalted	Salt and black pepper to taste
2 onions, peeled, chopped	3 tbsp olive oil	
1 zucchini, cut into slices	2 cups vegetable broth	

Preheat your Instant Pot to Sauté mode and warm the olive oil. Stir-fry the onions for 3-4 minutes until translucent. Add carrots, celery, zucchini, and ¼ cup of broth. Continue to cook for 10 more minutes, stirring constantly. Stir in potatoes, cayenne pepper, salt, pepper, bay leaves, remaining broth, and celery leaves. Seal the lid and cook on Meat/Stew mode for 30 minutes on High Pressure. Do a quick release and stir in 2 tbsp of butter until melted. Serve and enjoy!

211. Red Pollock & Tomato Stew

Serves: 4 | Ready in about: 50 minutes

1 lb pollock fillet	2 bay leaves, whole	1 onion, finely chopped
4 garlic cloves, crushed	2 cups fish stock	½ cup olive oil
1 lb tomatoes, peeled and diced	Salt and black pepper to taste	

Preheat your Instant Pot to Sauté mode and heat 2 tbsp olive oil. Add onion and sauté until translucent, stirring constantly, for about 3-4 minutes. Add tomatoes and cook until soft. Press Cancel. Add the remaining ingredients and seal the lid. Cook on High Pressure for 15 minutes. When ready, do a quick release. Serve warm.

212.   Greek-Inspired Chicken Stew

Serves: 4 | Ready in about: 50 minutes

2 tbsp olive oil
3 garlic cloves, minced
3 tbsp cilantro, chopped

Salt and black pepper to taste
2 cups chicken stock
2 shallots, thinly sliced

1 lb chicken breasts, cubed
5 oz dried pitted prunes, halved

Warm the olive oil in a pot over medium heat and cook shallots and garlic for 3 minutes. Add in chicken breasts and cook for another 5 minutes, stirring occasionally. Pour in chicken stock and prunes and season with salt and pepper. Cook for 30 minutes. Garnish with cilantro and serve.

213.   Kokkinisto (Greek Red Meat Stew)

Serves: 2 | Ready in about: 55 minutes

8 oz hot chicken sausage, removed from the casing
1 tbsp olive oil
½ onion, diced
1 garlic clove, minced

8 sundried tomatoes, diced
½ cup farro
1 cup chicken stock

2 cups arugula
5 fresh basil, sliced thin

Warm the olive oil in a pan over medium heat. Sauté the onion and garlic for 5 minutes. Add the sun-dried tomatoes and chicken sausage, stirring to break up the sausage. Cook for 7 minutes or until the sausage is no longer pink. Stir in the farro for about 2 minutes. Add the chicken stock and bring the mixture to a boil. Cover the pan and reduce the heat to low. Simmer for 30 minutes or until the farro is tender. Stir in arugula and let it wilt slightly, 2 minutes. Sprinkle with basil and serve.

214.   Cheesy Beef Stew with Eggplant

Serves: 6 | Ready in about: 50 minutes

9 oz beef neck, cut into bite-sized pieces
1 eggplant, chopped
2 cups fire-roasted tomatoes
½ tbsp fresh green peas

1 tbsp beef broth
4 tbsp olive oil
2 tbsp tomato paste

1 tbsp ground hot pepper
Salt to taste
Halloumi cheese for garnish

Preheat your Instant Pot to Sauté mode. Rub the meat with salt, cayenne, and hot pepper. Warm the olive oil in the pot and brown the meat for 5-7 minutes or until golden. Add all the remaining ingredients and seal the lid. Cook on Meat/Stew mode for 40 minutes on High. When ready, do a natural release for 10 minutes. Sprinkle with freshly grated Halloumi cheese. Serve warm, and enjoy!

215.   Creamy Pork Stew in Milky Broth

Serves: 4 | Ready in about: 50 minutes

1 tbsp olive oil oil
1 ½ cups buttermilk
1 ½ lb pork meat, cubed

1 red onion, chopped
1 garlic clove, minced
½ cup chicken stock

2 tbsp hot paprika
Salt and black pepper to taste
1 tbsp cilantro, chopped

Warm the oil in a pot over medium heat and sear the pork for 5 minutes. Put in onion and garlic and cook for 5 minutes. Stir in stock, paprika, salt, pepper, and buttermilk and bring to a boil; cook for 30 minutes. Top with cilantro.

216.   Sumptuous Seafood Stew

Serves: 6 | Ready in about: 30 minutes

2 lb codfish and seafood
¼ tbsp olive oil
2 onions, peeled, chopped

2 carrots, grated
2 tbsp fresh parsley, chopped
2 garlic cloves, crushed

3 cups water
1 tsp sea salt

Heat 3 tbsp olive oil on Sauté. Stir-fry onion and garlic for 3-4 minutes or until translucent. Add the remaining ingredients. Seal the lid, and cook on High Pressure for 10 minutes. Do a quick release. Serve and enjoy!

217. Beef Stifado (Greek Beef Stew)

Serves: 4 | Ready in about: 40 minutes

1 lb beef, cubed
2 tbsp olive oil
2 cups green peas
1 onion, diced

2 garlic cloves, minced
1 tomato, diced
3 cups beef broth
½ cup tomato paste

1 tsp hot pepper powder
1 tbsp flour
Salt to taste
½ tsp dried thyme

Warm the oil in your Instant Pot on Sauté. Sear the meat for 6-8 minutes, stirring often. Add the onion, garlic, and salt and sauté for 3 more minutes. Stir in flour, thyme, and pepper powder for 1-2 minutes. Add in the tomato and tomato paste, stir, and pour in the stock. Seal the lid, press Manual/Pressure Cook and cook for 20 minutes on High. When done, release the steam naturally for 10 minutes. Stir in the green peas, press Sauté, and cook for 4-5 minutes.

218. Arni Fricassee (Greek Lamb Fricassee)

Serves: 4 | Ready in about: 60 minutes

2 potatoes, peeled, cut into bite-sized pieces
2 tbsp olive oil
1 onion, chopped
1 lb lamb neck, boneless
2 large carrots, chopped

1 tomato, diced
1 red bell pepper, chopped
2 garlic cloves, minced
2 tbsp parsley, chopped

¼ cup lemon juice
Salt and black pepper to taste

Warm the olive oil in your Instant Pot on Sauté. Add the meat and brown for 4-6 minutes, stirring occasionally. Stir in onion, carrot, and garlic and cook for 3 more minutes until softened. Pour in the tomato and 2 cups of water. Season with salt and pepper. Seal the lid and cook on High Pressure for 45 minutes. When ready, do a quick pressure release. Sprinkle with parsley. Serve in bowls and enjoy!

219. Horta Yahni (Greek Vegetable Stew)

Serves: 4 | Ready in about: 25 minutes

3 zucchini, peeled, chopped
1 eggplant, peeled, chopped
3 red bell peppers, chopped

½ cup fresh tomato juice
2 tsp Greek seasoning
½ tsp salt

2 tbsp olive oil

Add all ingredients and give it a good stir. Pour 1 cup of water. Seal the lid and cook on High Pressure for 15 minutes. Do a quick release. Set aside to cool completely. Serve as a cold salad or a side dish.

220. Chickpea & Mushroom Stew

Serves: 4 | Ready in about: 20 minutes

½ tbsp button mushrooms, chopped
1 cup chickpeas, cooked
1 onion, peeled, chopped
1 lb string beans, trimmed
1 apple, cut into 1-inch cubes

½ cup raisins
2 carrots, chopped
2 garlic cloves, crushed
4 cherry tomatoes

2 tbsp fresh mint, chopped
1 tsp grated ginger
½ cup orange juice
½ tsp salt

Place all ingredients in the Instant Pot. Pour enough water to cover. Cook on High Pressure for 8 minutes. Do a natural release for 10 minutes.

221. Horta Yahni (Greek Vegetable Stew)

Serves: 4 | Ready in about: 25 minutes

3 zucchini, peeled, chopped
1 eggplant, peeled, chopped

3 red bell peppers, chopped
½ cup fresh tomato juice

2 tsp Greek seasoning
2 tbsp olive oil

Add all ingredients and give it a good stir. Pour 1 cup of water. Seal the lid and cook on High Pressure for 15 minutes. Do a quick release. Set aside to cool completely. Serve as a cold salad or a side dish.

BEANS, RICE & GRAINS

222. Freekeh Pilaf with Cranberry & Walnuts

Serves: 4 | Ready in about: 30 minutes

2 tbsp olive oil
2 ½ cups freekeh, soaked
2 medium onions, diced
¼ tsp ground cinnamon
¼ tsp ground allspice

¼ tsp ground nutmeg
5 cups chicken stock
½ cup walnuts, chopped
Salt and black pepper to taste
½ cup Greek yogurt

1 ½ tsp lemon juice
½ tsp garlic powder
1 tbsp dried cranberries

Warm the olive oil in a large skillet over medium heat. Add the onions and sauté them until fragrant. Add the freekeh, cinnamon, nutmeg, and allspice. Stir for 1 minute. Pour in the stock, cranberries, and walnuts and season with salt and pepper. Bring to a simmer. Cover and reduce the heat to low. Simmer for 15 minutes until the freekeh is tender. Remove from the heat and leave to sit for 5 minutes. In a small bowl, mix the yogurt, lemon juice, and garlic powder. Add the yogurt mixture to the freekeh and serve immediately.

223. Green Rice Delight

Serves: 4 | Ready in about: 35 minutes

2 tbsp butter
4 spring onions, sliced
1 leek, sliced
1 medium zucchini, chopped
5 oz broccoli florets

2 oz curly kale
½ cup frozen green peas
2 cloves garlic, minced
1 thyme sprig, chopped
1 rosemary sprig, chopped

1 cup white rice
2 cups vegetable broth
1 large tomato, chopped
2 oz Kalamata olives, sliced

Melt the butter in a saucepan over medium heat. Cook the spring onions, leek, and zucchini for about 4-5 minutes or until tender. Add in the garlic, thyme, and rosemary and continue to sauté for about 1 minute or until aromatic. Add in the rice, broth, and tomato. Bring to a boil, turn the heat to a gentle simmer, and cook for about 10-12 minutes. Stir in broccoli, kale, and green peas, and continue cooking for 5 minutes. Fluff the rice with a fork and garnish with olives.

224. One-Skillet Vegetable Quinoa & Garbanzo

Serves: 4 | Ready in about: 30 minutes

2 tbsp olive oil
1 shallot, chopped
2 garlic cloves, minced
1 tomato, chopped

1 cup quinoa
1 eggplant, cubed
¼ cup green olives, chopped
½ cup feta cheese, crumbled

1 cup canned garbanzo beans
Salt and black pepper to taste

Warm the olive oil in a skillet over medium heat and sauté garlic, shallot, tomato, and eggplant for 4-5 minutes until tender. Pour in quinoa and 2 cups of water. Season with salt and pepper and bring to a boil. Reduce the heat to low and cook for 15 minutes. Stir in olives, feta, and garbanzo beans.

225. Egg Noodles & Bean in Lemon Sauce

Serves: 4 | Ready in about: 20 minutes

3 tbsp olive oil
12 oz egg noodles
1 (14-oz) can diced tomatoes
1 (13-oz) can navy beans
½ cup heavy cream

1 cup vegetable stock
2 garlic cloves, minced
1 onion, chopped
1 cup spinach, chopped
1 tsp dill

1 tsp thyme
½ tsp red pepper, crushed
1 tsp lemon juice
1 tbsp fresh basil, chopped

Warm the olive oil in a pot over medium heat. Add in onion and garlic and cook for 3 minutes until softened. Stir in dill, thyme, and red pepper for 1 minute. Add in spinach, vegetable stock, and tomatoes. Bring to a boil, add the egg noodles, cover, and lower the heat. Cook for 5-7 minutes. Put in beans and cook until heated through. Combine the heavy cream, lemon juice, and basil. Serve the dish with creamy lemon sauce on the side.

226. Marinara Beanballs in Tasty Sauce

Serves: 4 | Ready in about: 45 minutes

1 (28-oz) can diced tomatoes with juice

3 tbsp olive oil	½ tsp dried thyme	½ cup bread crumbs
½ yellow onion, minced	½ tsp red pepper flakes	Salt and black pepper to taste
1 tsp coriander seeds	1 tsp garlic powder	3 garlic cloves, minced
½ tsp dried oregano	1 (15-oz) can white beans	2 tbsp basil leaves

Preheat the oven to 350 F. Warm 2 tbsp of olive oil in a skillet over medium heat. Sauté the onion for 3 minutes. Sprinkle with coriander seeds, oregano, thyme, pepper flakes, and garlic powder, then cook for 1 minute or until aromatic. Pour the sautéed mixture into a food processor and add the beans and bread crumbs. Sprinkle with salt and black pepper and pulse to combine well, and the mixture holds together. Shape the mixture into balls. Arrange them on a greased baking sheet. Bake for 30 minutes or until lightly browned. Flip the balls halfway through the cooking time.

Warm the remaining olive oil in a saucepan over medium heat and add the garlic cloves and basil. Sauté for 2 minutes or until fragrant. Fold in the tomatoes and juice. Bring to a boil. Reduce the heat to low. Put the lid on and simmer for 15 minutes. Sprinkle with salt. Transfer the beanballs to a large plate and drizzle with marinara sauce. Serve.

227. Traditional Bean Stew

Serves: 4 | Ready in about: 70 minutes

2 tbsp olive oil	2 tbsp parsley, chopped	1 tsp dried oregano
3 tomatoes, cubed	2 garlic cloves, minced	½ tsp dried thyme
1 yellow onion, chopped	1 cup lima beans, soaked	Salt and black pepper to taste
1 celery stalk, chopped	1 tsp paprika	

Cover the lima beans with water in a pot and place over medium heat. Bring to a boil and cook for 30 minutes. Drain and set aside. Warm olive oil in the pot over medium heat and cook the onion and garlic for 3 minutes. Stir in tomatoes, celery, oregano, thyme, and paprika and cook for 5 minutes. Pour in 3 cups of water and return the lima beans; season with salt and pepper. Simmer for 30 minutes. Top with parsley.

228. Sausage & Tomato Bean Casserole

Serves: 4 | Ready in about: 45 minutes

2 tbsp olive oil	1 onion, chopped	1 celery stalk, chopped
1 lb sausages	2 garlic cloves, minced	Salt and black pepper to taste
1 (15-oz) can navy beans	1 tsp paprika	
1 carrot, chopped	1 (14-oz) can tomatoes, diced	

Preheat oven to 350 F. Warm olive oil in a pot over medium heat. Sauté onion, garlic, celery, and carrot for 3-4 minutes, stirring often until softened. Add in sausages and cook for another 3 minutes, turning occasionally. Stir in paprika for 30 seconds. Heat off. Mix in tomatoes, beans, salt, and pepper. Pour into a baking dish and bake for 30 minutes.

229. Lettuce Rolls with Hummus & Beans

Serves: 4 | Ready in about: 20 minutes

2 tbsp extra-virgin olive oil	¼ tsp ground nutmeg	½ cup hummus
½ cup diced red onion	Salt and black pepper to taste	8 romaine lettuce leaves
2 chopped fresh tomatoes	1 (15-oz) can navy beans	
1 tsp paprika	¼ cup chopped fresh parsley	

Warm the olive oil in a skillet over medium heat. Add the onion and cook for 3 minutes, stirring occasionally. Add the tomatoes and paprika and cook for 3 more minutes, stirring occasionally. Add the beans and cook for 3 more minutes, stirring occasionally. Remove from the heat and sprinkle with salt, pepper, cumin, nutmeg, and parsley. Stir. Spread the hummus on the lettuce leaves. Spoon the warm bean mixture down the center of each leaf. Fold one side of the lettuce leaf over the filling lengthwise, then fold over the other side to make a wrap and serve.

230.   Spinach & Bean Stew

Serves: 4 | Ready in about: 40 minutes

2 tbsp olive oil
1 onion, chopped
1 (15-oz) can diced tomatoes
2 (15-oz) cans navy beans

1 cup carrots, chopped
1 celery stalk, chopped
4 cups vegetable broth
½ tsp dried thyme

1 lb baby spinach
Salt and black pepper to taste

Warm the olive oil in a saucepan over medium heat. Sauté the onion, celery, and carrots for 5 minutes until tender. Add the tomatoes, beans, carrots, broth, thyme, pepper, and salt. Stir and cook for 20 minutes. Add the spinach and cook for 5 minutes until the spinach wilts. Serve warm.

231.   Rustic Two-Bean Cassoulet

Serves: 4 | Ready in about: 40 minutes

2 tbsp olive oil
1 cup canned pinto beans
1 cup canned can kidney beans
2 red bell peppers, chopped

1 onion, chopped
1 celery stalk, chopped
2 garlic cloves, minced
1 (14-oz) can diced tomatoes

1 tbsp red pepper flakes
1 tsp ground cumin
Salt and black pepper to taste
¼ tsp ground coriander

Warm the olive oil in a pot over medium heat. Add the bell peppers, celery, garlic, and onion and stir. Sauté the vegetables for 5 minutes until tender. Stir in ground cumin, coriander, salt, and pepper for 1 minute. Pour in beans, tomatoes, and red pepper flakes. Bring to a boil, then decrease the heat and simmer for another 20 minutes. Serve.

232.   Cheesy Bean Rolls

Serves: 4 | Ready in about: 25 minutes

1 tbsp olive oil
1 red onion, chopped
2 garlic cloves, minced
1 green bell pepper, sliced

2 cups canned navy beans
1 red hot pepper, chopped
1 tbsp cilantro, chopped
1 tsp cumin, ground

Salt and black pepper to taste
4 whole-wheat tortillas
1 cup halloumi, shredded

Warm the olive oil in a skillet over medium heat and sauté onion for 3 minutes. Stir in garlic, bell pepper, navy beans, red hot pepper, cilantro, cumin, salt, and pepper and cook for 15 minutes. Spoon bean mixture on each tortilla and top with cheese. Roll up and serve right away.

233.   Bean Bell & Pepper Salad

Serves: 6 | Ready in about: 30 minutes

¼ cup extra-virgin olive oil
3 garlic cloves, minced
2 (15-oz) cans navy beans
Salt and black pepper to taste

2 tsp sherry vinegar
1 red onion, sliced
1 red bell pepper, chopped
¼ cup chopped fresh parsley

2 tsp chopped fresh chives
¼ tsp crushed red pepper

Warm 1 tbsp of olive oil in a saucepan over medium heat. Sauté the garlic until it turns golden but not brown, about 3 minutes. Add beans, 2 cups of water, and salt, and pepper, and bring to a simmer. Heat off. Let sit for 20 minutes. Mix the vinegar and red onion in a salad bowl. Drain the beans and remove the garlic. Add beans, remaining olive oil, bell pepper, parsley, crushed red pepper, chives, salt, and pepper to the onion mixture and gently toss to combine.

234.   Stuffed Sweet Potatoes with Beans

Serves: 4 | Ready in about: 50 minutes

4 sweet potatoes, pierced with a fork
2 tbsp olive oil
1 cup canned navy beans
1 small red pepper, chopped
1 tbsp lemon zest

2 tbsp lemon juice
1 garlic clove, minced
1 tbsp oregano, chopped
1 tbsp parsley, chopped

Salt and black pepper to taste
1 avocado, mashed
1 tbsp tahini paste

Preheat oven to 360 F. Line a baking sheet with parchment paper and place in the sweet potatoes. Bake for 40 minutes. Let cool and cut in half. Using a spoon, remove some flesh from the potatoes and place it in a bowl. Mix in beans, red pepper, lemon zest, half of the lemon juice, half of the oil, half of the garlic, oregano, half of the parsley, salt, and pepper. Divide the mixture between the potato halves. In another bowl, combine avocado, 2 tbsp of water, tahini, remaining lemon juice, remaining oil, remaining garlic, and remaining parsley and scatter over the stuffed potatoes. Serve.

235.   Lemon Cranberry Beans

Serves: 6 | Ready in about: 1 hour 45 minutes

¼ cup olive oil	2 carrots, chopped	½ tsp paprika
Salt and black pepper to taste	4 garlic cloves, sliced thin	½ cup dry white wine
1 lb cranberry beans, soaked	1 tbsp tomato paste	4 cups vegetable broth
1 onion, chopped	2 tomatoes, chopped	2 tbsp minced fresh mint

Preheat oven to 350 F. Warm the olive oil in a pot over medium heat. Sauté the onion and carrots until softened, about 5 minutes. Stir in garlic, tomato paste, tomatoes, paprika, salt, and pepper and cook until fragrant, about 1 minute. Stir in wine, scraping up any browned bits. Stir in broth, ½ cup of water, and beans and bring to a boil. Place in the oven and cook covered for about 1 ½ hours, stirring every 30 minutes until the beans are tender. Sprinkle with mint. Serve.

236.   Apricot-Infused Chickpeas with Couscous

Serves: 4 | Ready in about: 30 minutes

2 tbsp olive oil	14 oz canned chickpeas	½ cup dried apricots, chopped
1 red onion, chopped	2 cups veggie stock	Salt and black pepper to taste
2 garlic cloves, minced	2 cups couscous, cooked	

Warm the olive oil in a skillet over medium heat and cook the onion and garlic for 5 minutes. Put in chickpeas, stock, apricots, salt, and pepper and cook for 15 minutes. Ladle couscous into bowls. Top with chickpea mixture.

237.   Chickpeas with Lemon & Herbs

Serves: 4 | Ready in about: 30 minutes

¼ cup extra-virgin olive oil	Salt and black pepper to taste	2 tbsp minced fresh parsley
4 garlic cloves, sliced thin	1 tsp smoked paprika	2 tsp lemon juice
½ tsp red pepper flakes	2 (15-oz) cans chickpeas	
1 onion, chopped fine	1 cup chicken broth	

Warm 3 tbsp of olive oil in a skillet over medium heat. Cook garlic and pepper flakes until the garlic turns golden but not brown, about 3 minutes. Stir in onion and salt and cook until softened and lightly browned, 5 minutes. Stir in smoked paprika, chickpeas, and broth and bring to a boil. Simmer covered for 7 minutes until chickpeas are heated through.

Uncover, increase the heat to high, and continue to cook until nearly all liquid has evaporated, about 3 minutes. Remove and stir in parsley and lemon juice. Season with salt and pepper and drizzle with remaining olive oil. Serve.

238.   Hot Chicken Lentils

Serves: 4 | Ready in about: 1 hour 20 minutes

1 lb chicken thighs, skinless, boneless, and cubed

2 tbsp olive oil	2 carrots, chopped	½ tsp paprika
1 tbsp coriander seeds	1 onion, chopped	4 cups chicken stock
1 bay leaf	2 garlic cloves, chopped	1 cup brown lentils
1 tbsp tomato paste	½ tsp hot red pepper flakes	Salt and black pepper to taste

Warm the olive oil in a pot over medium heat and cook chicken, onion, and garlic for 6-8 minutes. Stir in carrots, tomato paste, coriander seeds, bay leaf, hot red pepper flakes, and paprika for 3 minutes. Pour in the chicken stock and bring to a boil. Simmer for 25 minutes. Add in lentils, season with salt and pepper and cook for another 15 minutes. Discard bay leaf and serve right away.

239.   Chickpea & Black Bean Burgers

Serves: 4 | Ready in about: 35 minutes

1 tsp olive oil
1 (15-ounce) can black beans
1 (15.5-ounce) can s
½ white onion, chopped
2 garlic cloves, minced

2 free-range eggs
1 tsp ground cumin
Salt and black pepper to taste
1 cup breadcrumbs
½ cup old-fashioned rolled oats

6 hamburger buns, halved
2 avocados
2 tbsp lemon juice
6 large lettuce leaves

Preheat oven to 380 F. Blitz the black beans, chickpeas, eggs, cumin, salt, and pepper in a food processor until smooth. Transfer the mixture to a bowl and add the onion and garlic and mix well. Stir in the bread crumbs and oats. Shape the mixture into 6 balls, and flatten them with your hands to make patties. Brush both sides of the burgers with oil. Arrange them on a parchment-lined baking sheet. Bake for 30 minutes, flipping once until slightly crispy on the edges.

Meanwhile, mash the avocado with the lemon juice and a pinch of salt with a fork until smooth; set aside. Toast the buns for 2-3 minutes. Spread the avocado mixture onto the base of each bun, then top with the burgers and lettuce leaves. Finish with the bun tops. Serve and enjoy!

240.   Spinach & Chickpea Bowl

Serves: 4 | Ready in about: 20 minutes

2 tbsp olive oil
1 lb canned chickpeas
10 oz spinach
1 tsp coriander seeds

1 red onion, finely chopped
2 tomatoes, pureed
1 garlic clove, minced
½ tbsp rosemary

½ tsp smoked paprika
Salt and white pepper to taste

Heat the olive oil in a pot over medium heat. Add in the onion, garlic, coriander seeds, salt, and pepper and cook for 3 minutes until translucent. Stir in tomatoes, rosemary, paprika, salt, and white pepper. Bring to a boil, then lower the heat, and simmer for 10 minutes. Add in chickpeas and spinach and cook covered until the spinach wilts. Serve.

241.   Garbanzo & Fava Beans

Serves: 6 | Ready in about: 20 minutes

3 tbsp extra-virgin olive oil
1 (16-oz) can garbanzo beans
1 (15-oz) can fava beans

½ tsp lemon zest
½ tsp dried oregano
½ cup lemon juice

3 cloves garlic, minced
Salt to taste

Place the garbanzo beans, fava beans, and 3 cups of water in a pot over medium heat. Cook for 10 minutes. Drain the beans reserving 1 cup of the liquid, and put them in a bowl. Mix the reserved liquid, lemon juice, lemon zest, oregano, minced garlic, and salt and add beans to the bowl. Mash up about half the beans in the bowl with a potato masher. Stir the mixture to combine. Drizzle the olive oil over the top. Serve with pita bread if desired.

242.   Revithada (Greek Chickpea Stew with Tomato & Onion)

Serves: 4 | Ready in about: 35 minutes

3 tbsp olive oil
3 tbsp capers, drained
1 lemon, juiced and zested

1 red onion, chopped
14 oz canned chickpeas
4 carrots, peeled and cubed

1 tbsp parsley, chopped
Salt and black pepper to taste

Warm the olive oil in a skillet over medium heat and cook the onion, lemon zest, lemon juice, and capers for 5 minutes. Stir in chickpeas, carrots, parsley, salt, and pepper and cook for another 20 minutes. Serve and enjoy!

243.   Lentils & Spinach

Serves: 6 | Ready in about: 30 minutes

2 tbsp olive oil
4 garlic cloves, sliced thin
Salt and black pepper to taste

1 onion, chopped
1 tsp ground coriander
1 tsp dried thyme

1 tsp ground cumin
1 cup lentils, rinsed
8 oz spinach, chopped

Warm the olive oil in a pot over medium heat. Sauté the garlic for 2-3 minutes, stirring often, until crisp and golden but not brown. Remove the garlic to a paper towel–lined plate and season lightly with salt; set aside. Add the onion to the pot and cook for 3 minutes until softened and lightly browned. Stir in salt, thyme, coriander, and cumin for 1 minute until fragrant.

Pour in 2 ½ cups of water and lentils and bring to a simmer. Lower the heat to low, cover, and simmer gently for 15 minutes, stirring occasionally until lentils are mostly tender but still intact. Stir in spinach and cook until spinach is wilted, about 5 minutes. Adjust the taste with salt and pepper. Sprinkle with toasted garlic and serve warm.

244. Sautéed Chickpeas with Asparagus

Serves: 4 | Ready in about: 25 minutes

2 tbsp olive oil	1 cup canned chickpeas	1 tsp ground coriander
2 garlic cloves, minced	Salt and black pepper to taste	2 tomatoes, chopped
2 potatoes, cubed	1 lb asparagus, chopped	2 tbsp parsley, chopped
1 yellow onion, chopped	1 tsp sweet paprika	½ cup ricotta cheese, crumbled

Warm the olive oil in a skillet over medium heat and sauté potatoes, onion, garlic, salt, and pepper for 7 minutes, stirring occasionally. Add in chickpeas, salt, pepper, asparagus, paprika, and coriander and sauté another 6-7 minutes. Remove to a bowl. Mix in tomatoes, parsley, and ricotta cheese and serve right away.

245. Faro & Chickpea Stew

Serves: 4 | Ready in about: 35 minutes

3 tbsp olive oil	1 yellow onion, chopped	2 tbsp harissa paste
1 cup faro	14 oz canned tomatoes, diced	2 tbsp cilantro, chopped
Salt and black pepper to taste	14 oz canned chickpeas	
1 eggplant, cubed	3 garlic cloves, minced	

Warm the olive oil in a skillet over medium heat and sauté eggplant, salt, and pepper for 10 minutes; reserve. In the same skillet, add and sauté onion for 3-4 minutes. Stir in garlic, salt, pepper, harissa paste, chickpeas, tomatoes, and faro, and 2 cups of water. Cook for 20 minutes. Stir in eggplant for 5 minutes. Garnish with cilantro and serve.

246. Easy Pork & Garbanzo Cassoulet

Serves: 4 | Ready in about: 50 minutes

2 tbsp olive oil	3 garlic cloves, minced	2 zucchini, chopped
2 lb pork stew meat, cubed	2 tsp sage	2 tbsp tomato paste
1 leek, chopped	4 oz canned garbanzo beans	2 tbsp parsley, chopped
1 red bell pepper, chopped	1 cup chicken stock	

Warm the olive oil in a pot over medium heat and sear pork meat for 10 minutes, stirring occasionally. Add in leek, bell pepper, garlic, and zucchini and sauté for 5 minutes. Stir in tomato paste and sage for 1 minute and pour in garbanzo beans and chicken stock. Cover and bring to a boil, then reduce the heat and simmer for 30 minutes. Adjust the seasoning and serve garnished with parsley.

247. Broccoli & Spinach Rice Bowl

Serves: 4 | Ready in about: 25 minutes

2 tbsp olive oil	1 ½ cups cooked brown rice	1 cup vegetable broth
12 oz broccoli cuts	1 onion, chopped	Salt and black pepper to taste
3 cups fresh baby spinach	1 garlic clove, minced	
1 red hot pepper, chopped	1 orange, juiced and zested	

Warm olive oil in a pan over medium heat and sauté onion for 5 minutes, then add in broccoli cuts and cook for 4-5 minutes until tender. Stir-fry garlic and hot pepper for 30 seconds. Pour in orange zest, orange juice, broth, salt, and pepper and bring to a boil. Stir in the rice and spinach and cook for 4 minutes until the liquid is reduced. Serve.

248. Green Pepper, Eggplant & Chickpea Casserole

Serves: 6 | Ready in about: 75 minutes

¼ cup olive oil
2 onions, chopped
1 green bell pepper, chopped
Salt and black pepper to taste

3 garlic cloves, minced
1 tsp dried oregano
½ tsp ground cumin
1 lb eggplants, cubed

1 (28-oz) can tomatoes, diced
2 (15-oz) cans chickpeas

Preheat oven to 400 F. Warm the olive oil in a skillet over medium heat. Add the onions, bell pepper, salt, and pepper. Cook for about 5 minutes until softened. Stir in garlic, oregano, and cumin for about 30 seconds until fragrant. Transfer to a baking dish and add the eggplants, tomatoes, and chickpeas and stir. Place in the oven and bake for 45-60 minutes, shaking the dish twice during cooking. Serve.

249. Cinnamon-Raspberry & Nut Quinoa

Serves: 4 | Ready in about: 5 minutes

1 tbsp honey
2 cups almond milk

2 cups quinoa, cooked
½ tsp cinnamon powder

1 cup raspberries
¼ cup walnuts, chopped

Combine quinoa, milk, cinnamon powder, honey, raspberries, and walnuts in a bowl. Serve in individual bowls.

250. Brown Rice Pilaf with Vegetables

Serves: 4 | Ready in about: 40 minutes

1 ½ tbsp olive oil
2 ¼ cups vegetable broth
½ cup green lentils
½ cup brown rice

½ cup diced carrots
½ cup diced celery
1 (2 ¼-oz) can sliced olives
¼ cup diced red onion

¼ cup cilantro, chopped
1 tbsp lemon juice
1 garlic clove, minced
Salt and black pepper to taste

In a saucepan over high heat, bring the broth and lentils to a boil, cover, and lower the heat to medium-low. Cook for 8 minutes. Raise the heat to medium, and stir in the rice. Cover the pot and cook the mixture for 14 minutes or until the liquid is absorbed. Remove the pot from the heat and let sit covered for 2 minutes, then stir.

While the lentils and rice are cooking, combine carrots, celery, olives, onion, and cilantro in a serving bowl. In a small bowl, whisk together the oil, lemon juice, garlic, salt, and black pepper. Set aside. Once the lentils and rice are done, add them to the serving bowl. Pour the dressing on top, and mix well. Serve warm.

251. Caper-Brown Rice Sautée

Serves: 4 | Ready in about: 30 minutes

2 tbsp olive oil
1 cup brown rice
1 onion, chopped

1 celery stalk, chopped
2 garlic cloves, minced
½ cup capers, rinsed

Salt and black pepper to taste
2 tbsp parsley, chopped

Warm the olive oil in a skillet over medium heat. Sauté celery, garlic, and onion for 10 minutes. Stir in rice, capers, 2 cups of water, salt, and pepper and cook for 25 minutes. Serve topped with parsley.

252. Lentil & Rice Salad with Caramelized Onions

Serves: 4 | Ready in about: 1 hour 15 minutes

¼ cup olive oil
2 cups lentils
1 cup brown rice

4 ½ cups water
½ tsp dried thyme
½ tsp dried tarragon

3 onions, peeled and sliced
Salt and black pepper to taste

Place the lentils and rice in a large saucepan with water. Bring to a boil, cover, and simmer for 23 minutes or until almost tender. Stir in the seasonings and cook for 25-30 minutes or until the rice is tender and the water is absorbed. In a separate saucepan, warm the olive oil over medium heat. Add the onions and cook slowly, stirring frequently, until the onions brown and caramelize, for 17-20 minutes. Top with the caramelized onions. Serve and enjoy!

253. Sun-Dried Tomato & Basil Pilaf

Serves: 4 | Ready in about: 35 minutes

10 oz sundried tomatoes in olive oil, drained and chopped

2 tbsp olive oil

2 cups chicken stock

1 onion, chopped

1 cup Arborio rice

Salt and black pepper to taste

1 cup Pecorino cheese, grated

¼ cup basil leaves, chopped

Warm the olive oil in a skillet over medium heat and cook the onion and sundried tomatoes for 5 minutes. Stir in rice, chicken stock, salt, pepper, and basil and bring to a boil. Cook for 20 minutes. Mix in Pecorino cheese and serve.

254. Cheesy Wild Rice with Mushrooms

Serves: 4 | Ready in about: 30 minutes

2 cups chicken stock

1 cup wild rice

1 onion, chopped

½ lb wild mushrooms, sliced

2 garlic cloves, minced

1 lemon, juiced and zested

1 tbsp chives, chopped

½ cup halloumi, grated

Salt and black pepper to taste

Warm chicken stock in a pot over medium heat and add in wild rice, onion, mushrooms, garlic, lemon juice, lemon zest, salt, and pepper. Bring to a simmer and cook for 20 minutes. Transfer to a baking tray and top with halloumi cheese. Place the tray under the broiler for 4 minutes until the cheese is melted. Sprinkle with chives and serve.

255. Cherry Tomato Rice Pilaf with Nuts

Serves: 4 | Ready in about: 30 minutes

2 tbsp olive oil

1 cup basmati rice

1 carrot, shredded

½ cup scallions, chopped

12 cherry tomatoes, halved

1 oz pistachios, crushed

2 cups vegetable broth

1 garlic clove, minced

1 tsp ground coriander

2 tbsp fresh parsley, chopped

Heat olive oil in a saucepan over medium heat. Add in the carrot, garlic, and scallions and cook for 3-4 minutes, stirring often. Stir in the rice for 1-2 minutes. Pour in the vegetable broth. Bring to a quick boil and sprinkle with ground coriander. Lower the heat and simmer covered for 10-12 minutes until the liquid has absorbed. Fluff the rice with a fork and transfer to a serving plate. Top with cherry tomatoes and pistachios and sprinkle with parsley. Serve.

256. Quick Instant Pot Pork with Rice

Serves: 4 | Ready in about: 35 minutes

3 tbsp olive oil

1 lb pork stew meat, cubed

Salt and black pepper to taste

2 chicken broth

1 leek, sliced

1 onion, chopped

1 carrot, sliced

1 cup brown rice

2 garlic cloves, minced

2 tbsp cilantro, chopped

Set your Instant Pot to Sauté and heat the olive oil. Place in pork and cook for 4-5 minutes, stirring often. Add in onion, leek, garlic, and carrot and sauté for 3 more minutes. Stir in brown rice for 1 minute and pour in chicken broth; return the pork. Lock the lid in place, select Manual, and cook for 20 minutes on High. When done, do a quick pressure release. Adjust the seasoning and serve topped with cilantro.

257. Rice & Pork

Serves: 4 | Ready in about: 8 hours 10 minutes

3 tbsp olive oil

2 lb pork loin, sliced

1 cup chicken stock

½ tbsp hot pepper powder

2 tsp thyme, dried

½ tbsp garlic powder

Salt and black pepper to taste

2 cups rice, cooked

Place pork, chicken stock, oil, hot pepper powder, garlic powder, salt, and pepper in your slow cooker. Cover with the lid and cook for 8 hours on Low. Share pork on plates with a side of rice and garnish with thyme to serve.

258. Paprika Brown Rice Bowl

Serves: 4 | Ready in about: 25 minutes

½ lb broccoli rabe, halved lengthways
2 tbsp olive oil
1 onion, sliced
1 red bell pepper, cut into strips
½ cup green peas

1 carrot, chopped
1 celery stalk, chopped
1 garlic clove, minced
½ cup brown rice
2 cups vegetable broth

Salt and black pepper to taste
½ tsp dried thyme
¾ tsp paprika
2 green onions, chopped

Warm the olive oil in a skillet over medium heat and sauté onion, garlic, carrot, celery, and bell pepper for 10 minutes. Stir in rice, vegetable broth, salt, pepper, thyme, paprika, and green onions and bring to a simmer. Cook for 15 minutes. Add in broccoli rabe and green peas and cook for 5 minutes.

259. Bell Peppers Filled with Rice

Serves: 4 | Ready in about: 35 minutes

1 tbsp olive oil
2 lb mixed bell peppers, halved
1 cup white rice, rinsed

½ cup ricotta cheese, crumbled
2 tomatoes, pureed
1 onion, chopped

1 tsp ground cumin
1 tsp ground fennel seeds
Salt and black pepper to taste

Blanch the peppers in a pot with salted water over medium heat for 1-2 minutes, drain and set aside. Add the rice to the pot, bring to a boil and simmer for 15 minutes. Drain and remove to a bowl. Add in olive oil, cumin, ground fennel seeds, onion, tomatoes, salt, and pepper and stir to combine. Divide the mixture between the pepper halves and top with ricotta cheese. Bake for 8-10 minutes. Serve right away.

260. Simple Brown Rice

Serves: 4 | Ready in about: 20 minutes

1 lb asparagus, steamed and chopped
2 tbsp olive oil
3 tbsp balsamic vinegar
1 cup brown rice

2 tsp mustard
Salt and black pepper to taste
5 oz baby spinach

½ cup parsley, chopped
1 tbsp tarragon, chopped

Bring to a boil a pot of salted water over medium heat. Add in brown rice and cook for 7-9 minutes until al dente. Drain and place in a bowl. Add the asparagus to the same pot and blanch them for 4-5 minutes. Remove them to the rice bowl. Mix in spinach, olive oil, balsamic vinegar, mustard, salt, pepper, parsley, and tarragon. Serve.

261. Feta Cheese & Asparagus Rice Salad

Serves: 4 | Ready in about: 35 minutes

3 tbsp olive oil
½ cups brown rice
Salt and black pepper to taste

½ lemon, zested and juiced
1 lb asparagus, chopped
1 shallot, minced

2 oz feta cheese, crumbled
¼ cup hazelnuts, toasted
¼ cup parsley, minced

In a pot, bring 2 cups of water to a boil. Add rice, a pinch of salt, and cook until tender, 15-18 minutes, stirring occasionally. Drain the rice, spread onto a rimmed baking sheet, and drizzle with 1 tbsp of lemon juice. Let cool completely.

Heat 1 tbsp of olive oil in a skillet over high heat. Add asparagus, salt, and pepper to taste and cook until asparagus is browned and crisp-tender, 4-5 minutes. Transfer to plate and let cool slightly. Whisk the remaining oil, lemon zest and juice, shallot in a bowl. Add rice, asparagus, half of the feta cheese, half of the hazelnuts, and half of the parsley. Toss to combine and let sit for 10 minutes. Season with salt and pepper. Sprinkle with the remaining feta, hazelnuts, and parsley.

262. Green Onion & Mushroom Rice Pilaf

Serves: 4 | Ready in about: 30 minutes

2 tbsp olive oil
1 cup rice, rinsed
2 greens onions, chopped

2 cups chicken stock
1 cup mushrooms, sliced
1 garlic clove, minced

Salt and black pepper to taste
½ cup Halloumi cheese, grated
2 tbsp cilantro, chopped

Warm the olive oil in a skillet over medium heat and cook the onion, garlic, and mushrooms for 5 minutes until tender. Stir in rice, salt, and pepper for 1 minute. Pour in chicken stock and cook for 15-18 minutes. Transfer to a platter, scatter Halloumi cheese all over, and sprinkle with cilantro to serve.

263.   Feta-Vegetable Millet

Serves: 6 | Ready in about: 35 minutes

6 oz okra, cut into 1-inch lengths

3 tbsp olive oil	2 tbsp lemon juice	3 tbsp chopped fresh dill
6 oz asparagus, chopped	2 tbsp minced shallot	2 oz feta cheese, crumbled
Salt and black pepper to taste	1 tsp mustard	
1 ½ cups whole millet	6 oz cherry tomatoes, halved	

In a large pot, bring 4 quarts of water to a boil. Add asparagus, snap peas, and salt and cook until crisp-tender, about 3 minutes. Using a slotted spoon, transfer vegetables to a large plate and let cool completely, about 15 minutes. Add millet to water, return to a boil, and cook until grains are tender, 15-20 minutes.

Drain millet, spread in rimmed baking sheet, and let cool completely, 15 minutes. Whisk oil, lemon juice, shallot, mustard, salt, and pepper in a large bowl. Add vegetables, millet, tomatoes, dill, and half of the feta cheese and toss gently to combine. Season with salt and pepper. Sprinkle with remaining feta cheese to serve.

264.   Cheesy Lamb Pilaf

Serves: 4 | Ready in about: 90 minutes

2 tbsp olive oil	1 lb lamb, cubed	1 cup arborio rice
2 garlic cloves, minced	Salt and black pepper to taste	2 tbsp mint, chopped
1 onion, chopped	2 cups vegetable stock	1 cup Halloumi, grated

Warm the olive oil in a skillet over medium heat and cook the onion for 5 minutes. Put in lamb and cook for another 5 minutes. Stir in garlic, salt, pepper, and stock and bring to a simmer; cook for 1 hour. Stir in rice and cook for 18-20 minutes. Top with Halloumi cheese and mint and serve.

265.   Halloumi-Roasted Pepper Brown Rice

Serves: 6 | Ready in about: 1 hour 50 minutes

2 tbsp halloumi cheese, grated	2 onions, finely chopped	1 ½ cups brown rice, rinsed
¾ cup roasted red peppers, chopped	Salt and black pepper to taste	1 lemon, cut into wedges
4 tsp olive oil	1 ½ cups vegetable broth	

Preheat oven to 375 F. Heat oil in a pot over medium heat until sizzling. Stir-fry the onions for 10-12 minutes until soft. Season with salt. Stir in 2 cups of water and broth and bring to a boil. Add in rice, cover, and transfer the pot to the oven. Cook until the rice is tender and liquid absorbed, 50-65 minutes. Remove from the oven. Sprinkle with red peppers and let sit for 5 minutes. Season to taste and stir in halloumi cheese. Serve with lemon wedges.

266.   Mushroom Millet

Serves: 6 | Ready in about: 35 minutes

10 oz cremini mushrooms, chopped	Salt and black pepper to taste	3 tbsp dry sherry
3 tbsp olive oil	1 shallot, minced	3 tbsp parsley, minced
1 ½ cups millet	½ tsp dried thyme	1 ½ tsp white wine

In a large pot, bring 4 quarts of water to a boil. Add millet and a pinch of salt, return to a boil and cook until tender, 15-20 minutes. Drain millet and cover to keep warm.

Warm 2 tablespoons of oil in a large skillet over medium heat. Add mushrooms, shallot, thyme, and salt and stir occasionally, until moisture has evaporated and vegetables start to brown, 10 minutes. Stir in wine, scraping off any browned bits from the bottom until the skillet is almost dry. Add the remaining oil and farro and keep stirring for 2 minutes. Stir in parsley and wine. Season with salt and pepper and serve.

267. Bulgur Pilaf with Almonds & Mushrooms

Serves: 2 | Ready in about: 45 minutes

3 scallions, minced
2 oz mushrooms, sliced
1 tbsp olive oil
1 garlic clove, minced

¼ cup almonds, sliced
½ cup bulgur
1 ½ cups chicken stock
½ tsp dried thyme

1 tbsp parsley, chopped
Salt to taste

Warm the olive oil in a saucepan over medium heat. Add garlic, scallions, mushrooms, and almonds, and sauté for 3 minutes. Pour the bulgur and cook, stirring, for 1 minute to toast it. Add the stock and thyme and bring the mixture to a boil. Cover and reduce the heat to low. Simmer the bulgur for 25 minutes or until the liquid is absorbed and the bulgur is tender. Sprinkle with parsley and season with salt to serve.

268. Tuna Barley with Okra

Serves: 4 | Ready in about: 50 minutes

2 tbsp olive oil
3 cups chicken stock
10 oz canned tuna, flaked

1 cup barley
Salt and black pepper to taste
12 cherry tomatoes, halved

½ cup pepperoncini, sliced
½ lb okra, blanched
½ lemon, juiced

Boil chicken stock in a saucepan over medium heat and add in barley. Cook covered for 40 minutes. Fluff the barley and remove to a bowl. Stir in tuna, salt, pepper, tomatoes, pepperoncini, olive oil, okra, and lemon juice. Serve.

269. Rosemary Barley with Walnuts

Serves: 4 | Ready in about: 45 minutes

2 tbsp olive oil
½ cup diced onion
½ cup diced celery
1 carrot, peeled and diced

3 cups water
1 cup barley
½ tsp thyme
½ tsp rosemary

¼ cup pine nuts
Salt and black pepper to taste

Warm the olive oil in a medium saucepan over medium heat. Sauté the onion, celery, and carrot over medium heat until tender. Add the water, barley, and seasonings, and bring to a boil. Reduce the heat and simmer for 23 minutes or until tender. Stir in the pine nuts and season to taste. Serve warm.

270. Energy-Boosting Green Barley Pilaf

Serves: 6 | Ready in about: 25 minutes

3 tbsp olive oil
1 small onion, chopped fine
Salt and black pepper to taste
1 ½ cups pearl barley, rinsed

2 garlic cloves, minced
½ tsp dried thyme
2 ½ cups water
¼ cup parsley, minced

2 tbsp cilantro, chopped
1 ½ tsp lemon juice

Warm the olive oil in a saucepan over medium heat. Stir-fry onion for 5 minutes until soft. Stir in barley, garlic, and thyme and cook, stirring frequently, until barley is lightly toasted and fragrant, 3-4 minutes. Stir in water and bring to a simmer. Reduce heat to low, cover, and simmer until barley is tender and water is absorbed, 25-35 minutes. Lay clean dish towel underneath the lid and let pilaf sit for 10 minutes. Add parsley, cilantro, and lemon juice and fluff gently with a fork to mix. Season with salt and pepper and serve warm.

271. Artichoke Hearts with Pearl Barley

Serves: 4 | Ready in about: 50 minutes

½ cup artichoke hearts, chopped
2 tbsp olive oil
1 cup pearl barley
2 tbsp grated Halloumi cheese
1 bay leaf

1 fresh cilantro sprig
1 fresh thyme sprig
1 onion, chopped
1 tbsp Greek seasoning

3 garlic cloves, minced
1 cup chicken broth
1 lemon, zested
Salt and black pepper to taste

Place barley, cilantro, bay leaf, and thyme in a pot over medium heat and cover with water. Bring to a boil, then lower the heat and simmer for 25 minutes. Drain, discard the bay leaf, rosemary, and thyme and reserve.

Warm the olive oil in a pan over medium heat. Sauté onion, artichoke, and Greek seasoning for 5 minutes. Add garlic and stir-fry for 40 seconds. Pour in some broth and cook until the liquid absorbs, add more, and keep stirring until absorbed. Mix in zest, salt, pepper, and cheese and stir for 2 minutes until the cheese has melted. Pour over the barley and serve.

272.　　Sage Farro

Serves: 4 | Ready in about: 50 minutes

2 tbsp olive oil	5 sage leaves	6 cups veggie stock
1 cup farro	1 garlic clove, minced	Salt and black pepper to taste
1 red onion, chopped	1 tbsp halloumi cheese, grated	

Warm the olive oil in a skillet over medium heat and cook the onion and garlic for 5 minutes. Stir in sage leaves, faro, veggie stock, salt, and pepper and bring to a simmer. Cook for 40 minutes. Mix in halloumi cheese and serve.

273.　　Herby Farro Pilaf

Serves: 6 | Ready in about: 30 minutes

3 tbsp olive oil	1 onion, chopped fine	¼ cup chopped fresh mint
1 ½ cups whole farro	1 garlic clove, minced	1 tbsp lemon juice
Salt and black pepper to taste	¼ cup chopped fresh cilantro	

Bring 4 quarts of water to boil in a pot. Add farro and season with salt and pepper, bring to a boil and cook until grains are tender with a slight chew, 20-25 minutes. Drain farro, return to the empty pot and cover to keep warm. Heat 2 tbsp of oil in a large skillet over medium heat. Stir-fry onion for 5 minutes. Stir in garlic and cook until fragrant, about 30 seconds. Add the remaining oil and farro and stir-fry for 2 minutes. Remove from heat, stir in cilantro, mint, and lemon juice. Season to taste and serve.

274.　　Zucchini Millet

Serves: 4 | Ready in about: 30 minutes

3 tbsp olive oil	1 cup millet	1 tsp hot pepper paste
2 tomatoes, chopped	2 spring onions, chopped	½ cup lemon juice
2 zucchini, chopped	½ cup cilantro, chopped	Salt and black pepper to taste

Warm the olive oil in a skillet over medium heat and sauté millet for 1-2 minutes. Pour in 2 cups of water, salt, and pepper and bring to a simmer. Cook for 15 minutes. Mix in spring onions, tomatoes, zucchini, hot pepper paste, and lemon juice. Serve topped with cilantro.

275.　　Buckwheat with Fresh Tarragon

Serves: 6 | Ready in about: 55 minutes

3 tbsp olive oil	1 garlic clove, minced	2 tbsp parsley, minced
1 ½ cups buckwheat, soaked	2 tsp fresh tarragon, minced	2 tsp lemon juice
3 cups vegetable broth	Salt and black pepper to taste	
½ onion, finely chopped	2 oz Halloumi cheese, grated	

Pulse buckwheat in your blender until about half of the grains are broken into smaller pieces. Bring broth and 3 cups of water to a boil in a medium saucepan over high heat. Reduce heat to low, cover, and keep warm. Heat 2 tablespoons oil in a pot over medium heat. Add onion and cook until softened, 5 minutes. Stir in garlic and cook until fragrant, about 30 seconds. Add farro and cook, stirring frequently, until grains are lightly toasted, 3 minutes.

Stir 5 cups warm broth mixture into farro mixture, reduce heat to low, cover, and cook until almost all liquid has been absorbed and farro is just al dente, about 25 minutes, stirring twice during cooking. Add tarragon, salt, and pepper and keep stirring for 5 minutes. Remove from heat and stir in Halloumi cheese, parsley, lemon juice, and the remaining olive oil. Adjust the seasoning and serve.

POULTRY

276. Baked Chicken with Fusilli

Serves: 4 | Ready in about: 55 minutes

2 tbsp olive oil
1 cup Provolone cheese, grated
16 oz fusilli pasta
1 lb ground chicken

1 shallot, thinly sliced
2 bell peppers, chopped
2 tomatoes, pureed
1 bay leaf

1 tbsp tomato paste
½ cup Greek yogurt
1 tsp Greek oregano
½ tsp salt

To a pot with salted boiling water, add the fusilli pasta and cook until al dente, 8-10 minutes. Reserve ½ cup of the cooking water and drain the pasta. Transfer to a bowl.

Preheat oven to 380 F. Warm the olive oil in a skillet over medium heat. Add in the chicken and brown for 3-4 minutes, stirring periodically. Add in shallot, bell peppers, oregano, and bay leaf and cook for 3-4 minutes. Remove the mixture to the pasta bowl and mix in the tomato puree and tomato paste. Sprinkle with the reserved cooking liquid and toss to coat. Transfer the pasta mixture to a baking dish. Spread the yogurt on top and sprinkle with the cheese. Cover with aluminum foil and bake for 20 minutes. Discard the foil and cook for another 5 minutes until the cheese is golden brown.

277. Chicken & Potato Greek Delight

Serves: 4 | Ready in about: 30 minutes

4 potatoes, peeled and quartered
4 boneless skinless chicken drumsticks
4 cups water
2 lemons, zested and juiced
1 tbsp olive oil
2 tsp fresh oregano

Salt and black pepper to taste
2 Serrano peppers, minced
3 tbsp finely chopped parsley
1 cup packed watercress
1 cucumber, thinly chopped
10 cherry tomatoes, quartered

16 Kalamata olives, pitted
¼ cup hummus
¼ cup feta cheese, crumbled
Lemon wedges for serving

Add water and potatoes to your Instant Pot. Set a trivet over them. In a baking bowl, mix lemon juice, olive oil, black pepper, oregano, zest, salt, and Serrano peppers. Add chicken drumsticks to the marinade and stir to coat.

Set the bowl with chicken on the trivet in the cooker. Seal the lid, select Manual and cook on High for 15 minutes. Do a quick release. Take out the bowl with chicken and the trivet from the pot. Drain potatoes and add parsley and salt. Split the potatoes among serving plates and top with watercress, cucumber slices, hummus, cherry tomatoes, chicken, olives, and feta cheese. Garnish with lemon wedges. Serve.

278. Hearty Greek-Style Chicken Stew

Serves: 4 | Ready in about: 30 minutes

¼ cup jarred roasted red peppers
3 tbsp olive oil
1 onion, chopped
2 garlic cloves, minced

2 tsp oregano, chopped
1 lb ground chicken
1 tbsp red wine vinegar
Salt and black pepper to taste

1 tsp red pepper flakes
1 ½ cups chicken stock
1 cup Kalamata olives, pitted
2 cups canned black eyed-peas

Warm the olive oil in a pot over medium heat and sauté ground chicken, onion, and garlic for 5 minutes, stirring occasionally. Put in roasted peppers, wine vinegar, salt, pepper, red pepper flakes, chicken stock, and black-eyed peas and bring to a boil. Simmer for 20 minutes. Serve topped with olives and oregano.

279. Herb-Infused Chicken with Asparagus Sauce

Serves: 4 | Ready in about: 40 minutes

1 chicken legs
4 garlic cloves, minced
4 fresh thyme, minced
3 fresh rosemary, minced
Salt and black pepper to taste

2 tbsp olive oil
8 oz asparagus, chopped
1 onion, chopped
1 cup chicken stock
1 tbsp soy sauce

1 fresh thyme sprig
1 tbsp flour
2 tbsp parsley, chopped

Warm the olive oil on Sauté in your Instant Pot. Add in onion and asparagus and sauté for 5 minutes until softened. Pour in chicken stock, 1 thyme sprig, black pepper, soy sauce, and salt, and stir. Insert a trivet over the asparagus mixture. Rub all sides of the chicken with garlic, rosemary, black pepper, lemon zest, thyme, and salt. Arrange the chicken legs on the trivet. Seal the lid, select Manual, and cook for 20 minutes on High Pressure. Do a quick release. Remove the chicken to a serving platter. In the inner pot, sprinkle flour over the asparagus mixture and blend the sauce with an immersion blender until desired consistency. Top the chicken with asparagus sauce and garnish with parsley. Serve and enjoy!

280. Mushroom Pappardelle with Greek-Style Chicken

Serves: 2 | Ready in about: 30 minutes

4 oz cremini mushrooms, sliced	8 oz chicken breasts, cubed	6 oz pappardelle pasta
2 tbsp olive oil	2 tsp tomato paste	¼ cup Greek yogurt
½ onion, minced	2 tsp dried tarragon	Salt and black pepper to taste
2 garlic cloves, minced	2 cups chicken stock	¼ tsp red pepper flakes

Warm 1 tablespoon of olive oil in a pan over medium heat. Suté the onion, garlic, and mushrooms for 5 minutes. Move the vegetables to the edges of the pan and add the remaining 1 tablespoon of olive oil to the center of the pan. Place the chicken cubes in the center and let them cook for about 6 minutes, stirring often until golden brown.

Mix in the tomato paste and tarragon. Add the stock and stir well to combine everything. Bring the mixture to a boil. Add the pappardelle. Simmer covered for 9-11 minutes, stirring occasionally, until the pasta is cooked and the liquid is mostly absorbed. Remove the pan from the heat. Stir 2 tbsp of the hot liquid from the pan into the yogurt. Pour the tempered yogurt into the pan and stir well to mix it into the sauce. Season with salt and pepper. Top with pepper flakes.

281. Syrupy Chicken with Green Peas

Serves: 4 | Ready in about: 40 minutes

2 tbsp olive oil	Salt and black pepper to taste	1 cup green peas
1 tsp dried thyme	1 cup chicken stock	2 tbsp chives, chopped
1 lb chicken breasts, cubed	½ cup tomato sauce	

Warm the olive oil in a pot over medium heat and sauté the chicken for 8 minutes, stirring occasionally. Season with thyme, salt, and pepper. Pour in chicken stock and tomato sauce and bring to a boil. Simmer for 20 minutes. Add in green peas and cook for 4-5 minutes. Top with chives.

282. Creamy Green Bean & Chicken Bake

Serves: 4 | Ready in about: 35 minutes

1 lb green beans, trimmed and halved	½ cup sour cream	1 tbsp dill, chopped
1 lb boneless chicken thighs, skinless	Salt and black pepper to taste	1 tbsp thyme, chopped
2 tsp turmeric powder	1 tbsp lime juice	

Preheat the oven to 380 F. Place chicken, turmeric, green beans, sour cream, salt, pepper, lime juice, thyme, and dill in a roasting pan and mix well. Bake for 25 minutes. Serve.

283. Chicken & Egg Casserole

Serves: 4 | Ready in about: 45 minutes

½ lb Halloumi cheese, grated	1 tsp dry mustard	2 tomatoes, chopped
1 tbsp olive oil	2 cloves garlic, crushed	1 tsp sweet paprika
1 lb chicken breasts, cubed	2 red bell peppers, sliced	½ tsp dried basil
4 eggs, beaten	1 red onion, sliced	Salt to taste

Preheat oven to 360 F. Warm the olive oil in a skillet over medium heat. Add the bell peppers, garlic, onion, and salt and cook for 3 minutes. Stir in tomatoes for an additional 5 minutes. Put in chicken breasts, paprika, dry mustard, and basil. Cook for another 6-8 minutes. Transfer the mixture to a greased baking pan and pour over the beaten eggs; season with salt. Bake for 15-18 minutes. Remove and spread the cheese over the top. Let cool for a few minutes. Serve sliced.

284.   Chicken Rice Bowls with Dried Apricots

Serves: 4 | Ready in about: 30 minutes

2 cups cooked chicken breasts, chopped
½ cup dried apricots, chopped
2 cups peeled and chopped cucumber
2 tbsp chicken broth
1 cup instant brown rice

¼ cup tahini
¼ cup Greek yogurt
2 tbsp scallions, chopped
1 tbsp lemon juice
1 tsp ground cumin

¾ tsp ground cinnamon
¼ tsp kosher or sea salt
4 tsp sesame seeds
1 tbsp fresh mint leaves

Place the broth in a pot over medium heat and bring to a boil. Reduce the heat and add the brown rice cook. Simmer for 10 minutes or until rice is cooked through. In a bowl, mix the tahini, yogurt, scallions, lemon juice, 1 tbsp of water, cumin, cinnamon, and salt. Transfer half the tahini mixture to another medium bowl.

Mix the chicken into the first bowl. When the rice is done, place it into the second bowl of tahini. Divide the chicken between 4 bowls. Spoon the rice mixture next to the chicken. Next to the chicken, place the dried apricots, and in the remaining empty section, add the cucumbers. Sprinkle with sesame seeds and fresh mint.

285.   Saucy Chicken with Grapes

Serves: 4 | Ready in about: 80 min + chilling time

4 tbsp olive oil
2 tbsp butter
3 garlic cloves, minced
1 tbsp lemon zest

2 tbsp fresh thyme, chopped
2 tbsp fresh parsley, chopped
Salt and black pepper to taste
4 bone-in chicken legs

2 cups red grapes (in clusters)
1 red onion, sliced
1 cup red wine
1 cup chicken stock

Toss the chicken with 2 tbsp of olive oil, garlic, thyme, parsley, lemon zest, salt, and pepper in a bowl. Refrigerate for 1 hour. Preheat oven to 400 F. Heat the remaining olive oil in a saucepan over medium heat. Sear the chicken for 3–4 minutes per side. Top the chicken with grapes. Transfer to the oven and bake for 20–30 minutes or until internal temperature registers 180 F on an instant-read thermometer.

Melt the butter in another saucepan and sauté the onion for 3–4 minutes. Add the wine and stock, stir, and simmer the sauce for about 30 minutes until it is thickened. Plate the chicken and grapes and pour the sauce over to serve.

286.   Ground Chicken Balls with Yogurt-Cucumber Sauce

Serves: 4 | Ready in about: 40 minutes

3 tbsp olive oil
2 garlic cloves, minced
1 lb ground chicken
1 egg

1 red onion, chopped
¼ tsp red pepper flakes
½ tsp dried oregano
1 cup Greek yogurt

1 cucumber, shredded
¼ tsp garlic powder
2 tbsp lemon juice
2 tbsp dill, chopped

In a bowl, combine ground chicken, egg, red onion, garlic, oregano, and red pepper flakes. Mix to combine well and shape the mixture into 1-inch balls.

Preheat the oven to 360 F. Warm 2 tbsp of olive oil in a skillet over medium heat and brown the meatballs for 10 minutes on all sides. Transfer the meatballs to a baking dish and bake for another 15 minutes. Combine Greek yogurt, cucumber, remaining olive oil, garlic powder, lemon juice, and dill in a bowl. Serve the meatballs with yogurt sauce.

287.   Chicken Breasts with Chickpeas & Olives

Serves: 4 | Ready in about: 45 minutes

2 tbsp avocado oil
1 lb chicken breasts, cubed
Salt and black pepper to taste

1 red onion, chopped
15 oz canned chickpeas
15 oz canned tomatoes, diced

1 cup pitted Kalamata olives, halved
2 tbsp lime juice
1 tsp cilantro, chopped

Warm the olive oil in a pot over medium heat and sauté chicken and onion for 5 minutes. Put in salt, pepper, chickpeas, tomatoes, olives, lime juice, cilantro, and 2 cups of water. Cover with a lid and bring to a boil, then reduce the heat and simmer for 30 minutes. Serve warm.

288.   Chicken & Vegetable Stir-Fry

Serves: 4 | Ready in about: 30 minutes

2 tbsp olive oil
1 lb chicken breasts, chopped
Salt and black pepper to taste

2 cloves garlic, minced
2 red bell pepper, chopped
1 onion, chopped

½ lemon, juiced and zested
½ cup feta cheese, crumbled
2 tbsp fresh dill, chopped

Warm the olive oil in a skillet over medium heat. Season the chicken with salt and pepper. Add the chicken and sear for about 4 minutes; reserve. Add the onion, garlic, and bell pepper to the same skillet and stir-fry for 6-8 minutes until crisp-tender. Return the chicken to the skillet and sprinkle with lemon zest and juice. Cook for 1 more minute. Sprinkle with feta cheese and dill and remove from the heat. Cover and allow to sit for 2–3 minutes until the cheese melts. Serve.

289.   Tomato-Glazed Chicken

Serves: 4 | Ready in about: 90 minutes

3 tbsp olive oil
1 (32-oz) can diced tomatoes,
4 chicken breast halves
2 whole cloves

¼ cup chicken broth
2 tbsp tomato paste
¼ tsp hot pepper flakes
1 tsp ground allspice

½ tsp dried mint
1 cinnamon stick
Salt and black pepper to taste

Place tomatoes, chicken broth, olive oil, tomato paste, hot pepper flakes, mint, allspice, cloves, cinnamon stick, salt, and pepper in a pot over medium heat and bring just to a boil. Then, lower the heat and simmer for 30 minutes. Strain the sauce through a fine-mesh sieve and discard the cloves and cinnamon stick. Let it cool completely.

Preheat oven to 350 F. Lay the chicken on a baking dish and pour the sauce over. Bake covered with aluminum foil for 40-45 minutes. Uncover and continue baking for 5 more minutes.

290.   Chicken Loaf with Tzatziki Sauce

Serves: 4 | Ready in about: 70 min + chilling time

1 lb ground chicken
1 onion, chopped
1 tsp garlic powder

1 cup tzatziki sauce
½ tsp dried Greek oregano
½ tsp dried cilantro

½ tsp sweet paprika
Salt and black pepper to taste

Preheat oven to 350 F. In a bowl, add chicken, paprika, onion, Greek oregano, cilantro, garlic, salt, and pepper and mix well with your hands. Shape the mixture into a greased loaf pan and bake in the oven for 55-60 minutes. Let sit for 15 minutes and slice. Serve topped with tzatziki sauce.

291.   Nutty-Topped Chicken Breasts

Serves: 4 | Ready in about: 40 minutes

2 tbsp olive oil
1 ½ lb chicken breasts, cubed
4 spring onions, chopped

2 carrots, peeled and sliced
¼ cup mayonnaise
½ cup Greek yogurt

1 cup toasted cashews, chopped
Salt and black pepper to taste

Warm the olive oil in a skillet over medium heat and brown chicken for 8 minutes on all sides. Stir in spring onions, carrots, mayonnaise, yogurt, salt, and pepper and bring to a simmer. Cook for 20 minutes. Top with cashews to serve.

292.   Yummy Chicken with Creamy Yogurt Sauce

Serves: 4 | Ready in about: 40 minutes

2 tbsp olive oil
1/3 cup Greek yogurt
1 lb chicken breasts, halved

2 garlic cloves, minced
2 tbsp lemon juice
1 tbsp red wine vinegar

2 tbsp dill, chopped
Salt and black pepper to taste

Preheat the oven to 380 F. In a food processor, blend garlic, lemon juice, vinegar, yogurt, dill, salt, and pepper until smooth. Warm olive oil in a skillet over medium heat. Sear chicken for 6 minutes on both sides. Pour yogurt sauce over the chicken and bake for 25 minutes. Serve.

293. Wine Chicken with Green Beans

Serves: 4 | Ready in about: 8 hours 10 minutes

12 oz green beans, chopped
1 lb chicken breasts, cubed
1 cup chicken stock

1 onion, chopped
1 tbsp white wine vinegar
1 cup Kalamata olives, chopped

1 tbsp curry powder
2 tsp basil, dried
Salt and black pepper to taste

Place chicken, green beans, chicken stock, onion, vinegar, olives, curry powder, basil, salt, and pepper in your slow cooker. Cover with the lid and cook for 8 hours on Low.

294. Oven Baked Chicken with Root Vegetables

Serves: 6 | Ready in about: 50 minutes

2 sweet potatoes, peeled and cubed
½ cup pitted green olives, smashed
¼ cup olive oil
2 lb chicken breasts, sliced

2 tbsp harissa seasoning
1 lemon, zested and juiced
Salt and black pepper to taste
2 carrots, chopped

1 onion, chopped
½ cup feta cheese, crumbled
½ cup parsley, chopped

Preheat the oven to 390 F. Place chicken, harissa seasoning, lemon juice, lemon zest, olive oil, salt, pepper, carrots, sweet potatoes, and onion in a roasting pan and mix well. Bake for 40 minutes. Combine feta cheese and green olives in a bowl. Share chicken mixture on plates and top with olive mixture. Top with parsley and parsley and serve.

295. Feta-Topped Chicken Breasts

Serves: 4 | Ready in about: 35 minutes

1 lb chicken breasts, cut into strips
2 tbsp olive oil
1 fennel bulb, chopped

Salt and black pepper to taste
2 tbsp balsamic vinegar
2 cups tomatoes, cubed

1 tbsp chives, chopped
¼ cup feta cheese, crumbled

Warm the olive oil in a skillet over medium heat and sear chicken for 5 minutes, stirring often. Mix in fennel, salt, pepper, vinegar, and tomatoes and cook for 20 minutes. Top with feta cheese and chives and serve.

296. Halloumi Cheese & Chicken

Serves: 4 | Ready in about: 40 minutes

2 tbsp butter
1 cup Halloumi cheese, cubed
Salt and black pepper to taste
1 hard-boiled egg yolk

½ cup olive oil
6 black olives, halved
1 tbsp fresh cilantro, chopped
1 tbsp balsamic vinegar

1 tbsp garlic, finely minced
1 tbsp fresh lemon juice
1 ½ lb chicken wings

Melt the butter in a saucepan over medium heat. Sear the chicken wings for 5 minutes per side. Season with salt and pepper to taste. Place the chicken wings on a parchment-lined baking pan. Mash the egg yolk with a fork and mix in the garlic, lemon juice, balsamic vinegar, olive oil, and salt until creamy, uniform, and smooth.

Preheat oven to 380 F. Spread the egg mixture over the chicken. Bake for 15-20 minutes. Top with the cheese and bake an additional 5 minutes until hot and bubbly. Scatter cilantro and olives on top of the chicken wings. Serve.

297. Almond Chicken with Eggplants

Serves: 4 | Ready in about: 40 minutes

2 tbsp olive oil
1 lb eggplants, cubed
Salt and black pepper to taste
1 onion, chopped

2 garlic cloves, minced
1 tsp hot paprika
1 tbsp oregano, chopped
1 cup chicken stock

1 lb chicken breasts, cubed
1 cup half and half
3 tsp toasted chopped almonds

Warm the olive oil in a skillet over medium heat and sauté chicken for 8 minutes, stirring often. Mix in eggplants, onion, and garlic and cook for another 5 minutes. Season with salt, pepper, hot paprika, and oregano and pour in the stock. Bring to a boil and simmer for 16 minutes. Stir in half and half for 2 minutes. Serve topped with almonds.

298.   Wine-Braised Chicken Breasts with Capers

Serves: 4 | Ready in about: 25 minutes

2 tbsp butter
1 lb chicken breasts
½ cup flour
½ tsp ground nutmeg

½ cup chicken broth
½ cup dry white wine
1 lemon, juiced and zested
1 tbsp capers

2 tbsp chopped fresh cilantro
Salt and black pepper to taste

Cut the chicken into 4 pieces and pound them to ¼-inch thickness using a meat mallet. Combine flour, nutmeg, salt, and pepper in a bowl. Roll the chicken in the mixture and shake off the excess flour. Warm butter in a skillet over medium heat and brown the chicken for 6-8 minutes on both sides; set aside. Scrape the bottom of the pot with white wine. Add in broth, lemon juice, lemon zest, and capers. Simmer for 3-4 minutes until the mixture thickens. Pour the sauce over the chicken and sprinkle with cilantro to serve.

299.   Baby Potatoes & Chicken Traybake

Serves: 4 | Ready in about: 50 minutes

4 fresh prunes, cored and quartered
2 tbsp olive oil
4 chicken legs

1 lb baby potatoes, halved
1 carrot, julienned

2 tbsp chopped fresh parsley
Salt and black pepper to taste

Preheat oven to 420 F. Combine potatoes, carrots, prunes, olive oil, salt, and pepper in a bowl. Transfer to a baking dish. Top with chicken. Season with salt and pepper. Roast for about 40-45 minutes. Serve topped with parsley.

300.   Sautéed Asparagus & Chicken

Serves: 4 | Ready in about: 30 minutes

2 tbsp olive oil
1 lb chicken breasts, sliced
Salt and black pepper to taste

1 lb asparagus, chopped
6 sundried tomatoes, diced
3 tbsp capers, drained

2 tbsp lemon juice

Warm the olive oil in a skillet over medium heat. Cook asparagus, tomatoes, salt, pepper, capers, and lemon juice for 10 minutes. Remove to a bowl. Brown chicken in the same skillet for 8 minutes on both sides. Put veggies back into skillet and cook for another 2-3 minutes. Serve and enjoy!

301.   Chicken Souvlaki with Vegetables

Serves: 6 | Ready in about: 20 minutes

2 tbsp olive oil
1 ½ lb chicken breasts, cubed
1 tbsp fresh chives, chopped

1 zucchini, sliced thick
1 tbsp Greek seasoning
1 cup bell peppers, sliced

1 red onion, cut into wedges
1 ½ cups cherry tomatoes

Preheat the grill to high. Toss the chicken with olive oil and Greek seasoning. Thread them onto skewers, alternating with the vegetables. Grill the skewers for 10 minutes, turning them occasionally to ensure even cooking. Top with chives.

302.   Creamy Drunken Chicken with Mushrooms

Serves: 4 | Ready in about: 30 minutes

4 chicken breasts, pounded thin
¼ cup olive oil
Salt and black pepper to taste
¼ cup whole-wheat flour

½ lb mushrooms, sliced
2 carrots, chopped
1 cup white wine

1 cup chicken broth
¼ cup parsley, chopped

Warm the oil in a saucepan on medium heat. Season the chicken with salt and pepper, then dredge them in the flour. Fry until golden brown on both sides, about 4-6 minutes; reserve. Sauté the mushrooms and carrots in the same pan. Add the wine and chicken broth and bring to a simmer. Cook for 10 minutes or until the sauce is reduced and thickened slightly. Return the chicken to the pan, and cook it in the sauce for 10 minutes. Top with parsley and serve.

303. Chicken & Bean Cassoulet

Serves: 4 | Ready in about: 35 minutes

2 tbsp olive oil	2 garlic cloves, minced	1 tbsp Greek seasoning
4 chicken breast halves	½ cup Marsala wine	1 cup baby spinach
1 onion, chopped	1 (14-oz) can diced tomatoes	⅛ tsp red pepper flakes
1 green bell pepper, chopped	1 (14-oz) can white beans	Salt and black pepper to taste

Pound the chicken to ¾-inch thickness using a meat mallet. Warm the olive oil in a pan over medium heat and brown the chicken for 6 minutes on both sides; set aside. In the same pan, sauté the onion, garlic, and bell pepper for 5 minutes. Pour in the wine and scrape any bits from the bottom. Simmer for 1 minute. Stir in tomatoes, beans, Greek seasoning, salt, pepper, and pepper flakes. Bring just to a boil, then lower the heat and simmer for 5 minutes. Stir in spinach and put back the reserved chicken; cook for 3-4 more minutes. Serve.

304. Mushroom & Chicken Kabobs

Serves: 4 | Ready in about: 50 minutes

1 red bell pepper, cut into squares	2 tsp sweet paprika	¼ tsp ground cardamom
2 tbsp olive oil	1 tsp ground nutmeg	1 lemon, juiced
2 chicken breasts, cubed	1 tsp Greek seasoning	3 garlic cloves, minced
1 red onion, cut into squares	¼ tsp smoked paprika	
1 cup mushrooms, quartered	Salt and black pepper to taste	

Combine chicken, onion, mushrooms, bell pepper, smoked paprika, nutmeg, Greek seasoning, sweet paprika, salt, pepper, cardamom, lemon juice, garlic, and olive oil in a bowl. Transfer to the fridge covered for 30 minutes.

Preheat your grill to high. Alternate chicken cubes, peppers, mushrooms, and onions on each of 8 metal skewers. Grill them for 16 minutes on all sides, turning frequently. Serve.

305. Hot Chicken Sausages with Pepper Sauce

Serves: 4 | Ready in about: 30 minutes

2 tbsp olive oil	1 onion, thinly sliced	½ cup dry white wine
4 chicken sausage links	1 red bell pepper, sliced	Salt and black pepper to taste
2 garlic cloves, minced	1 green bell pepper, sliced	½ dried hot pepper, minced

Warm the olive oil in a pan over medium heat and brown the sausages for 6 minutes, turning periodically. Set aside. In the same pan, sauté onion and bell peppers and garlic for 5 minutes until tender. Deglaze with the wine and stir in salt, pepper, and hot pepper. Simmer for 4 minutes until the sauce reduces by half. Serve sausages topped with bell peppers.

306. Delectable Chicken Pot

Serves: 4 | Ready in about: 35 minutes

1 lb skinless and boneless chicken thighs	1 tsp smoked paprika	14 oz canned tomatoes, diced
2 tbsp olive oil	1 tsp hot pepper powder	½ cup capers
1 onion, chopped	½ tsp fennel seeds, ground	
2 garlic cloves, minced	2 tsp oregano, dried	

Warm the oil in a skillet over medium heat and sauté the onion, garlic, paprika, hot pepper powder, fennel seeds, and oregano for 3 minutes. Put in chicken, tomatoes, 1 cup of water, and capers. Bring to a boil and simmer for 20-25 minutes.

307. Mushroom Chicken Breasts

Serves: 4 | Ready in about: 40 minutes

2 tbsp olive oil	1 celery stalk chopped	1 cup Bella mushrooms, sliced
4 chicken breasts, cubed	Salt and black pepper to taste	1 cup heavy cream
1 onion, chopped	1 tbsp thyme, chopped	2 tbsp chives, chopped
2 garlic cloves, minced	3 cups chicken stock	1 tbsp parsley, chopped

Warm the oil in a pot over medium heat and cook the onion and garlic for 3 minutes. Put in chicken and mushrooms and cook for another 10 minutes, stirring occasionally. Stir in celery, salt, pepper, thyme, and stock and bring to a boil; cook for 15 minutes. Stir in heavy cream for 3-4 minutes. Sprinkle with chives and parsley. Serve and enjoy!

308. Juicy Chicken Breasts

Serves: 4 | Ready in about: 30 minutes

2 tbsp olive oil
2 cups peaches, cubed
1 tbsp smoked paprika

1 lb chicken breasts, cubed
2 cups chicken broth
Salt and black pepper to taste

1 tbsp chives, chopped

Warm the olive oil in a skillet over medium heat and sauté chicken, salt, and pepper for 8 minutes, stirring occasionally. Stir in peaches, paprika, and chicken broth and cook for another 15 minutes. Serve topped with chives.

309. Herby Chicken Bake

Serves: 4 | Ready in about: 80 minutes

2 tbsp butter, melted
1 (3 ½-lb) chicken
2 lemons, halved

4 rosemary sprigs
1 bay leaf
6 thyme sprigs

1 tsp lemon juice
Salt and black pepper to taste

Preheat oven to 420 F and fit a rack into a roasting tray. Brush the chicken with butter on all sides. Put the lemons, herbs, and bay leaf inside the cavity. Drizzle with lemon juice and sprinkle with salt and pepper. Roast for 60-65 minutes. Let rest for 10 minutes before carving.

310. Balsamic Chicken & Spinach Dish

Serves: 4 | Ready in about: 60 minutes

2 tbsp olive oil
2 cups baby spinach
1 lb chicken sausage, sliced

1 red bell pepper, chopped
1 onion, sliced
2 tbsp garlic, minced

Salt and black pepper to taste
½ cup chicken stock
1 tbsp balsamic vinegar

Preheat oven to 380 F. Warm olive oil in a skillet over medium heat. Cook sausages for 6 minutes on all sides. Remove to a bowl. Add the bell pepper, onion, garlic, salt, and pepper to the skillet and sauté for 5 minutes. Pour in stock and vinegar and return the sausages. Bring to a boil and cook for 10 minutes. Add in the spinach and cook until wilts, about 4 minutes. Serve and enjoy!

311. Lemony Chicken Meatballs with Peach Topping

Serves: 4 | Ready in about: 25 minutes

2 tbsp olive oil
1 lb ground chicken
2 peaches, cubed

½ red onion, finely chopped
1 lemon, juiced
1 garlic clove, minced

½ jalapeño pepper, minced
2 tbsp chopped fresh cilantro
Salt and black pepper to taste

Season the ground chicken with salt and pepper. Shape the mixture into meatballs. Warm olive oil in a pan over medium heat and brown-fry the meatballs for 8-10 minutes on all sides until golden brown. In a bowl, combine peaches, lemon juice, garlic, red onion, jalapeño pepper, cilantro, and salt. Top the meatballs with the salsa and serve.

312. Bell Peppers & Chicken Skillet

Serves: 4 | Ready in about: 65 minutes

2 tbsp olive oil
2 lb chicken breasts, cubed
2 garlic cloves, minced

1 red onion, chopped
2 red bell peppers, chopped
¼ tsp cumin, ground

2 cups corn
½ cup chicken stock
1 tsp hot pepper powder

Warm the olive oil in a skillet over medium heat and sear chicken for 8 minutes on both sides. Put in onion and garlic and cook for another 5 minutes. Stir in bell peppers, cumin, corn, stock, and hot pepper powder. Cook for 45 minutes.

313. Chicken with Spinach & Chickpeas

Serves: 4 | Ready in about: 25 minutes

2 tbsp olive oil
1 lb chicken breasts, cubed
10 oz spinach, chopped
1 cup canned chickpeas

1 onion, chopped
2 garlic cloves, minced
½ cup chicken stock
2 tbsp Halloumi cheese, grated

1 tbsp parsley, chopped
Salt and black pepper to taste

Warm the olive oil in a skillet over medium heat and brown chicken for 5 minutes. Season with salt and pepper. Stir in onion and garlic for 3 minutes. Pour in stock and chickpeas and bring to a boil. Cook for 20 minutes. Mix in spinach and cook until wilted, about 5 minutes. Top with Halloumi cheese and parsley. Serve and enjoy!

314. Creamy Chicken Breasts with White Sauce

Serves: 4 | Ready in about: 30 minutes

1 cup canned cream of onion soup
2 tbsp olive oil
1 lb chicken breasts, cubed
½ tsp dried basil

½ cup flour
½ cup white wine
1 cup heavy cream
4 garlic cloves, minced

¼ tsp hot pepper flakes, crushed
Salt and black pepper to taste
2 tbsp parsley, chopped

In a bowl, combine salt, black pepper, hot pepper flakes, basil, and flour. Add in chicken and toss to coat. Warm the olive oil in a skillet over medium heat. Add in the chicken and cook for 5 minutes, stirring occasionally. Pour in the white wine to scrape any bits from the bottom. Stir in garlic, onion soup, and ½ cup of water. Bring to a boil, then lower the heat, and simmer covered for 15-18 minutes. Stir in heavy cream, top with parsley and serve.

315. Thyme Chicken Casserole

Serves: 4 | Ready in about: 65 minutes

1 tbsp butter, softened
1 lb chicken drumsticks
2 garlic cloves, minced

1 tsp paprika
1 lemon, zested
1 tbsp chopped fresh thyme

Salt and black pepper to taste

Preheat oven to 350 F. Mix butter, thyme, paprika, salt, garlic, pepper, and lemon zest in a bowl. Rub the mixture all over the chicken drumsticks and arrange them on a baking dish. Add in ½ cup of water and roast in the oven for 50-60 minutes. Remove the chicken from the oven and let it sit covered with foil for 10 minutes. Serve and enjoy!

316. Oven Roasted Peppery Chicken

Serves: 4 | Ready in about: 70 minutes

3 tbsp olive oil
1 lb chicken breasts, sliced
2 lb cherry tomatoes, halved

1 onion, chopped
3 garlic cloves, minced
3 red hot peppers, chopped

½ lemon, zested
Salt and black pepper to taste

Warm the olive oil in a skillet over medium heat and brown chicken for 8 minutes on both sides. Remove to a roasting pan. In the same skillet, add onion, garlic, and hot peppers and cook for 2 minutes. Pour the mixture over the chicken and toss to coat. Add in tomatoes, lemon zest, 1 cup of water, salt, and pepper. Bake for 45 minutes.

317. Cilantro Chicken Bowl

Serves: 4 | Ready in about: 50 minutes

4 chicken things, skinless and boneless
2 tbsp olive oil
Salt and black pepper to taste

1 celery stalk, chopped
2 leeks, chopped
2 cups chicken stock

2 tbsp cilantro, chopped
1 cup quinoa
1 tsp lemon zest

Warm the olive oil in a pot over medium heat and cook the chicken for 6-8 minutes on all sides. Stir in leeks and celery and cook for another 5 minutes until tender. Season with salt and pepper. Stir in quinoa and lemon zest for 1 minute and pour in the chicken stock. Bring to a boil and simmer for 35 minutes. Serve topped with cilantro.

318.   Chicken White Bean Casserole

Serves: 4 | Ready in about: 40 minutes

1 ½ lb skinless, boneless chicken thighs, cubed
½ cup canned artichokes, drained and chopped

2 tbsp olive oil
2 garlic cloves, minced
1 tbsp oregano, chopped

2 shallots, sliced
1 tsp paprika
1 cup canned white beans

½ cup parsley, chopped
1 cup halloumi, shredded
Salt and black pepper to taste

Preheat the oven to 390 F. Warm the olive oil in a skillet over medium heat and sauté the chicken for 5 minutes. Transfer to a baking pan and garlic, oregano, artichokes, paprika, shallots, beans, parsley, salt, and pepper. Top with halloumi cheese and bake for 25 minutes. Serve and enjoy!

319.   Stir-Fried Chicken with Zucchini

Serves: 4 | Ready in about: 40 minutes

2 tbsp olive oil
2 cups tomatoes, crushed
1 lb chicken breasts, cubed

Salt and black pepper to taste
2 shallots, sliced
3 garlic cloves, minced

2 zucchini, sliced
2 tbsp thyme, chopped
1 cup chicken stock

Warm the olive oil in a skillet over medium heat. Sear chicken for 6 minutes, stirring occasionally. Add in shallots and garlic and cook for another 4 minutes. Stir in tomatoes, salt, pepper, zucchini, and stock and bring to a boil; simmer for 20 minutes. Garnish with thyme and serve.

320.   Herbed Chicken with Tomatoes

Serves: 4 | Ready in about: 50 minutes

2 tbsp olive oil
1 lb chicken breasts, sliced
1 onion, chopped
1 carrot, chopped

2 garlic cloves, minced
½ cup chicken stock
1 tsp oregano, dried
1 tsp tarragon, dried

1 tsp rosemary, dried
1 cup canned tomatoes, diced
Salt and black pepper to taste

Warm the olive oil in a pot over medium heat and cook the chicken for 8 minutes on both sides. Put in carrot, garlic, and onion and cook for 3 minutes. Season with salt and pepper. Pour in stock, oregano, tarragon, rosemary, and tomatoes and bring to a boil; simmer for 25 minutes. Serve.

321.   Cheesy Chicken Breasts

Serves: 4 | Ready in about: 65 minutes

2 tbsp canola oil
1 lb chicken breasts, halved
½ tsp hot paprika
1 cup chicken stock

2 tbsp hazelnuts, chopped
2 spring onions, chopped
2 garlic cloves, minced
¼ cup Halloumi cheese, grated

2 tbsp cilantro, chopped
2 tbsp parsley, chopped
Salt and black pepper to taste

Preheat the oven to 370 F. Combine chicken, canola oil, hot paprika, stock, hazelnuts, spring onions, garlic, salt, and pepper in a greased baking pan and bake for 40 minutes. Sprinkle with Halloumi cheese and bake for an additional 5 minutes until the cheese melts. Top with cilantro and parsley.

322.   Greek-Style Chicken Wings

Serves: 6 | Ready in about: 50 minutes

2 tbsp canola oils
12 chicken wings, halved
2 garlic cloves, minced

1 lime, juiced and zested
1 cup raisins, soaked
1 tsp cumin, ground

Salt and black pepper to taste
½ cup chicken stock
1 tbsp chives, chopped

Preheat the oven to 340 F. Combine chicken wings, garlic, lime juice, lime zest, canola oil, raisins, cumin, salt, pepper, stock, and chives in a baking pan. Bake for 40 minutes.

323. Chicken Breasts with Greek Sauce

Serves: 4 | Ready in about: 25 min + marinating time

½ cup olive oil
2 tbsp rosemary, chopped
2 tbsp parsley, chopped

1 tsp minced garlic
1 lemon, zested and juiced
Salt and black pepper to taste

4 chicken breasts
2 tsp basil, chopped

Combine the olive oil, rosemary, garlic, lemon juice, lemon zest, parsley, salt, and pepper in a plastic bag. Add the chicken and shake to coat. Refrigerate for 2 hours.

Heat your grill to medium heat. Remove the chicken breasts from the marinade and grill them for 6-8 minutes per side. Pour the marinade into a saucepan, add 2 tbsp of water and simmer for 2-3 minutes until the sauce thickens. Sprinkle with basil and serve the grilled chicken. Enjoy!

324. Zucchini & Chicken Dish

Serves: 4 | Ready in about: 70 minutes

3 tbsp canola oil
1 lb turkey breast, sliced
Salt and black pepper to taste

3 garlic cloves, minced
2 zucchini, sliced
1 cup chicken stock

¼ cup heavy cream
2 tbsp parsley, chopped

Warm the olive oil in a pot over medium heat. Cook the turkey for 10 minutes on both sides. Put in garlic and cook for 1 minute. Season with salt and pepper. Stir in zucchini for 3-4 minutes and pour in the chicken stock. Bring to a boil and cook for 40 minutes. Stir in heavy cream and parsley.

325. Potato, Carrot & Chicken Bake

Serves: 4 | Ready in about: 60 minutes

2 tbsp olive oil
1 lb chicken breasts, cubed
1 carrot, chopped
2 garlic cloves, minced

Salt and black pepper to taste
2 tsp thyme, dried
1 baby potatoes, halved
1 onion, sliced

¾ cup chicken stock
2 tbsp basil, chopped

Preheat the oven to 380 F. Grease a baking dish with oil. Put carrot, potatoes, chicken, garlic, salt, pepper, thyme, onion, stock, and basil in the dish and bake for 50 minutes. Serve.

326. Walnut Chicken with Tomatoes

Serves: 4 | Ready in about: 35 minutes

2 tbsp olive oil
1 lb chicken breast halves
Salt and black pepper to taste

2 tbsp walnuts, chopped
1 tbsp chives, chopped
½ cup tomato sauce

½ cup chicken stock

Warm the olive oil in a skillet over medium heat and cook chicken for 8 minutes, flipping once. Season with salt and pepper. Stir in walnuts, tomato sauce, and stock and bring to a boil. Cook for 16 minutes. Serve sprinkled with chives.

327. Carrot Chicken with Farro

Serves: 4 | Ready in about: 50 minutes

2 tbsp olive oil
3 carrots, chopped
1 cup farro, soaked
1 lb chicken breasts, cubed

1 red onion, chopped
4 garlic cloves, minced
2 tbsp dill, chopped
2 tbsp tomato paste

2 cups vegetable stock
Salt and black pepper to taste

Warm olive oil in your pressure cooker on Sauté and sear the chicken for 10 minutes on all sides, stirring occasionally. Remove to a plate. Add onion, garlic, and carrots to the cooker and sauté for 3 minutes. Stir in tomato paste, farro, and vegetable stock and return the chicken. Seal the lid, select Pressure Cook, and cook for 30 minutes on High. Do a natural pressure release for 10 minutes. Adjust the taste with salt and pepper. Sprinkle with dill and serve.

328.   Chicken with Caper Sauce

Serves: 4 | Ready in about: 35 minutes

2 tbsp canola oil
4 chicken breast halves
Salt and black pepper to taste

1 tbsp sweet paprika
1 onion, chopped
1 tbsp balsamic vinegar

2 tbsp parsley, chopped
1 avocado, peeled and cubed
2 tbsp capers

Preheat the grill over medium heat. Rub chicken halves with half of the canola oil, paprika, salt, and pepper and grill them for 14 minutes on both sides. Share into plates. Combine onion, remaining oil, vinegar, parsley, avocado, and capers in a bowl. Pour the sauce over the chicken and serve.

329.   Orange Chicken Thighs

Serves: 4 | Ready in about: 40 minutes

2 tbsp olive oil
2 tbsp sweet hot pepper sauce
2 lb chicken thighs, cubed
Salt and black pepper to taste

1 ½ tsp orange extract
¼ cup orange juice
2 tbsp cilantro, chopped
1 cup chicken stock

¼ tsp red pepper flakes
2 cups cooked white rice

Warm the olive oil in a skillet over medium heat and sear chicken for 8 minutes on all sides. Season with salt and pepper and stir in orange extract, orange juice, stock, sweet hot pepper sauce, and red pepper flakes. Bring to a boil. Cook for 20 minutes. Top with cilantro and serve over cooked rice.

330.   Tasty Chicken with Green Peas

Serves: 4 | Ready in about: 35 minutes

2 tbsp olive oil
1 lb chicken breasts, halved
1 tsp hot pepper powder
Salt and black pepper to taste

1 tsp garlic powder
1 tbsp smoked paprika
½ cup chicken stock
2 tsp sherry vinegar

3 tsp hot sauce
2 tsp cumin, ground
1 cup green peas
1 carrot, chopped

Warm the olive oil in a skillet over medium heat and cook chicken for 6 minutes on both sides. Sprinkle with hot pepper powder, salt, pepper, garlic powder, and paprika. Pour in the chicken stock, vinegar, hot sauce, cumin, carrot, and green peas and bring to a boil; cook for an additional 15 minutes.

331.   Hot Chicken Lentils with Artichokes

Serves: 4 | Ready in about: 50 minutes

2 tbsp olive oil
4 chicken breasts, halved
1 lemon, juiced and zested
2 garlic cloves, crushed

1 tbsp thyme, chopped
6 oz canned artichokes hearts
1 cup canned lentils, drained
1 cup chicken stock

1 tsp hot pepper
Salt and black pepper to taste

Warm the olive oil in a skillet over medium heat and cook chicken for 5-6 minutes until browned, flipping once. Mix in lemon zest, garlic, lemon juice, salt, pepper, thyme, artichokes, lentils, stock, and hot pepper and bring to a boil. Cook for 35 minutes. Serve immediately.

332.   Lemony Chicken Breasts

Serves: 4 | Ready in about: 8 hours 10 minutes

2 tbsp olive oil
2 chicken breasts, halved
Juice of ½ lemon
Zest of ½ lemon, grated

2 tsp cardamom, ground
Salt and black pepper to taste
2 spring onions, chopped
2 tbsp tomato paste

2 garlic cloves, minced
1 cup pineapple juice
½ cup chicken stock
¼ cup cilantro, chopped

Place chicken, lemon juice, lemon zest, cardamom, salt, pepper, olive oil, spring onions, tomato paste, garlic, pineapple juice, and stock in your slow cooker. Cover with the lid and cook for 8 hours on Low. Garnish with cilantro.

333.   Almond Chicken Balls

Serves: 4 | Ready in about: 30 minutes

2 tbsp olive oil
1 lb ground chicken
2 tsp toasted chopped almonds
1 egg, whisked

2 tsp turmeric powder
2 garlic cloves, minced
Salt and black pepper to taste
1 ¼ cups heavy cream

¼ cup parsley, chopped
1 tbsp chives, chopped

Place chicken, almonds, egg, turmeric powder, garlic, salt, pepper, parsley, and chives in a bowl and toss to combine. Form meatballs out of the mixture. Warm olive oil in a skillet over medium heat. Brown meatballs for 8 minutes on all sides. Stir in cream and cook for another 10 minutes.

334.   Traditional Chicken Souvlaki

Serves: 4 | Ready in about: 20 min + cooling time

1 red bell pepper, cut into chunks
2 chicken breasts, cubed
2 tbsp olive oil

2 cloves garlic, minced
8 oz cipollini onions
½ cup lemon juice

Salt and black pepper to taste
1 tsp rosemary, chopped
1 cup tzatziki sauce

In a bowl, mix oil, garlic, salt, pepper, and lemon juice and add the chicken, cipollini, rosemary, and bell pepper. Refrigerate for 2 hours. Preheat your grill to high heat. Thread chicken, bell pepper, and cipollini onto skewers and grill them for 6 minutes per side. Serve with tzatziki sauce.

335.   Peach Glazed Chicken Drumsticks

Serves: 4 | Ready in about: 35 minutes

2 tbsp olive oil
8 chicken drumsticks, skinless
3 peaches, peeled and chopped

¼ cup honey
¼ cup cider vinegar
1 sweet onion, chopped

1 tsp minced fresh rosemary
Salt to taste

Warm the olive oil in a large skillet over medium heat. Sprinkle chicken with salt and pepper and brown it for about 7 minutes per side. Remove to a plate. Add onion and rosemary to the skillet and sauté for 1 minute or until lightly golden. Add honey, vinegar, salt, and peaches and cook for 10-12 minutes or until peaches are softened. Add the chicken back to the skillet and heat just until warm, brushing with the sauce. Serve chicken thighs with peach sauce.

336.   Basil Tomato Chicken Breasts

Serves: 4 | Ready in about: 30 minutes

2 tbsp olive oil
1 lb chicken breasts
½ tsp garlic powder
¼ tsp hot pepper powder

Salt and black pepper to taste
1 large tomato, sliced thinly
1 cup halloumi, shredded
1 (14-oz) can diced tomatoes

2 tbsp fresh basil leaves, torn
4 tsp balsamic vinegar

Preheat oven to 450 F. Flatten the chicken breasts with a rolling pin. Add the chicken, olive oil, garlic powder, hot pepper powder, black pepper, and salt to a resealable bag. Seal the bag and massage the ingredients into the chicken. Take the chicken out of the bag and place it on a greased baking sheet.

Bake the chicken for 15-18 minutes or until the meat reaches an internal temperature of 160 F and the juices run clear. Layer the tomato slices on each chicken breast and top with halloumi cheese. Broil the chicken for another 2-3 minutes or until the cheese melts. Remove the chicken from the oven. Microwave the crushed tomatoes for 1 minute. Divide the tomatoes between plates and top with chicken breasts. Scatter with basil and a drizzle of balsamic vinegar.

337.   Roasted Artichokes & Chicken Thighs

Serves: 4 | Ready in about: 25 minutes

2 artichoke hearts, halved lengthwise
2 tbsp butter, melted

3 tbsp olive oil
2 lemons, zested and juiced

½ tsp salt
4 chicken thighs

Preheat oven to 450 F. Place a large, rimmed baking sheet in the oven. Whisk the olive oil, lemon zest, and lemon juice in a bowl. Add the artichoke hearts and turn them to coat on all sides. Lay the artichoke halves flat-side down in the center of 4 aluminum foil sheets and close up loosely to create packets. Put the chicken in the remaining lemon mixture and toss to coat. Carefully remove the hot baking sheet from the oven and pour on the butter; tilt the pan to coat.

Arrange the chicken thighs, skin-side down, on the sheet, and add the artichoke packets. Roast for about 20 minutes or until the chicken is cooked through and the skin is slightly charred. Check the artichokes for doneness and bake for another 5 minutes if needed. Serve and enjoy!

338. Easy Chicken with Olive Tapenade

Serves: 4 | Ready in about: 35 minutes

½ cup olive oil
2 tbsp capers, canned
2 chicken breasts
1 cup black olives, pitted

Salt and black pepper to taste
½ cup parsley, chopped
½ cup rosemary, chopped
Salt and black pepper to taste

2 garlic cloves, minced
½ lemon, juiced and zested

In a food processor, blend olives, capers, half of the oil, salt, pepper, parsley, rosemary, garlic, lemon zest, and lemon juice until smooth; set aside. Warm the remaining oil in a skillet over medium heat. Brown the chicken for 8-10 minutes on both sides. Top with tapenade. Serve and enjoy!

339. Quick One-Pan Turkey

Serves: 4 | Ready in about: 35 minutes

1 tbsp sunflower seeds, toasted
3 tbsp avocado oil
1 turkey breast, sliced

1 ¼ cups chicken stock
Salt and black pepper to taste
¼ cup parsley, chopped

4 oz feta cheese, crumbled
¼ cup red onion, chopped
1 tbsp lemon juice

Warm the avocado oil in a skillet over medium heat and sear turkey for 8 minutes on both sides. Mix in stock, salt, pepper, parsley, onion, and lemon juice and bring to a boil. Cook for 15 minutes. Remove to a serving plate and top with feta cheese and sunflower seeds to serve.

340. Turkey Ham Stuffed Peppers

Serves: 4 | Ready in about: 10 minutes

1 cup Greek yogurt
1 lb turkey ham, chopped
2 tbsp mustard
Salt and black pepper to taste

1 celery stalk, chopped
2 tbsp balsamic vinegar
1 bunch scallions, sliced
¼ cup parsley, chopped

1 cucumber, sliced
4 red bell peppers, halved
1 tomato, sliced

Preheat the oven to 360 F. Combine turkey ham, celery, balsamic vinegar, salt, pepper, mustard, yogurt, scallions, parsley, cucumber, and tomatoes in a bowl. Fill bell peppers with the mixture and arrange them on a greased baking dish. Bake in the oven for about 20 minutes. Serve warm.

341. Turkey with Green Veggies

Serves: 4 | Ready in about: 40 minutes

3 tbsp olive oil
1 lb asparagus, halved
1 lb turkey breast, sliced
1 cup chicken stock

Salt and black pepper to taste
1 cup canned artichoke hearts
2 tomatoes, chopped
10 Kalamata olives, sliced

1 shallot, chopped
3 garlic cloves, minced
3 tbsp dill, chopped

Warm the olive oil in a pot over medium heat and cook turkey and garlic for 8 minutes or until the meat is golden brown. Stir in the asparagus, chopped tomatoes, chicken stock, salt, black pepper, artichoke hearts, Kalamata olives, and shallot and bring to a boil. Lower the heat and simmer for 20 minutes. Garnish with dill and serve.

PORK, BEEF & LAMB

342.   Cheesy Pork Chops

Serves: 6 | Ready in about: 20 minutes

2 tbsp butter
3 tbsp olive oil
6 pork chops, boneless

2 fresh eggs
2 tbsp chicken stock
½ cup grated Halloumi cheese

1 cup bread crumbs
1 tsp Greek seasoning
½ tsp dried basil

Flatten the chops with a meat tenderizer. In a bowl, beat the eggs with chicken stock. Mix the Halloumi cheese, crumbs, Greek seasoning, and basil on a shallow plate. Dip each pork chop into the egg mixture, then coat with the cheese mixture. Warm the butter and olive oil in a large skillet over medium heat. Sear the pork chops for 6-8 minutes on both sides until brown and crisp. Serve immediately.

343.   Pork Souvlaki with Apricot Glaze

Serves: 6 | Ready in about: 50 minutes

2 lb pork tenderloin, cubed
1 cup apricot jam

½ cup apricot nectar
1 cup dried whole apricots

2 onions, cut into wedges
½ tsp dried rosemary

Coat the pork cubes with apricot jam, cover, and set aside for 10-15 minutes. Bring to a boil the apricot nectar, rosemary, and dried apricots in a saucepan over medium heat. Lower the heat and simmer for 2-3 minutes. Remove the apricots with a perforated spoon and pour the hot liquid over the pork. Stir and drain the pork, reserving the marinade.

Preheat your grill to medium-high. Alternate pork cubes, onion wedges, and apricots onto 6 metal skewers. Brush them with some marinade and grill for 10-12 minutes, turning and brushing with some more marinade until the pork is slightly pink and the onions are crisp-tender. Simmer the remaining marinade for 3-5 minutes. Serve the skewers with marinade on the side. Enjoy!

344.   Garlicky Pork in Spicy Sauce

Serves: 4 | Ready in about: 20 minutes

2 tbsp olive oil
½ tsp garlic, minced
For the Sauce:
1 cup cherry tomatoes
2 tbsp fresh basil, chopped
1 tsp rosemary

Salt and black pepper to taste
¼ cup vegetable broth

½ cup red onion, chopped
1 tsp oregano
2 tbsp olive oil

4 pork chops

1 cloves garlic, minced
1 hot pepper, minced
Salt and black pepper to taste

Warm the olive oil in a pan over medium heat. Sauté the garlic until aromatic. Add in the pork chops, broth, salt, and pepper and cook for 2-3 minutes per side; remove to a plate. Puree the sauce ingredients in your food processor until smooth and creamy. Pour the sauce into a pan over medium heat and cook for 5-6 minutes. Pour the sauce over the pork.

345.   Onion & Bell Pepper Pork Chops

Serves: 4 | Ready in about: 30 minutes

2 tbsp olive oil
4 pork chops
Salt and black pepper to taste
1 tsp fennel seeds

1 red bell pepper, sliced
1 green bell pepper, sliced
1 yellow onion, thinly sliced
2 tsp Greek seasoning

2 garlic cloves, minced
1 tbsp balsamic vinegar

Warm the oil in a large skillet over medium heat. Season the pork chops with salt and pepper and add them to the skillet. Cook for 6-8 minutes on both sides or until golden brown; reserve. Sauté the garlic, sliced bell peppers, onions, fennel seeds, and herbs in the skillet for 6-8 minutes until tender, stirring occasionally. Return the pork, cover, and lower the heat to low. Cook for another 3 minutes or until the pork is cooked through. Transfer the pork and vegetables to a serving platter. Add the vinegar to the skillet and stir to combine for 1-2 minutes. Drizzle the sauce over the pork.

346.   Cheesy Spinach-Filled Pork Loin Delight

Serves: 6 | Ready in about: 55 minutes

1 ½ lb pork tenderloin
6 slices pancetta, chopped

1 cup mushrooms, sliced
5 sundried tomatoes, diced

Salt and black pepper to taste

Place a skillet over medium heat and stir-fry the pancetta for 5 minutes until crispy. Add the mushrooms and sauté for another 4-5 minutes until tender, stirring occasionally. Stir in sundried tomatoes and season with salt and pepper; set aside. Preheat the oven to 350F. Using a sharp knife, cut the pork tenderloin in half lengthwise, leaving about a 1-inch border; be careful not to cut through to the other side. Open the tenderloin like a book to form a large rectangle.

Flatten it to about ¼-inch thickness with a meat tenderizer. Season the pork generously with salt and pepper. Top all over with pancetta filling. Roll up pork tenderloin and tightly secure it with kitchen twine. Place on a greased baking sheet. Bake for 60-75 minutes until the pork is cooked through, depending on the thickness of the pork. Remove from the oven and let rest for 10 minutes at room temperature. Remove the twine and discard. Slice the pork into medallions and serve.

347.   Almond-Smothered Cocktail Meatballs

Serves: 4 | Ready in about: 30 minutes

3 tbsp olive oil
8 oz ground pork
8 oz ground beef
½ cup finely minced onions
1 large egg, beaten

1 potato, shredded
Salt and black pepper to taste
1 tsp garlic powder
½ tsp oregano
2 tbsp chopped parsley

¼ cup ground almonds
1 cup chicken broth
¼ cup butter

Place the ground meat, onions, egg, potato, salt, garlic powder, pepper, and oregano in a large bowl. Shape the mixture into small meatballs, about 1 inch in diameter, and place on a plate. Let sit for 10 minutes at room temperature.

Warm the olive oil in a skillet over medium heat. Add the meatballs and brown them for 6-8 minutes on all sides; reserve. In the hot skillet, melt the butter and add the almonds and broth. Cook for 3-5 minutes. Add the meatballs to the skillet, cover, and cook for 8-10 minutes. Top with parsley.

348.   Pork Chops with Apricot Chutney

Serves: 4 | Ready in about: 40 minutes

1 tbsp olive oil
½ tsp garlic powder
4 pork loin chops, boneless
For the chutney
3 cups apricots, peeled and chopped
½ cup red sweet pepper, chopped
1 tsp olive oil

Salt and black pepper to taste
¼ tsp ground cumin
½ tsp sage, dried

¼ cup shallot, minced
½ jalapeno pepper, minced
1 tbsp balsamic vinegar

1 tsp hot pepper powder

2 tbsp cilantro, chopped

Warm the olive oil in a skillet over medium heat and cook the shallot for 5 minutes. Stir in sweet pepper, apricots, jalapeño pepper, vinegar, and cilantro and cook for 10 minutes. Remove from heat.

In the meantime, sprinkle pork chops with olive oil, salt, pepper, garlic powder, cumin, sage, and hot pepper powder. Preheat the grill to medium heat. Grill pork chops for 12-14 minutes on both sides. Serve topped with chutney.

349.   Pork Loin stuffed with Vegetables

Serves: 4 | Ready in about: 30 minutes

2 tbsp canola oil
2 carrots, chopped
2 garlic cloves, minced

1 lb pork loin, cubed
4 oz snow peas
¾ cup beef stock

1 onion, chopped
Salt and white pepper to taste

Warm the oil in a skillet over medium heat and sear pork for 5 minutes. Stir in snow peas, carrots, garlic, stock, onion, salt, and pepper and bring to a boil; cook for 15 minutes.

350. Melt-in-your-mouth Pork Shoulder

Serves: 4 | Ready in about: 2 hours 10 minutes

3 tbsp olive oil
2 lb pork shoulder
1 onion, chopped

2 tbsp garlic, minced
1 tbsp hot paprika
1 tbsp basil, chopped

1 cup chicken broth
Salt and black pepper to taste

Preheat oven to 350 F. Heat olive oil in a skillet and brown the pork on all sides for about 8-10 minutes; remove to a baking dish. Add onion and garlic to the skillet and sauté for 3 minutes until softened. Stir in hot paprika, salt, and pepper for 1 minute and pour in chicken broth. Transfer to the baking dish, cover with aluminium foil and bake for 90 minutes. Then remove the foil and continue baking for another 20 minutes until browned on top. Let the pork cool for a few minutes, slice, and sprinkle with basil. Serve topped with the cooking juices.

351. Savory Rosemary Pork Chops with Veggie Medley

Serves: 4 | Ready in about: 35 minutes

½ green cabbage head, shredded
2 tsp olive oil
4 pork chops
4 bell peppers, chopped

1 tsp rosemary
2 tbsp wine vinegar
2 spring onions, chopped

Salt and black pepper to taste

Warm half of oil in a skillet over medium heat. Cook spring onions for 3 minutes. Stir in vinegar, cabbage, bell peppers, salt, and pepper and simmer for 10 minutes. Heat off.

Preheat the grill over medium heat. Sprinkle pork chops with remaining oil, salt, pepper, and rosemary and grill for 10 minutes on both sides. Share chops into plates with cabbage mixture on the side. Serve immediately.

352. Pork Sausage & Herby Eggs

Serves: 2 | Ready in about: 20 minutes

2 tbsp olive oil
½ cup leeks, chopped
½ lb pork sausage, crumbled
4 eggs, whisked

1 thyme sprig, chopped
1 tsp habanero pepper, minced
½ tsp dried marjoram
1 tsp garlic puree

½ cup green olives, sliced
Salt and black pepper to taste

Warm the olive oil in a skillet over medium heat. Sauté the leeks until they are just tender, about 4 minutes. Add the garlic, habanero pepper, salt, black pepper, and sausage; cook for 8 minutes, stirring frequently. Pour in the eggs and sprinkle with thyme and marjoram. Cook for an additional 4 minutes, stirring with a spoon. Garnish with olives.

353. One-Tray Baked Pork Chops

Serves: 4 | Ready in about: 45 minutes

1 tbsp olive oil
4 pork loin chops, boneless

Salt and black pepper to taste
4 garlic cloves, minced

1 tbsp thyme, chopped

Preheat the oven to 390 F. Place pork chops, salt, pepper, garlic, thyme, and olive oil in a roasting pan and bake for 10 minutes. Decrease the heat to 360 F and bake for 25 minutes.

354. Roast Pork Loin with Green Onions

Serves: 4 | Ready in about: 50 minutes

2 lb pork loin roast, boneless and cubed
2 tbsp olive oil
2 garlic cloves, minced

Salt and black pepper to taste
1 cup tomato sauce

1 tsp rosemary, chopped
4 green onions, chopped

Preheat the oven to 360 F. Heat olive oil in a skillet over medium heat and cook pork, garlic, and green onions for 6-7 minutes, stirring often. Add in tomato sauce, rosemary, and 1 cup of water. Season with salt and pepper. Transfer to a baking dish and bake for 40 minutes. Serve warm.

355. Sweet-Mustard Pork Chops

Serves: 4 | Ready in about: 40 minutes

2 tbsp olive oil	2 tbsp wholegrain mustard	4 pork loin chops, boneless
½ cup vegetable stock	1 tbsp honey	Salt and black pepper to taste

Preheat oven to 380 F. Mix honey, mustard, salt, pepper, paprika, and olive oil in a bowl. Add in the pork and toss to coat. Transfer to a greased baking sheet and pour in the vegetable stock. Bake covered with foil for 30 minutes. Remove the foil and bake for 6-8 minutes until golden brown.

356. Creamy Pork Tenderloin with Caraway Seeds

Serves: 4 | Ready in about: 30 minutes

2 tbsp olive oil	Salt and black pepper to taste	1/3 cup heavy cream
1 lb pork tenderloin, sliced	3 tbsp ground caraway seeds	½ cup dill, chopped

Warm the olive oil in a skillet over medium heat and sear pork for 8 minutes on all sides. Stir in salt, pepper, ground caraway seeds, heavy cream, and dill and bring to a boil. Cook for another 12 minutes. Serve warm.

357. Bell Pepper Pork Stew

Serves: 4 | Ready in about: 8 hours 10 minutes

2 tbsp olive oil	Salt and black pepper to taste	1 red bell pepper, chopped
1 lb pork stew meat, cubed	2 cups tomatoes, chopped	1 green bell pepper, chopped
½ cup chicken stock	2 carrots, chopped	1 tbsp parsley, chopped

Place oil, chicken stock, bell peppers, salt, pepper, pork meat, tomatoes, and carrots in your slow cooker. Cover with the lid and cook for 8 hours on Low. Scatter with parsley.

358. Skordalia Pork Shoulder

Serves: 4 | Ready in about: 35 minutes

¼ cup olive oil	2 lb pork shoulder, cubed	½ cup skordalia sauce
1 tsp red pepper flakes	2 tsp dried marjoram	Salt and black pepper to taste
2 garlic cloves, minced	¼ cup lemon juice	

Warm the oil in a skillet over medium heat and sear pork for 5 minutes. Mix in marjoram, red pepper flakes, lemon juice, garlic, salt, and pepper and cook for another 20 minutes, stirring often. Serve with skordalia sauce on the side.

359. Pork Loin in Oregano Tomato Sauce

Serves: 4 | Ready in about: 50 minutes

2 tbsp olive oil	1 red onion, chopped	2 tsp turmeric powder
1 lb pork loin, sliced	Salt and black pepper to taste	1 tsp dried oregano
3 garlic cloves, chopped	3 cups chicken stock	2 tbsp parsley, chopped
3 carrots, sliced	2 tbsp tomato paste	

Preheat the oven to 360 F. Warm the olive oil in a pot over medium heat and cook pork, onion, and garlic for 8 minutes. Stir in carrots, salt, pepper, stock, tomato paste, turmeric, and oregano and transfer to a baking dish. Bake for 30 minutes. Serve topped with parsley.

360. Rosemary Pork Chops in Tomato Sauce

Serves: 4 | Ready in about: 40 minutes

2 tbsp olive oil	½ cup tomato puree	1 tbsp Greek seasoning
4 pork chops	Salt and black pepper to taste	1 tbsp rosemary, chopped

Preheat the oven to 380 F. Warm olive oil in a skillet over medium heat. Sear pork. Stir in salt, pepper, tomato purée, Greek seasoning, and rosemary and bake for 20 minutes.

361. Quick & Easy Pork Skewers

Serves: 6 | Ready in about: 20 min + marinating time

3 tbsp olive oil
1 onion, grated
3 garlic cloves, minced

1 tsp ground cumin
Salt and black pepper to taste
2 tsp dried oregano

2 lb boneless pork butt, cubed
2 lemons, cut into wedges

In a large bowl, whisk the olive oil, onion, garlic, cumin, salt, pepper, and oregano. Add pork and toss to coat. Cover and place in the refrigerator for at least 2 hours or overnight.

Preheat your grill to medium-high. Thread the pork cubes onto bamboo skewers. Place the pork on the grill and cook for about 10 minutes on all sides or until the pork is cooked through. Serve with lemon wedges.

362. Tangy Mustard Pork Tenderloin

Serves: 4 | Ready in about: 30 minutes

2 tbsp olive oil
1 (1 ½-oz) pork tenderloin
2 garlic cloves, minced
½ cup fresh parsley, chopped

1 tbsp rosemary, chopped
1 tbsp tarragon, chopped
3 tbsp stone-ground mustard
½ tsp cumin powder

½ hot pepper, minced
Salt and black pepper to taste

Preheat oven to 400 F. In a food processor, blend parsley, tarragon, rosemary, mustard, olive oil, hot pepper, cumin, salt, garlic, and pepper until smooth. Rub the mixture all over the pork and transfer onto a lined baking sheet. Bake in the oven for 20-25 minutes. Slice and serve.

363. Cilantro-Mustard-Glazed Pork Loin

Serves: 4 | Ready in about: 35 minutes

2 tbsp olive oil
1 onion, chopped
2 lb pork loin, cut into strips

½ cup vegetable stock
Salt and black pepper to taste
2 tsp mustard

1 tbsp cilantro, chopped

Warm the olive oil in a skillet over medium heat and cook the onion for 5 minutes. Put in pork loin and cook for another 10 minutes, stirring often. Stir in vegetable stock, salt, pepper, mustard, and cilantro and cook for an additional 10 minutes. Serve and enjoy!

364. Slow Cooker Flavorful Pork Loin

Serves: 4 | Ready in about: 8 hours 10 minutes

1 tbsp olive oil
2 lb pork loin, sliced
1 lb pearl onions

Salt and white pepper to taste
1 tsp Greek seasoning
1 cup vegetable stock

1 tbsp tomato paste
2 bay leaves

Place pork, olive oil, salt, pepper, pearl onions, Greek seasoning, stock, tomato paste, and bay leaves in your slow cooker. Cover with the lid and cook for 8 hours on Low. Discard the bay leaves and serve.

365. Green Vegetable Pork Chops

Serves: 4 | Ready in about: 70 minutes

2 tbsp olive oil, divided
½ lb green beans, trimmed
½ lb asparagus spears

½ cup frozen peas, thawed
2 tomatoes, chopped
1 lb pork chops

1 tbsp tomato paste
1 onion, chopped
Salt and black pepper to taste

Warm olive oil in a saucepan over medium heat. Sprinkle the chops with salt and pepper. Place in the pan and brown for 8 minutes in total; set aside. In the same pan, sauté onion for 2 minutes until soft. In a bowl, whisk the tomato paste and 1 cup of water and pour into the saucepan. Bring to a simmer and scrape any bits from the bottom. Add the chops back and bring to a boil. Then lower the heat and simmer for 40 minutes. Add in green beans, asparagus, peas, tomatoes, salt, and pepper and cook for 10 minutes until the greens are soft.

366.   Effortless Pork Stew

Serves: 4 | Ready in about: 50 minutes

1 tbsp olive oil
1 lb pork stew meat, cubed
2 shallots, chopped
14 oz canned tomatoes, diced

1 garlic clove, minced
3 cups beef stock
2 tbsp paprika
1 tsp coriander seeds

1 tsp dried thyme
Salt and black pepper to taste
2 tbsp parsley, chopped

Warm the olive oil in a pot over medium heat and cook pork meat for 5 minutes until brown, stirring occasionally. Add in shallots and garlic and cook for an additional 3 minutes. Stir in beef stock, tomatoes, paprika, thyme, coriander seeds, salt, and pepper and bring to a boil; cook for 30 minutes. Serve warm, topped with parsley.

367.   Leek Pork Butt Delight

Serves: 4 | Ready in about: 1 hour and 40 minutes

2 lb boneless pork butt roast, cubed
3 tbsp olive oil
Salt and black pepper to taste
2 lb leeks, sliced

2 garlic cloves, minced
1 (14-oz) can diced tomatoes
1 cup dry white wine

½ cup chicken broth
1 bay leaf
2 tsp chopped fresh parsley

Season the pork with salt and pepper. Warm the oil in a saucepan over medium heat. Brown the pork on all sides, about 8 minutes; transfer to a bowl. Add the leeks, salt, and pepper to the fat left in a saucepan and sauté for 5-7 minutes, stirring occasionally, until softened and lightly browned. Stir in garlic and cook until fragrant, about 30 seconds. Pour in tomatoes and their juice, scraping up any browned bits, and cook until tomato liquid is nearly evaporated, 10-12 minutes.

Preheat oven to 325 F. Add the wine, broth, and bay leaf to the saucepan and return the pork with any accumulated juices; bring to a simmer. Cover, transfer to the oven and cook for about 60 minutes until the pork is tender and falls apart when prodded with a fork. Remove and discard the bay leaf. Sprinkle with parsley. Serve and enjoy!

368.   One-Skillet Pork Chops in Tomato-Olive Sauce

Serves: 4 | Ready in about: 20 minutes

2 tbsp olive oil
4 pork loin chops, boneless
6 tomatoes, crushed

3 tbsp basil, chopped
10 black olives, halved
1 yellow onion, chopped

1 garlic clove, minced

Warm the olive oil in a skillet over medium heat and brown pork chops for 6 minutes on all sides. Share into plates. In the same skillet, stir tomatoes, basil, olives, onion, and garlic and simmer for 4 minutes. Drizzle tomato sauce over it.

369.   Thyme Pork Chops

Serves: 4 | Ready in about: 30 minutes

2 tbsp olive oil
½ tsp cayenne powder

4 pork chops, boneless
¼ cup peach preserves

1 tbsp thyme, chopped

In a bowl, mix peach preserves, olive oil, and cayenne powder. Preheat your grill to medium. Rub pork chops with some peach glaze and grill for 10 minutes. Turn the chops, rub more glaze and cook for 10 minutes. Top with thyme.

370.   Chestnut & Pork Millet

Serves: 6 | Ready in about: 30 minutes

2 cups pork roast, cooked and shredded
½ cup sour cream

1 cup millet
3 oz water chestnuts, sliced

Salt and white pepper to taste

Place millet and salted water in a pot over medium heat and cook for 20 minutes. Drain and remove to a bowl to cool. When ready, add in pork, chestnuts, cream, salt, and pepper and mix to combine. Serve.

371. Succulent Pan-Seared Pork Chops

Serves: 4 | Ready in about: 30 minutes

3 tbsp olive oil
4 pork chops
Salt and black pepper to taste

5 tbsp chicken broth
6 garlic cloves, minced
¼ cup honey

2 tbsp apple cider vinegar
2 tbsp parsley, chopped

Warm the olive oil in a large skillet over medium heat. Season the pork chops with salt and pepper and add them to the skillet. Cook for 10 minutes on both sides or until golden brown; reserve. Lower the heat and add 3 tablespoons of broth, scraping the bits and flavors from the bottom of the skillet; cook for 2 minutes until the broth evaporates. Add the garlic and cook for 30 seconds. Stir in honey, vinegar, and the remaining broth. Cook for 3-4 minutes until the sauce thickens slightly. Return the pork chops and cook for 2 minutes. Top with parsley and serve.

372. Fiery Pork Meatballs

Serves: 4 | Ready in about: 30 minutes

3 tbsp olive oil
1 lb ground pork
2 tbsp parsley, chopped

2 green onions, chopped
4 garlic cloves, minced
1 red hot pepper, chopped

1 cup veggie stock
2 tbsp hot paprika

Combine pork, parsley, green onions, garlic, and red hot pepper in a bowl and form medium balls out of the mixture. Warm olive oil in a skillet over medium heat. Sear meatballs for 8 minutes on all sides. Stir in stock and hot paprika and simmer for another 12 minutes. Serve warm.

373. Mushroom Mix & Beef Stew

Serves: 4 | Ready in about: 60 minutes

1 lb cremini mushrooms, sliced
2 tbsp olive oil
2 tbsp tomato paste
1 ½ lb beef meat, cubed
1 carrot, chopped

2 garlic cloves, chopped
1 large onion, chopped
2 cups beef stock
1 tsp thyme, chopped

2 bay leaves
1 oz dried button mushrooms
Salt and black pepper to taste

Soak the button mushrooms in water for 10 minutes. Warm the olive oil in a pot over medium heat. Season the beef with salt and pepper, and cook for 5 minutes, stirring often. Add the onion and garlic, and cook for another 3 minutes. Stir in the carrot, tomato paste, thyme, bay leaves, and mushrooms, and cook for 5 minutes. Pour the soaked button mushrooms with the water and beef stock into the pot, then simmer for 40 minutes. Adjust the seasoning, and serve.

374. Wine-Infused Pork Chops

Serves: 4 | Ready in about: 30 minutes

2 tbsp olive oil
4 pork chops
1 cup red onion, sliced

10 black peppercorns, crushed
¼ cup vegetable stock
¼ cup dry white wine

2 garlic cloves, minced
Salt to taste

Warm the oil in a skillet over medium heat and sear pork chops for 8 minutes on both sides. Put in onion and garlic and cook for another 2 minutes. Mix in stock, wine, salt, and peppercorns and cook for 10 minutes, stirring often.

375. Flavorful Pork Stew

Serves: 4 | Ready in about: 50 minutes

3 tbsp olive oil
1 ½ lb pork stew meat, cubed
Salt and black pepper to taste

1 cup red onions, chopped
1 cup dried apricots, chopped
2 garlic cloves, minced

1 cup canned tomatoes, diced
2 tbsp parsley, chopped

Warm oil in a skillet over medium heat. Sear pork meat for 5 minutes. Put in onions and cook for another 5 minutes. Stir in salt, pepper, apricots, garlic, tomatoes, and parsley and bring to a simmer and cook for 30 minutes.

376. Apple-Glazed Roasted Pork Tenderloin

Serves: 4 | Ready in about: 35 minutes

2 tbsp olive oil
1 lb pork tenderloin
Salt and black pepper to taste

¼ cup apple jelly
¼ cup apple juice
2 tbsp wholegrain mustard

3 fresh thyme sprigs
½ tbsp cornstarch
½ tbsp heavy cream

Preheat oven to 330 F. Warm the oil in a skillet over medium heat. Season the pork with salt and pepper. Sear it for 6-8 minutes on all sides. Transfer to a baking sheet. To the same skillet, add the apple jelly, juice, and mustard and stir for 5 minutes over low heat, stirring often. Top with the pork and thyme sprigs. Place the skillet in the oven and bake for 15-18 minutes, brushing the pork with the apple-mustard sauce every 5 minutes. Remove the pork and let it rest for 15 minutes. Place a small pot over low heat. Blend the cornstarch with heavy cream and cooking juices and pour the mixture into the pot. Stir for 2 minutes until it thickens. Drizzle the sauce over the pork. Serve sliced, and enjoy!

377. No-fuss Pork Stew

Serves: 4 | Ready in about: 35 minutes

2 tbsp olive oil
1 lb pork shoulder, cubed
Salt and black pepper to taste

1 onion, chopped
2 garlic cloves, minced
1 tbsp hot pepper paste

2 tbsp balsamic vinegar
¼ cup chicken stock
¼ cup mint, chopped

Warm the oil in a skillet over medium heat and cook the onion for 3 minutes. Put in pork cubes and cook for another 3 minutes. Stir in salt, pepper, garlic, hot pepper paste, vinegar, stock, and mint and cook for 20-25 minutes.

378. Hearty Mushroom Pork Stew

Serves: 4 | Ready in about: 8 hours 10 minutes

2 tbsp olive oil
2 lb pork stew meat, cubed
1 lb mushrooms, chopped
Salt and black pepper to taste

2 cups chicken stock
1 carrot, chopped
1 yellow onion, chopped
2 garlic cloves, minced

2 cups tomatoes, chopped
½ cup parsley, chopped

Place pork meat, salt, pepper, stock, olive oil, onion, carrot, garlic, mushrooms, and tomatoes in your slow cooker. Cover with the lid and cook for 8 hours on Low. Top with parsley.

379. Greek Pork Au Gratin

Serves: 4 | Ready in about: 40 minutes

3 tbsp olive oil
1 lb pork chops
½ cup basil leaves, chopped
½ cup mint leaves, chopped

1 tbsp rosemary, chopped
2 garlic cloves, minced
1 eggplant, cubed
2 zucchini, cubed

1 bell pepper, chopped
2 oz feta, crumbled
8 oz cherry tomatoes, halved

Preheat the oven to 380 F. Place pork chops, basil, mint, rosemary, garlic, olive oil, eggplant, zucchini, bell pepper, and tomatoes in a roasting pan and bake covered with foil for 27 minutes. Uncover, sprinkle with the feta cheese, and bake for another 5-10 minutes until the cheese melts.

380. Luscious Pork in Cilantro Sauce

Serves: 4 | Ready in about: 30 minutes

½ cup olive oil
1 lb pork stew meat, cubed
1 tbsp walnuts, chopped

2 tbsp cilantro, chopped
2 tbsp basil, chopped
2 garlic cloves, minced

Salt and black pepper to taste
2 cups Greek yogurt

In a food processor, blend cilantro, basil, garlic, walnuts, yogurt, salt, pepper, and half of the oil until smooth. Warm the remaining oil in a skillet over medium heat. Brown pork meat for 5 minutes. Pour sauce over meat and bring to a boil. Cook for another 15 minutes. Serve.

381.   Party Pork Chops with Squash & Zucchini

Serves: 4 | Ready in about: 40 minutes

2 tbsp olive oil
4 pork loin chops, boneless
1 tsp Greek seasoning
1 zucchini, sliced

1 yellow squash, cubed
10 cherry tomatoes, halved
½ tsp oregano, dried
Salt and black pepper to taste

3 garlic cloves, minced
10 Kalamata olives, halved
¼ cup ricotta cheese, crumbled

Preheat the oven to 370 F. Place pork chops, salt, pepper, Greek seasoning, zucchini, squash, tomatoes, oregano, olive oil, garlic, and olives in a roasting pan and bake covered for 30 minutes. Serve topped with ricotta cheese.

382.   Peppery Parsnip & Pork

Serves: 4 | Ready in about: 90 minutes

2 tbsp olive oil
2 lb pork loin, sliced
2 parsnips, chopped

5 black peppercorns, crushed
2 red onions, chopped
2 cups Greek yogurt

1 tsp mustard
Salt and black pepper to taste

Preheat oven to 360 F. Warm the olive oil in a skillet over medium heat and sear pork for 8 minutes on all sides. Remove to a bowl. In the same skillet, cook the onions, parsnips, and peppercorns and cook for 5 minutes. Put the pork back along with the yogurt, mustard, salt, and pepper. Bake for 1 hour.

383.   Orecchiette Pasta with Mushroom & Sausage

Serves: 2 | Ready in about: 30 minutes

½ cup cremini mushrooms, sliced
1 tbsp olive oil
½ medium onion, diced
2 garlic cloves, minced

4 oz sausage
½ tsp Greek seasoning
8 oz dry orecchiette pasta
2 cups chicken stock

1 cup baby spinach
¼ cup heavy cream
1 tbsp basil, chopped

Warm the olive oil in a pan over medium heat. Add the onion, garlic, and mushrooms and sauté for 5 minutes until tender. Remove the sausage from its casing and add it to the pan, breaking it up well. Stir-fry for 5 more minutes or until the sausage is no longer pink. Season with Greek seasoning and add the pasta and chicken stock; bring the mixture to a boil. Lower the heat to medium-low and t simmer for 9-11 minutes or until the pasta is cooked. Remove from the heat. Add the spinach and stir until it wilts, 3 minutes. Stir in the heavy cream. Serve topped with basil.

384.   Minty Fried Beef Meatballs

Serves: 4 | Ready in about: 20 min + chilling time

2 bread slices, soaked in water, squeezed, and crumbled
4 tbsp olive oil
2 lb ground beef
2 medium onions, grated
1 tbsp minced garlic

2 large eggs, beaten
2 tsp dried Greek oregano
2 tbsp fresh parsley, chopped
1 tsp fresh mint, chopped

1/8 tsp ground cumin
Salt and black pepper to taste

Mix well all the ingredients, except for the olive oil, in a large bowl. Shape the mixture into balls and place them on a tray. Cover with plastic wrap and place in the fridge for at least 2 hours. Warm the olive oil in a skillet over medium heat and sear the keftedes for 6-8 minutes until they are browned on all sides. Work in batches as needed. Serve.

385.   Flavorful Spiced Beef Meatballs

Serves: 4 | Ready in about: 25 minutes

¼ cup feta cheese, crumbled
1 lb ground beef
¼ cup breadcrumbs
Salt and black pepper to taste
1 red onion, grated

2 tbsp parsley, chopped
2 garlic cloves, minced
1 lemon, juiced and zested
1 egg

½ tsp ground cumin
½ tsp ground coriander
¼ tsp cinnamon powder

Preheat oven to 390 F. Line a baking sheet with parchment paper. Combine beef, breadcrumbs, salt, pepper, onion, parsley, garlic, lemon juice, lemon zest, egg, cumin, coriander, cinnamon powder, and fresh feta cheese in a bowl and form balls out of the mixture. Place meatballs on the sheet and bake for 15 minutes. Serve warm.

386.   Beef Gyro with Veggies

Serves: 2 | Ready in about: 30 minutes

Beef

1 tbsp olive oil	2 garlic cloves, minced	1 tsp dried oregano
½ medium onion, minced	6 oz lean ground beef	

Yogurt Sauce

⅓ cup plain Greek yogurt	1 tbsp minced fresh dill	1 tbsp lemon juice
1 oz crumbled feta cheese	1 tbsp minced scallions	Garlic salt to taste

Sandwiches

2 Greek-style pitas, warm	1 cucumber, sliced
6 cherry tomatoes, halved	Salt and black pepper to taste

Warm the 1 tbsp olive oil in a pan over medium heat. Sauté the onion, garlic, and ground for 5-7 minutes, breaking up the meat well. When the meat is no longer pink, drain off any fat and stir in oregano. Turn off the heat. In a small bowl, combine the yogurt, feta, dill, scallions, lemon juice, and garlic salt. Divide the yogurt sauce between the warm pitas. Top with ground beef, cherry tomatoes, and diced cucumber. Season with salt and pepper. Serve.

387.   Skirt Steak with Mushroom Mustard Sauce

Serves: 4 | Ready in about: 30 min + marinating time

For the steak

2 tbsp olive oil	2 garlic cloves, minced	1 tsp yellow mustard
1 lb beef skirt steak	1 tbsp Worcestershire sauce	
1 cup red wine	1 tbsp dried thyme	

For the mushroom sauce

1 lb mushrooms, sliced	2 garlic cloves, minced	Salt and black pepper to taste
1 tsp dried dill	1 cup dry red wine	

Combine wine, garlic, Worcestershire sauce, 2 tbsp of olive oil, thyme, and mustard in a bowl. Place in the steak, cover with plastic wrap and let it marinate for at least 3 hours in the refrigerator. Remove the steak and pat dry with paper towels. Warm olive oil in a pan over medium heat and sear steak for 8 minutes on all sides; set aside. In the same pan, sauté mushrooms, dill, salt, and pepper for 6 minutes, stirring periodically. Add in garlic and sauté for 30 seconds. Pour in the wine and scrape off any bits from the bottom. Simmer for 5 minutes until the liquid reduces. Slice the steak and top with the mushroom sauce. Serve hot.

388.   Classic Greek Meatballs

Serves: 4 | Ready in about: 25 minutes

2 tbsp olive oil	1 onion, chopped	1 garlic clove, minced
1 lb ground beef meat	3 tbsp cilantro, chopped	Salt and black pepper to taste

Combine beef, onion, cilantro, garlic, salt, and pepper in a bowl and form meatballs out of the mixture. Sprinkle with oil. Preheat the grill over medium heat and grill them for 14 minutes on all sides. Serve with salad.

389.   Baked Beef Ribs

Serves: 4 | Ready in about: 2 hours 10 minutes

2 tbsp olive oil	2 garlic cloves, minced	½ cup chicken stock
2 lb beef ribs	1 onion, chopped	1 tbsp ground fennel seeds

Preheat oven to 360 F. Mix garlic, onion, stock, olive oil, fennel seeds, and beef ribs in a roasting pan and bake for 2 hours. Serve hot with salad.

390. Tasty Slow Cooker Beef Stew

Serves: 4 | Ready in about: 8 hours 10 minutes

2 tbsp canola oil
2 lb beef stew meat, cubed
Salt and black pepper to taste
2 cups beef stock

2 shallots, chopped
2 tbsp thyme, chopped
2 garlic cloves, minced
1 carrot, chopped

3 celery stalks, chopped
28 oz canned tomatoes, diced
2 tbsp parsley, chopped

Place the beef meat, salt, pepper, beef stock, canola oil, shallots, thyme, garlic, carrot, celery, and tomatoes in your slow cooker. Put the lid and cook for 8 hours on Low. Sprinkle with parsley and serve warm.

391. Greek-Inspired Burgers

Serves: 4 | Ready in about: 20 minutes

¼ tsp mustard powder
¼ tsp cumin
1 ¼ lb ground beef

½ tsp garlic salt
¼ tsp red pepper flakes
½ tsp Greek seasoning

1 cup tomato sauce
8 halloumi cheese slices

Preheat your grill to medium. In a large bowl, lightly mix with your hands the ground beef, mustard powder, cumin, garlic salt, pepper flakes, and Greek seasoning. Shape the mixture into 4 patties. Grill the burgers for about 10 minutes, turning them occasionally to ensure even cooking. In the last 2 minutes of cooking, top each burger with a generous tablespoon of tomato sauce and 2 slices of cheese per burger. Remove and let sit for 1–2 minutes. Serve.

392. Zesty & Spicy Beef Zoodles

Serves: 4 | Ready in about: 20 minutes

2 tbsp olive oil
1 lb beef steaks, sliced
2 zucchini, spiralized

½ cup sweet hot pepper sauce
1 cup carrot, grated
3 tbsp water

Salt and black pepper to taste

Warm the olive oil in a skillet over medium heat and brown beef steaks for 8 minutes on both side; reserve and cover with foil to keep warm. Stir zucchini noodles, hot pepper sauce, carrot, water, salt, and pepper and cook for an additional 3-4 minutes. Remove the foil from the steaks and pour the zucchini mix over to serve.

393. Fragrant Aromatic Beef Stew

Serves: 4 | Ready in about: 80 minutes

3 tbsp olive oil
2 lb beef shoulder, cubed
Salt and black pepper to taste
1 onion, chopped

2 garlic cloves, minced
3 tomatoes, grated
1 tsp hot red pepper flakes
2 cups chicken stock

1 cup couscous
10 green olives, sliced
1 tbsp cilantro, chopped

Warm the oil in a pot over medium heat and cook beef for 5 minutes until brown, stirring often. Add in onion and garlic and cook for 5 minutes. Stir in tomatoes, salt, pepper, stock, olives, and hot red pepper flakes. Bring to a boil and simmer for 1 hour. Cover the couscous with boiling water in a bowl, cover, and let sit for 4-5 minutes until the water has been absorbed. Fluff with a fork and season with salt and pepper. Pour the stew over and scatter with cilantro.

394. Bell Pepper & Beef Casserole

Serves: 4 | Ready in about: 1 hour 40 minutes

2 tbsp olive oil
1 lb beef steaks
1 red bell pepper, sliced

1 green bell pepper, sliced
1 yellow bell pepper, sliced
2 tbsp oregano, chopped

4 garlic cloves, minced
½ cup chicken stock
Salt and black pepper to taste

Preheat oven to 360 F. Warm olive oil in a skillet over medium heat. Sear the beef steaks for 8 minutes on both sides. Stir in bell peppers, oregano, garlic, stock, salt, and pepper and bake for 80 minutes. Serve warm.

395.   Tender Beef Filet Mignon in Savory Mushroom Sauce

Serves: 2 | Ready in about: 25 minutes

8 oz cremini mushrooms, quartered

2 tbsp olive oil	½ cup red wine	Salt and black pepper to taste
2 filet mignon steaks	1 cup chicken stock	¼ tsp garlic powder
1 shallot, minced	½ tsp dried thyme	¼ tsp shallot powder
2 tsp flour	1 fresh rosemary sprig	¼ tsp mustard powder
2 tsp tomato paste	1 tsp herbes de Provence	

Warm 1 tablespoon of olive oil in a saucepan over medium heat. Add the mushrooms and shallot and stir-fry for 5-8 minutes. Stir in the flour and tomato paste and cook for another 30 seconds. Pour in the wine and scrape up any browned bits from the sauté pan. Add the chicken stock, thyme, and rosemary. Bring it to a boil and cook until the sauce thickens, 2-4 minutes. In a small bowl, mix the herbes de Provence, salt, garlic powder, shallot powder, mustard powder, salt, and pepper. Rub the beef with the herb mixture on both sides. Warm the remaining olive oil in a sauté over medium heat. Sear the beef for 2-3 minutes on each side. Serve topped with mushroom sauce.

396.   Orange Flank Steak

Serves: 4 | Ready in about: 25 minutes

8 tbsp olive oil	¼ cup fresh basil, chopped	1 tsp red pepper flakes
1 lb flank steak	2 garlic cloves, minced	1 tbsp red wine vinegar
Salt and black pepper to taste	½ tsp celery seeds	
½ cup parsley, chopped	1 orange, zested and juiced	

Place the parsley, basil, garlic, orange zest and juice, celery seeds, salt, pepper, and red pepper flakes, and pulse until finely chopped in your food processor. With the processor running, stream in the red wine vinegar and 6 tbsp of olive oil until well combined. Set aside until ready to serve.

Preheat your grill. Rub the steak with the remaining olive oil, salt, and pepper. Place the steak on the grill and cook for 6-8 minutes on each side. Remove and leave to sit for 10 minutes. Slice the steak and drizzle with pistou. Serve.

397.   Savory Spiced Beef Meatballs

Serves: 4 | Ready in about: 30 minutes

1 tsp olive oil	½ tsp ground cinnamon	1 lb ground beef
¼ cup finely chopped onions	¼ tsp smoked paprika	⅓ cup bread crumbs
¼ cup raisins, chopped	¼ tsp nutmeg	1 (28-oz) can diced tomatoes
1 tsp ground cumin	1 large egg	

Place the ground beef, bread crumbs, onions, raisins, cumin, cinnamon, nutmeg, smoked paprika, and egg in a bowl and mix gently with your hands. Shape the mixture into 20 meatballs.

Warm the olive oil in a large skillet over medium heat. Sear the meatballs for 8 minutes, rolling around every minute or so with a fork to brown them on most sides. Place the meatballs on a paper towel–lined plate. Discard the fat from the pan and wipe it out with paper towels. Add in the meatballs and pour the tomatoes over. Cover and cook until the sauce begins to bubble. Lower the heat to medium, cover partially and cook for 7-8 more minutes. Serve and enjoy!

398.   Hearty Beef Stew

Serves: 4 | Ready in about: 35 minutes

2 tbsp olive oil	1 onion, chopped	2 tbsp balsamic vinegar
1 lb beef stew, ground	2 garlic cloves, minced	¼ cup chicken stock
Salt and black pepper to taste	1 tbsp hot pepper paste	¼ cup mint, chopped

Warm the olive oil in a skillet over medium heat and cook the onion for 3 minutes. Put in beef stew and cook for another 3 minutes. Stir in salt, pepper, garlic, hot pepper paste, vinegar, stock, and mint and cook for 20-25 minutes.

399.   Allspice Beef Stuffed Peppers

Serves: 4 | Ready in about: 50 minutes

2 tbsp olive oil
2 red bell peppers
1 lb ground beef
1 shallot, finely chopped

2 garlic cloves, minced
2 tbsp fresh sage, chopped
Salt and black pepper to taste
1 tsp ground allspice

½ cup fresh parsley, chopped
½ cup baby arugula leaves
½ cup pine nuts, chopped
1 tbsp orange juice

Warm the olive oil in a large skillet over medium heat. Sauté the beef, garlic, and shallot for 8-10 minutes until the meat is browned and cooked through. Season with sage, allspice, salt, and pepper; remove from the heat to cool slightly. Stir in parsley, arugula, pine nuts, and orange juice and mix. Preheat oven to 390 F. Slice the peppers in half lengthwise and remove the seeds and membranes. Spoon the filling into the pepper halves. Bake in the oven for 25-30 minutes.

400.   Beef Steak with Kale Slaw & Bell Peppers

Serves: 4 | Ready in about: 35 minutes

2 tsp olive oil
1 lb skirt steak
4 cups kale slaw

1 tbsp garlic powder
Salt and black pepper to taste
1 small red onion, sliced

10 sundried tomatoes, halved
½ red bell pepper, sliced

Preheat the broiler. Brush steak with olive oil, salt, garlic powder, and pepper and place under the broiler for 10 minutes, turning once. Remove to a cutting board and let rest for 10 minutes, then cut the steak diagonally. In the meantime, place sun-dried tomatoes, kale slaw, onion, and bell pepper in a bowl and mix to combine. Transfer to a serving plate and top with steak slices to serve.

401.   Hearty Beef & Vegetable Stew

Serves: 6 | Ready in about: 35 minutes

2 sweet potatoes, cut into chunks
2 lb beef meat for stew
¾ cup red wine
1 tbsp butter

6 oz tomato paste
6 oz baby carrots, chopped
1 onion, finely chopped
Salt to taste

4 cups beef broth
½ cup green peas
1 tsp dried thyme
3 garlic cloves, crushed

Heat the butter on Sauté in your Instant Pot. Add beef and brown for 5-6 minutes. Add onions and garlic, and keep stirring for 3 more minutes. Add the remaining ingredients and seal the lid. Cook on Meat/Stew for 20 minutes on High pressure. Do a quick release and serve immediately.

402.   Savory Shallot & Beef Dish

Serves: 4 | Ready in about: 50 minutes

2 tbsp olive oil
1 lb beef meat, cubed
1 lb shallots, chopped

1 tbsp sweet paprika
Salt and black pepper to taste
1 ½ cups chicken stock

4 garlic cloves, minced
1 cup balsamic vinegar

Warm the olive oil in a pot over medium heat and sauté shallots, balsamic vinegar, salt, and pepper for 10 minutes. Stir in beef, paprika, chicken stock, and garlic and bring to a simmer. Cook for 30 minutes. Serve immediately.

403.   Kalogeros (Beef with Tomato Sauce)

Serves: 4 | Ready in about: 30 minutes

3 tbsp olive oil
2 garlic cloves, minced
1 lemon, juiced and zested

1 ½ lb ground beef
Salt and black pepper to taste
1 lb cherry tomatoes, halved

1 red onion, chopped
2 tbsp tomato paste
1 tbsp mint leaves, chopped

Warm the olive oil in a skillet over medium heat and cook beef and garlic for 5 minutes. Stir in lemon zest, lemon juice, salt, pepper, cherry tomatoes, onion, tomato paste, and mint and cook for 15 minutes. Serve right away.

404. Scallion Beef with Walnuts

Serves: 4 | Ready in about: 30 minutes

3 tbsp olive oil
1 ½ lb beef meat, cubed
2 tbsp lime juice

1 tbsp balsamic vinegar
5 garlic cloves, minced
Salt and black pepper to taste

2 tbsp walnuts, chopped
2 scallions, chopped

Warm the olive oil in a skillet over medium heat and sear the beef for 8 minutes on both sides. Put in scallions and garlic and cook for another 2 minutes. Stir in lime juice, vinegar, salt, pepper, and walnuts and cook for 10 minutes.

405. Best-Ever Rich Beef Meal

Serves: 4 | Ready in about: 40 minutes

1 tbsp olive oil
1 lb beef meat, cubed
1 red onion, chopped
1 garlic clove, minced

1 celery stalk, chopped
Salt and black pepper to taste
14 oz canned tomatoes, diced
1 cup vegetable stock

½ tsp ground nutmeg
2 tsp dill, chopped

Warm the oil in a skillet over medium heat and cook the onion and garlic for 5 minutes. Put in beef and cook for 5 more minutes. Stir in celery, salt, pepper, tomatoes, stock, nutmeg, and dill and bring to a boil. Cook for 20 minutes.

406. Seared Peach Lamb

Serves: 4 | Ready in about: 70 minutes

2 tbsp olive oil
1 lb lamb, cubed
2 cups Greek yogurt

2 peaches, peeled and cubed
1 onion, chopped
2 tbsp parsley, chopped

½ tsp red pepper flakes
Salt and black pepper to taste

Warm the olive oil in a skillet over medium heat and sear the lamb for 5 minutes. Put in onion and cook for another 5 minutes. Stir in yogurt, peaches, parsley, red pepper flakes, salt, and pepper, and bring to a boil. Cook for 45 minutes.

407. Traditional Greek Roasted Lamb & Potatoes

Serves: 6 | Ready in about: 3 hours 10 minutes

3 lb red potatoes, cut into 1-inch chunks
1 (4-lb) leg of lamb
2 tbsp olive oil
1 lemon, juiced

1 tsp dried Greek oregano
½ tsp dried rosemary
2 garlic cloves, minced

Salt and black pepper to taste
3 tbsp butter, melted

Preheat oven to 300 F. Season the lamb leg with oregano, rosemary, garlic, salt, and pepper and place it in a roasting pan, fat-side up. Brush with olive oil and sprinkle with some lemon juice. Bake for about 2 hours, brushing it occasionally. Increase the oven temperature to 350 F. Spread the potatoes around the lamb. Season them with salt and pepper and drizzle with butter. Add ½ cup of water. Return the pan to the oven and roast for about 50-60 minutes until the lamb is cooked and the potatoes are tender. Remove, slice the lamb, and serve with the potatoes.

408. Creamy Fig & Yogurt Lamb Stew

Serves: 4 | Ready in about: 2 hours

2 tbsp olive oil
Salt and black pepper to taste
1 ½ lb stewing lamb, cubed
1 carrot, chopped

1 onion, chopped
1 celery rib, chopped
14 oz canned tomatoes, diced
1 garlic clove, minced

1 cup dried figs, chopped
6 tbsp Greek yogurt

Warm 2 tbsp of oil in a pot over medium heat and cook lamb for 5 minutes until browned, stirring occasionally. Stir in carrot, onion, celery, and garlic for another 5 minutes. Pour in tomatoes, figs, and 2 cups of water. Season with salt and pepper and bring to a boil. Reduce the heat and simmer for 90 minutes. Serve topped with yogurt.

409.   Succulent Lamb Kebabs with Yogurt Sauce

Serves: 4 | Ready in about: 25 minutes

2 tbsp olive oil
1 lb ground lamb
2 tbsp chopped fresh mint
¼ cup flour
¼ cup chopped red onions

¼ cup toasted pine nuts
2 tsp ground cumin
Salt to taste
1 tsp ground cinnamon
½ tsp ground nutmeg

½ tsp black pepper
1 cup Greek yogurt
1 lemon, zested and juiced

In a small bowl, whisk the yogurt, olive oil, salt, lemon zest, and lemon juice. Keep in the refrigerator until ready to serve. Warm the olive oil in a pot over low heat. In a large bowl, combine the lamb, mint, flour, red onions, pine nuts, cumin, salt, cinnamon, ginger, nutmeg, and pepper and mix well with your hands. Shape the mixture into 12 patties. Thread the patties onto skewers and place them on a lined cookie sheet. Set under your preheated broiler for about 12 minutes, flipping once halfway through cooking. Serve the skewers with yogurt sauce.

410.   Basil Leg Lamb

Serves: 4 | Ready in about: 7 hours 10 minutes

2 cups stewed tomatoes, drained
3 ½ lb leg of lamb, cubed
1 lb small potatoes, cubed

1 grapefruit, zested and juiced
4 garlic cloves, minced

Salt and black pepper to taste
½ cup basil, chopped

Place potatoes, tomatoes, grapefruit juice, grapefruit zest, garlic, leg of lamb, salt, and pepper in your slow cooker. Cover with a lid and cook for 8 hours on Low. Top with basil.

411.   Lamb with Broccoli

Serves: 4 | Ready in about: 70 minutes

2 tbsp olive oil
1 lb lamb meat, cubed
1 garlic clove, minced

1 onion, chopped
1 tsp rosemary, chopped
1 cup vegetable stock

2 cups broccoli florets
2 tbsp sweet paprika
Salt and black pepper to taste

Warm the olive oil in a skillet over medium heat and cook the onion and garlic for 5 minutes. Put in lamb meat and cook for another 5-6 minutes. Stir in rosemary, stock, broccoli, paprika, salt, and pepper and cook for 50 minutes.

412.   Festive Holiday Leg of Lamb Delight

Serves: 4 | Ready in about: 2 hours 20 minutes

½ cup butter
2 lb leg of lamb, boneless
2 tbsp tomato paste

2 tbsp yellow mustard
2 tbsp basil, chopped
2 garlic cloves, minced

Salt and black pepper to taste
1 cup white wine
½ cup sour cream

Preheat oven to 360 F. Warm butter in a skillet over medium heat. Sear the leg of lamb for 10 minutes on all sides. Stir in mustard, basil, tomato paste, garlic, salt, pepper, wine, and sour cream and bake for 2 hours. Serve right away.

413.   Paprika-Spiced Lamb with Hearty Beans

Serves: 4 | Ready in about: 50 minutes

1 (28-oz) can white beans
2 tbsp olive oil, divided
1 lb lamb shoulder, cubed
Salt and black pepper to taste

2 garlic cloves, minced
1 large onion, diced
1 celery stalk, chopped
1 cup tomatoes, chopped

1 carrot, chopped
⅓ cup tomato paste
1 tsp paprika
1 tsp dried oregano

Warm the olive oil in a pot over medium heat. Season the lamb with salt and pepper and sauté for 3-4 minutes until brown, stirring occasionally. Stir in the onion, celery, tomatoes, and carrots and cook for 4-5 minutes.

Add the paprika and tomato paste and stir to combine. Pour in the beans and 2 cups water. Bring the mixture to a boil and simmer for 20-25 minutes until the lamb is cooked. Season with salt, pepper, and oregano and serve.

414.　　Hot Lamb with Fluffy Couscous & Chickpeas

Serves: 6 | Ready in about: 50 minutes

1 lb lamb shoulder, halved

3 tbsp olive oil

1 cup couscous

Salt and black pepper to taste

1 onion, finely chopped

10 (2-inch) orange zest strips

1 tsp ground coriander

¼ tsp ground cinnamon

½ tsp cayenne pepper

½ cup dry white wine

2 ½ cups chicken broth

1 (15-oz) can s

½ cup dates, chopped

½ cup sliced almonds, toasted

Cover the couscous in a bowl with 1 ½ cups of boiling water and put a lid. Let stand for 5 min to absorb the water.

Preheat oven to 330 F. Heat 2 tablespoons oil in a pot over medium heat. Season the lamb with salt and pepper and brown it for 4 minutes per side; set aside.

Stir-fry onion into the fat left in the pot, 3 minutes. Stir in orange zest, coriander, cinnamon, cayenne, and pepper until fragrant, 30 seconds. Stir in wine, scraping off any browned bits. Stir in broth and chickpeas and bring to a boil.

Make a nestle of lamb into the pot along with any accumulated juices. Cover, transfer the pot to the oven, and cook until a fork slips easily in and out of the lamb, 1 hour.

Transfer the lamb to a cutting board, let cool slightly, then shred using 2 forks, discarding excess fat and bones. Strain cooking liquid through a fine mesh strainer set over the bowl. Return solids and 1 ½ cups of cooking liquid to the pot and bring to a simmer over medium heat; discard the remaining liquid. Stir in couscous and dates. Add shredded lamb and almonds. Season to taste and serve.

415.　　Lamb Eggplant Moussaka

Serves: 4 | Ready in about: 55 minutes

5 tbsp olive oil

1 lb ground lamb

1 (14-oz) can diced tomatoes

1 cup Greek yogurt

2 small eggplants, sliced

2 shallots, chopped

2 garlic cloves, minced

2 tbsp tomato paste

1 tsp dried oregano

1 egg, beaten

Salt and black pepper to taste

¼ tsp ground coriander

2 oz grated Halloumi cheese

2 tbsp chopped fresh parsley

Preheat oven to 400 F. Warm olive oil in a pan over medium heat and cook the eggplant slices for 6-8 minutes on both sides. Remove to paper towels. In the same pan, sauté shallots and garlic for 3 minutes, stirring often. Add in ground lamb and cook for 5 minutes until no longer pink. Stir in tomato paste, tomatoes, oregano, ground coriander, salt, and pepper; cook for 4-5 minutes.

Combine yogurt, egg, salt, and pepper in a bowl. Spread half of the lamb mixture on a baking dish, add a layer of eggplant, then the remaining meat, and finally the remaining eggplants. Bake for 15 minutes. Remove and top with the yogurt mixture. Sprinkle with the cheese and return in the oven for 5-8 minutes until the cheese melts. Top with parsley.

416.　　Succulent Eggplant Lamb

Serves: 4 | Ready in about: 70 minutes

2 tbsp olive oil

1 cup chicken stock

1 ½ lb lamb meat, cubed

2 eggplants, cubed

2 onions, chopped

2 tbsp tomato paste

2 tbsp parsley, chopped

4 garlic cloves, minced

Warm the olive oil in a skillet over medium heat and cook the onions and garlic for 4 minutes. Put in lamb and cook for 6 minutes. Stir in eggplants and tomato paste for 5 minutes. Pour in the stock and bring to a boil. Cook for another 50 minutes, stirring often. Serve garnished with parsley.

FISH & SEAFOOD

417. Roasted Salmon with Parsley

Serves: 4 | Ready in about: 20 minutes

2 tbsp olive oil
1 lb salmon fillets
¼ fresh parsley, chopped

1 garlic clove, minced
¼ tsp dried dill
¼ tsp hot pepper powder

¼ tsp garlic powder
1 lemon, grated
Salt and black pepper to taste

Preheat oven to 350 F. Sprinkle the salmon with dill, hot pepper powder, garlic powder, salt, and pepper. Warm olive oil in a pan over medium heat and sear salmon skin-side down for 5 minutes. Transfer to the oven and bake for another 4-5 minutes. Combine parsley, lemon zest, garlic, and salt in a bowl. Serve salmon topped with the mixture.

418. Juicy Salmon in Thyme Tomato Sauce

Serves: 4 | Ready in about: 25 minutes

2 tbsp olive oil
4 salmon fillets, boneless

1 tsp thyme, chopped
Salt and black pepper to taste

1 lb cherry tomatoes, halved

Warm the olive oil in a skillet over medium heat and sear salmon for 6 minutes, turning once; set aside. In the same skillet, stir in cherry tomatoes for 3-4 minutes and sprinkle with thyme, salt, and pepper. Pour the sauce over the salmon.

419. Skillet Salmon with Olives & Escarole

Serves: 4 | Ready in about: 25 minutes

3 tbsp olive oil
1 head escarole, torn
4 salmon fillets, boneless

1 lime, juiced
Salt and black pepper to taste
¼ cup fish stock

¼ cup pitted green olives, chopped
¼ cup fresh chives, chopped

Warm half of the olive oil in a skillet over medium heat and sauté escarole, lime juice, salt, pepper, fish stock, and olives for 6 minutes. Share into plates. Warm the remaining oil in the same skillet. Sprinkle salmon with salt and pepper and fry for 8 minutes on both sides until golden brown. Transfer to the escarole plates and serve, topped with chives.

420. Savory Fennel & Bell Pepper Salmon

Serves: 4 | Ready in about: 30 minutes

2 tbsp olive oil
4 salmon fillets, boneless
1 fennel bulb, sliced

Salt and black pepper to taste
½ tsp hot pepper powder
1 yellow bell pepper, diced

1 red bell pepper, chopped
1 green bell pepper, chopped

Warm olive oil in a skillet over medium heat. Season the salmon with hot pepper powder, salt, and pepper and cook for 6-8 minutes, turning once. Remove to a serving plate. Add fennel and peppers to the skillet and cook for another 10 minutes until tender. Top the salmon with the mixture.

421. Wholesome Cod & Potato Dish

Serves: 4 | Ready in about: 35 minutes

1 tbsp olive oil
2 cod fillets
1 tbsp basil, chopped

Salt and black pepper to taste
2 potatoes, peeled and sliced
2 tsp turmeric powder

1 garlic clove, minced

Preheat the oven to 360F. Spread the potatoes on a greased baking dish and season with salt and pepper. Bake for 10 minutes. Arrange the cod fillets on top of the potatoes, sprinkle with salt and pepper, and drizzle with some olive oil. Bake for 10-12 more minutes until the fish flakes easily.

Warm the remaining olive oil in a skillet over medium heat and sauté garlic for 1 minute. Stir in basil, salt, pepper, turmeric powder, and 3-4 tbsp of water; cook for another 2-3 minutes. Pour the sauce over the cod fillets and serve.

422. Deliciously Seasoned Cod

Serves: 2 | Ready in about: 40 minutes

2 cod fillets, cut into 4 portions
¼ tsp paprika
¼ tsp onion powder
3 tbsp olive oil
4 medium scallions
2 tbsp fresh chopped basil

3 tbsp minced garlic
Salt and black pepper to taste
¼ tsp dry marjoram
6 sun-dried tomato slices
½ cup dry white wine
½ cup ricotta cheese, crumbled

1 (15-oz) can artichoke hearts
1 lemon, sliced
1 cup pitted black olives
1 tsp capers

Preheat oven to 375 F. Warm the olive oil in a skillet over medium heat. Sprinkle the cod with paprika and onion powder. Sear it for about 1 minute per side or until golden; reserve. Add the scallions, basil, garlic, salt, pepper, marjoram, tomatoes, and wine to the same skillet. Bring to a boil. Remove the skillet from the heat. Arrange the fish on top of the sauce and sprinkle with ricotta cheese. Place the artichokes in the pan and top with lemon slices. Sprinkle with black olives and capers. Place the skillet in the oven. Bake for 15-20 minutes until it flakes easily with a fork.

423. Simple Salmon Parcels

Serves: 4 | Ready in about: 25 minutes

2 tbsp olive oil
½ cup apple juice

4 salmon fillets
4 tsp lemon zest

4 tbsp chopped parsley
Salt and black pepper to taste

Preheat oven to 380F. Brush salmon with olive oil and season with salt and pepper. Cut four pieces of nonstick baking paper and divide the salmon between them. Top each one with apple juice, lemon zest, and parsley. Wrap the paper to make packets and arrange them on a baking sheet. Cook for 15 minutes until the salmon is cooked through. Remove the packets to a serving plate, open them, and drizzle with cooking juices to serve.

424. Flavorful Oven-Baked Salmon

Serves: 4 | Ready in about: 30 minutes

15 green pimiento-stuffed olives
2 small red onions, sliced
1 cup fennel bulbs shaved
1 cup cherry tomatoes

Salt and black pepper to taste
1 tsp cumin seeds
½ tsp smoked paprika
4 salmon fillets

½ cup chicken broth
3 tbsp olive oil
2 cups cooked farro

Preheat oven to 375 F. In a bowl, combine the onions, fennel, tomatoes, and olives. Season with salt, pepper, cumin, and paprika, and mix well. Spread out on a greased baking dish. Arrange the fish fillets over the vegetables, season with salt, and gently pour the broth over. Drizzle with olive oil and bake for 20 minutes. Serve over farro.

425. Roasted Salmon with Asparagus

Serves: 4 | Ready in about: 20 minutes

2 tbsp olive oil
4 salmon fillets, skinless

2 tbsp balsamic vinegar
1 lb asparagus, trimmed

Salt and black pepper to taste

Preheat the oven to 380F. In a roasting pan, arrange the salmon fillets and asparagus spears. Season with salt and pepper and drizzle with olive oil and balsamic vinegar; roast for 12-15 minutes. Serve warm.

426. Cod Poached in Oil

Serves: 4 | Ready in about: 20 minutes

4 cod fillets, skins removed
3 cups olive oil

Salt and black pepper to taste
1 lemon, zested and juiced

3 fresh thyme sprigs

Heat the olive oil with thyme sprigs in a pot over low heat. Gently add the cod fillets and poach them for about 6 minutes or until the fish is completely opaque. Using a slotted spoon, carefully remove the fish to a plate lined with paper towels. Sprinkle with lemon zest, salt, and pepper. Drizzle with lemon juice and serve immediately.

427.   Creamy Fettuccine with Cod

Serves: 4 | Ready in about: 30 minutes

1 lb cod fillets, cubed
16 oz fettuccine
3 tbsp olive oil

1 onion, finely chopped
Salt and lemon pepper to taste
1 ½ cups heavy cream

1 cup Halloumi cheese, grated

Boil salted water in a pot over medium heat and stir in fettuccine. Cook according to package directions and drain. Heat the olive oil in a large saucepan over medium heat and add the onion. Stir-fry for 3 minutes until tender. Sprinkle cod with salt and lemon pepper and add to saucepan; cook for 4–5 minutes until fish fillets and flakes easily with a fork. Stir in heavy cream for 2 minutes. Add in the pasta, tossing gently to combine. Cook for 3–4 minutes until sauce is slightly thickened. Sprinkle with Halloumi cheese.

428.   Salmon Coated in Walnut Crust

Serves: 4 | Ready in about: 25 minutes

2 tbsp olive oil
4 salmon fillets, boneless
2 tbsp mustard

5 tsp honey
1 cup walnuts, chopped
1 tbsp lemon juice

2 tsp parsley, chopped
Salt and pepper to the taste

Preheat the oven to 380F. Line a baking tray with parchment paper. In a bowl, whisk the olive oil, mustard, and honey. In a separate bowl, combine walnuts and parsley. Sprinkle salmon with salt and pepper and place them on the tray. Rub each fillet with mustard mixture and scatter with walnut mixture; bake for 15 minutes. Drizzle with lemon juice.

429.   Easy Salmon with Balsamic Haricots Vert

Serves: 4 | Ready in about: 25 minutes

2 tbsp olive oil
3 tbsp balsamic vinegar
1 garlic clove, minced

½ tsp red pepper flakes
1 ½ lb haricots vert, chopped
Salt and black pepper to taste

1 red onion, sliced
4 salmon fillets, boneless

Warm half of the oil in a skillet over medium heat and sauté vinegar, onion, garlic, red pepper flakes, haricots vert, salt, and pepper for 6 minutes. Share into plates. Warm the remaining oil. Sprinkle salmon with salt and pepper and sear for 8 minutes on all sides. Serve with haricots vert.

430.   Cheesy Tomato Cod

Serves: 4 | Ready in about: 35 minutes

2 tbsp olive oil
4 cod fillets, boneless
Salt and black pepper to taste

12 cherry tomatoes, halved
1 red hot pepper, chopped
1 tbsp cilantro, chopped

2 tbsp balsamic vinegar
1 oz feta, torn

Preheat the oven to 380 F. Drizzle the cod fillets with some olive oil and season with salt and pepper. Place them on a roasting tray, top with feta cheese, and bake for 15 minutes until golden and crispy. Warm the remaining oil in a skillet over medium heat and cook the cherry tomatoes for 5 minutes. Stir in red hot pepper, cilantro, and balsamic vinegar for 1-2 minutes. Serve the fish with sautéed veggies.

431.   Cod with Luscious Calamari Rings

Serves: 4 | Ready in about: 20 minutes

1 lb cod, skinless and cubed
2 tbsp olive oil
1 mango, peeled and cubed
½ lb calamari rings

1 tbsp garlic hot pepper sauce
¼ cup lime juice
½ tsp smoked paprika
½ tsp cumin, ground

2 garlic cloves, minced
Salt and black pepper to taste

Warm the olive oil in a skillet over medium heat and cook hot pepper sauce, lime juice, paprika, cumin, garlic, salt, pepper, and mango for 3 minutes. Stir in cod and calamari and cook for another 7 minutes. Serve warm.

432.   Cabbage-Roasted Cod

Serves: 4 | Ready in about: 30 minutes

2 tbsp olive oil
1 white cabbage head, shredded
1 tsp garlic powder

1 tsp smoked paprika
4 cod fillets, boneless
½ cup tomato sauce

1 tsp Greek seasoning
1 tbsp chives, chopped

Preheat the oven to 390F. Mix cabbage, garlic powder, paprika, olive oil, tomato sauce, Greek seasoning, and chives in a roasting pan. Top with cod fillets and bake covered with foil for 20 minutes. Serve immediately.

433.   Fiery Cod Fillets

Serves: 4 | Ready in about: 35 minutes

2 tbsp olive oil
1 tsp lime juice
Salt and black pepper to taste
1 tsp sweet paprika

1 tsp hot pepper powder
1 onion, chopped
2 garlic cloves, minced
4 cod fillets, boneless

1 tsp ground coriander
½ cup fish stock
½ lb cherry tomatoes, cubed

Warm oil in a skillet over medium heat. Season the cod with salt, pepper, and hot pepper powder and cook in the skillet for 8 minutes on all sides; set aside. In the same skillet, cook the onion and garlic for 3 minutes. Stir in lime juice, paprika, coriander, fish stock, and cherry tomatoes and bring to a boil. Simmer for 10 minutes. Serve topped with cod fillets.

434.   Mushroom-Smothered Cod Fillets

Serves: 4 | Ready in about: 45 minutes

2 cups cremini mushrooms, sliced
¼ cup olive oil
4 cod fillets
½ cup shallots, chopped
2 garlic cloves, minced

2 cups canned diced tomatoes
½ cup clam juice
¼ tsp hot pepper flakes
¼ tsp sweet paprika

1 tbsp capers
¼ cup raisins, soaked
1 lemon, cut into wedges
Salt to taste

Heat the oil in a skillet over medium heat. Sauté shallots and garlic for 2-3 minutes. Add in mushrooms and cook for 4 minutes. Stir in tomatoes, clam juice, pepper flakes, paprika, capers, and salt. Bring to a boil and simmer for 15 minutes.

Preheat oven to 380 F. Arrange the cod fillets on a greased baking pan. Cover with the mushroom mixture and top with the soaked raisins. Bake for 18-20 minutes. Serve garnished with lemon wedges.

435.   Cod Skewers Bursting with Fresh Herbs

Serves: 4 | Ready in about: 30 minutes

1 lb cod fillets, cut into chunks
2 sweet peppers, cut into chunks
2 tbsp olive oil
2 oranges, juiced

1 tbsp mustard
1 tbsp fresh dill

1 tsp fresh parsley
Salt and black pepper to taste

Mix olive oil, orange juice, dill, parsley, mustard, salt, and pepper in a bowl. Stir in cod to coat. Allow sitting for 10 minutes. Heat the grill over medium heat. Thread the cod and peppers onto skewers. Grill for 7-8 minutes, turning regularly until the fish is cooked through.

436.   Tarragon Haddock with Capers

Serves: 4 | Ready in about: 25 minutes

2 tbsp olive oil
4 haddock fillets, boneless
¼ cup capers, drained

1 tbsp tarragon, chopped
Salt and black pepper to taste
2 tbsp parsley, chopped

1 tbsp lemon juice

Warm the olive oil in a skillet over medium heat and sear haddock for 6 minutes on both sides. Stir in capers, tarragon, salt, pepper, parsley, and lemon juice and cook for another 6-8 minutes. Serve right away.

437. Hearty Herbed Cod Stew

Serves: 4 | Ready in about: 35 minutes

4 cod fillets, boneless, skinless, cubed

2 tbsp olive oil	2 garlic cloves, minced	1 carrot, sliced
2 tbsp parsley, chopped	½ tsp paprika	1 red bell pepper, chopped
2 tomatoes, chopped	2 cups chicken stock	½ cup black olives, pitted and halved
2 tbsp cilantro, chopped	Salt and black pepper to taste	1 red onion, sliced

Warm olive oil in a saucepan over medium heat and cook garlic, carrot, bell pepper, and onion for 5 minutes. Stir in cod fillets, parsley, tomatoes, and paprika for 3-4 minutes. Pour in chicken stock and olives and bring to a boil. Cook for 15 minutes. Adjust the seasoning and sprinkle with cilantro.

438. Cod Casserole with Leeks & Olives

Serves: 4 | Ready in about: 30 minutes

½ cup olive oil	4 leeks, trimmed and sliced	Salt and black pepper to taste
1 lb fresh cod fillets	1 cup breadcrumbs	
1 cup black olives, chopped	¾ cup chicken stock	

Preheat oven to 350 F. Brush the cod with some olive oil, season with salt and pepper, and bake for 5-7 minutes. Let it cool, then cut it into 1-inch pieces. Warm the remaining olive oil in a skillet over medium heat. Stir-fry the olives and leeks for 4 minutes until the leeks are tender. Add the breadcrumbs and chicken stock, stirring to mix. Fold in the pieces of cod. Pour the mixture into a greased baking dish and bake for 15 minutes or until cooked through.

439. Cod Fillets in White Wine Sauce

Serves: 4 | Ready in about: 40 minutes

4 cod fillets	1 tbsp olive oil	2 garlic cloves, minced
Salt and black pepper to taste	½ cup dry white wine	1 tsp chopped fresh sage
½ fennel seeds, ground	½ cup vegetable stock	4 rosemary sprigs

Preheat oven to 375 F. Season the cod fillets with salt, pepper, and ground fennel seeds and place them in a greased baking dish. Add the wine, stock, garlic, and sage and drizzle with olive oil. Cover with foil and bake for 20 minutes until the fish flakes easily with a fork. Remove the fillets from the dish. Place the liquid in a saucepan over high heat and cook, stirring frequently, until reduced by half, about 10 minutes. Serve the fish topped with sauce and fresh rosemary sprigs.

440. Rosemary Baked Haddock

Serves: 6 | Ready in about: 35 min + marinating time

1 cup milk	2 tbsp rosemary, chopped	1 lemon, zested
Salt and black pepper to taste	1 garlic clove, minced	1 ½ lb haddock fillets

In a large bowl, coat the fish with milk, salt, pepper, and 1 tablespoon of rosemary. Refrigerate for 2 hours. Preheat oven to 380 F. Carefully remove the haddock from the marinade, drain thoroughly, and place in a greased baking dish. Cover and bake for15–20 minutes until the fish is flaky. Remove the fish from the oven and let it rest for 5 minutes. Mix the remaining rosemary, lemon zest, and garlic to make the gremolata. Sprinkle the fish with gremolata.

441. Tomato-Dill Baked Haddock

Serves: 4 | Ready in about: 20 minutes

4 haddock fillets, boneless	2 garlic cloves, minced	Salt and black pepper to taste
1 cup vegetable stock	2 cups cherry tomatoes, halved	2 tbsp dill, chopped

Put a greased skillet over medium heat, add the cherry tomatoes, garlic, salt, and pepper and cook them for 5 minutes. Stir in haddock fillets and vegetable stock and bring to a simmer. Cook covered for 10-12 minutes. Top with dill.

442. Capered Tarragon Haddock

Serves: 4 | Ready in about: 40 minutes

4 haddock fillets
Salt and black pepper to taste

2 garlic cloves, minced
½ cup dry white wine

½ cup seafood stock
4 rosemary sprigs for garnish

Preheat oven to 380 F. Sprinkle haddock fillets with salt and black pepper and arrange them on a baking dish. Pour in the wine, garlic, and stock. Bake covered for 20 minutes until the fish is tender; remove to a serving plate. Pour the cooking liquid into a pot over high heat. Cook for 10 minutes until reduced by half. Place on serving dishes and top with the reduced poaching liquid. Serve garnished with rosemary.

443. Tilapia with Fresh Parsley & Tomato

Serves: 4 | Ready in about: 20 minutes

2 tbsp olive oil
4 tilapia fillets, boneless

½ cup tomato sauce
2 tbsp parsley, chopped

Salt and black pepper to taste

Warm olive oil in a skillet over medium heat. Sprinkle tilapia with salt and pepper and cook until golden brown, flipping once, about 6 minutes. Pour in the tomato sauce and parsley and cook for an additional 4 minutes. Serve.

444. Flavorful Tilapia Pilaf

Serves: 2 | Ready in about: 45 minutes

3 tbsp olive oil
2 tilapia fillets, boneless
½ tsp Greek seasoning

½ cup brown rice
½ cup green bell pepper, diced
½ cup white onions, chopped

½ tsp garlic powder
Salt and black pepper to taste

Warm 1 tbsp of olive oil in a saucepan over medium heat. Cook the onions, bell pepper, garlic powder, Greek seasoning, salt, and pepper for 3 minutes. Stir in brown rice and 2 cups of water and bring to a simmer. Cook for 18 minutes. Warm the remaining oil in a skillet over medium heat. Season the tilapia with salt and pepper. Fry for 10 minutes on both sides. Share the rice among plates and top with the tilapia fillets.

445. Creamy Avocado & Onion Tilapia

Serves: 4 | Ready in about: 10 minutes

1 tbsp olive oil
1 tbsp orange juice
¼ tsp kosher salt

½ tsp ground coriander seeds
4 tilapia fillets, skin-on
¼ cup chopped red onions

1 avocado, skinned and sliced

In a bowl, mix together the olive oil, orange juice, ground coriander seeds, and salt. Add the fish and turn to coat on all sides. Arrange the fillets on a greased microwave-safe dish. Top with onion and cover the dish with plastic wrap, leaving a small part open at the edge to vent the steam. Microwave on high for about 3 minutes. The fish is done when it just begins to separate into chunks when pressed gently with a fork. Top the fillets with the avocado.

446. Halibut with Roasted Pepper & Parsley Garnish

Serves: 4 | Ready in about: 45 minutes

3 tbsp olive oil
1 tsp butter
2 red peppers, cut into wedges

4 halibut fillets
2 shallots, cut into rings
2 garlic cloves, minced

¾ cup breadcrumbs
2 tbsp chopped fresh parsley
Salt and black pepper to taste

Preheat oven to 450 F. Combine red peppers, garlic, shallots, 1 tbsp of olive oil, salt, and pepper in a bowl. Spread on a baking sheet and bake for 40 minutes. Warm the remaining olive oil in a pan over medium heat and brown the breadcrumbs for 4-5 minutes, stirring constantly. Set aside. Clean the pan and add in the butter to melt. Sprinkle the fish with salt and pepper. Add to the butter and cook for 8-10 minutes on both sides. Divide the pepper mixture between 4 plates and top with halibut fillets. Spread the crunchy breadcrumbs all over and top with parsley. Serve.

447. Zesty Flounder with Vibrant Pasta Salad

Serves: 4 | Ready in about: 25 minutes

2 tbsp olive oil
4 flounder fillets, boneless
1 tsp rosemary, dried
2 tsp cumin, ground
1 tbsp coriander, ground

2 tsp cinnamon powder
2 tsp oregano, dried
Salt and black pepper to taste
2 cups macaroni, cooked
1 cup cherry tomatoes, halved

1 avocado, peeled and sliced
1 cucumber, cubed
½ cup black olives, sliced
1 lemon, juiced

Preheat the oven to 390 F. Combine rosemary, cumin, coriander, cinnamon, oregano, salt, and pepper in a bowl. Add in the flounder and toss to coat. Warm olive oil in a skillet over medium heat. Brown the fish fillets for 4 minutes on both sides. Transfer to a baking tray and bake in the oven for 7-10 minutes. Combine macaroni, tomatoes, avocado, cucumber, olives, and lemon juice in a bowl; toss to coat. Serve the fish with pasta salad on the side.

448. Halibut Baked with Savory Eggplant Topping

Serves: 4 | Ready in about: 35 minutes

2 tbsp olive oil
¼ cup tomato sauce
4 halibut fillets, boneless

2 eggplants, sliced
Salt and black pepper to taste
2 tbsp balsamic vinegar

2 tbsp chives, chopped

Preheat the oven to 380F. Warm the olive oil in a skillet over medium heat and fry the eggplant slices for 5-6 minutes, turning once; reserve. Add the tomato sauce, salt, pepper, and vinegar to the skillet and cook for 5 minutes. Return the eggplants to the skillet and cook for 2 minutes. Remove to a plate. Place the halibut fillets on a greased baking tray and bake for 12-15 minutes. Serve the halibut over the eggplants sprinkled with chives.

449. Sautéed Leeks & Halibut Confit

Serves: 4 | Ready in about: 45 minutes

1 tsp fresh lemon zest
¼ cup olive oil
4 skinless halibut fillets

Salt and black pepper to taste
1 lb leeks, sliced
1 tsp Dijon mustard

¾ cup dry white wine
1 tbsp fresh cilantro, chopped
4 lemon wedges

Warm the olive oil in a skillet over medium heat. Season the halibut with salt and pepper. Sear in the skillet for 6-7 minutes until cooked through. Carefully transfer the halibut to a large plate. Add leeks, mustard, salt, and pepper to the skillet and sauté for 10-12 minutes, stirring frequently, until softened. Pour in the wine and lemon zest and bring to a simmer. Top with halibut. Reduce the heat to low, cover, and simmer for 6-10 minutes. Carefully transfer halibut to a serving platter, tent loosely with aluminum foil, and let rest while finishing leeks. Increase the heat and cook the leeks for 2-4 minutes until the sauce is slightly thickened. Adjust the seasoning with salt and pepper. Pour the leek mixture around the halibut, sprinkle with cilantro, and serve with lemon wedges.

450. Golden Crispy Sole Fillets

Serves: 4 | Ready in about: 10 minutes

¼ cup olive oil
½ cup flour

½ tsp paprika
8 skinless sole fillets

Salt and black pepper to taste
4 lemon wedges

Warm the olive oil in a skillet over medium heat. Mix the flour with paprika in a shallow dish. Coat the fish with the flour, shaking off any excess. Sear the sole fillets for 2-3 minutes per side until lightly browned. Serve with lemon wedges.

451. Bean & Canned Tuna Bowl

Serves: 6 | Ready in about: 30 minutes

3 tbsp olive oil
1 lb kale, chopped
1 onion, chopped
3 garlic cloves, minced

1 (2 ¼-oz) can sliced olives
¼ cup capers
¼ tsp red pepper flakes
2 (6-oz) cans tuna in olive oil

1 (15-oz) can white beans
½ cup chicken broth
Salt and black pepper to taste

Steam the kale for approximately 4 minutes or until crisp-tender and set aside. Warm the olive oil in a saucepan over medium heat. Sauté the onion and garlic for 4 minutes, stirring often. Add the chicken broth, olives, capers, and crushed red pepper flakes and cook for 4-5 minutes, stirring often. Add the kale and stir. Remove to a bowl and mix in the tuna, beans, pepper, and salt. Serve and enjoy!

452. Spicy Flounder Parcels

Serves: 4 | Ready in about: 20 minutes

2 tbsp olive oil
4 flounder fillets
¼ tsp red pepper flakes
4 fresh rosemary sprigs

2 garlic cloves, thinly sliced
1 cup cherry tomatoes, halved
½ chopped onion
2 tbsp capers

8 black olives, sliced
2 tbsp dry white wine
Salt and black pepper to taste

Preheat oven to 420 F. Drizzle the flounder with olive oil and season with salt, pepper, and red pepper flakes. Divide fillets between 4 pieces of aluminium foil. Top each one with garlic, cherry tomatoes, capers, onion, and olives. Fold the edges to form packets with opened tops. Add in a rosemary sprig in each one and drizzle with the white wine. Seal the packets and arrange them on a baking sheet. Bake for 10 minutes or until the fish is cooked. Serve warm.

453. Creamy Potato & Halibut Chowder

Serves: 4 | Ready in about: 25 minutes

3 gold potatoes, peeled and cubed
4 oz halibut fillets, boneless and cubed
2 tbsp olive oil
2 carrots, chopped
1 red onion, chopped

Salt and white pepper to taste
4 cups fish stock
½ cup heavy cream

1 tbsp dill, chopped

Warm the olive oil in a skillet over medium heat and cook the onion for 3 minutes. Put in potatoes, salt, pepper, carrots, and stock and bring to a boil. Cook for an additional 5-6 minutes. Stir in halibut, cream, and dill and simmer for another 5 minutes. Serve right away.

454. Citrus-Crusted Roasted Red Snapper

Serves: 2 | Ready in about: 35 minutes

2 tbsp olive oil
1 tsp fresh cilantro, chopped
½ tsp grated lemon zest
½ tbsp lemon juice

½ tsp grated grapefruit zest
½ tbsp grapefruit juice
½ tsp grated orange zest
½ tbsp orange juice

½ shallot, minced
¼ tsp red pepper flakes
Salt and black pepper to taste
1 whole red snapper, cleaned

Preheat oven to 380F. Whisk the olive oil, cilantro, lemon juice, orange juice, grapefruit juice, shallot, and pepper flakes together in a bowl. Season with salt and pepper. Set aside the citrus topping until ready to serve.

In a separate bowl, combine lemon zest, orange zest, grapefruit zest, salt, and pepper. With a sharp knife, make 3-4 shallow slashes, about 2 inches apart, on both sides of the snapper. Spoon the citrus mixture into the fish cavity and transfer to a greased baking sheet. Roast for 25 minutes until the fish flakes. Serve drizzled with citrus topping.

455. Yummy Mustard Sardine Cakes

Serves: 4 | Ready in about: 20 minutes

3 tbsp olive oil
1 tsp mustard powder
1 tsp hot pepper powder
20 oz canned sardines, mashed

2 garlic cloves, minced
2 tbsp dill, chopped
1 onion, chopped
1 cup breadcrumbs

1 egg, whisked
Salt and black pepper to taste
2 tbsp lemon juice

Combine sardines, garlic, dill, onion, breadcrumbs, egg, mustard powder, hot pepper powder, salt, pepper, and lemon juice in a bowl and form medium patties. Warm the olive oil in a skillet over medium heat and fry the cakes for 10 minutes on both sides. Serve with aioli.

456. Tzatziki Tuna Gyros

Serves: 4 | Ready in about: 15 minutes

4 oz tzatziki
½ lb canned tuna, drained
½ cup tahini

4 sundried tomatoes, diced
2 garlic cloves, minced
1 tbsp lemon juice

4 pita wraps
5 black olives, chopped
Salt and black pepper to taste

In a bowl, combine the tahini, 2 tbsp warm water, garlic, lemon juice, salt, and black pepper. Warm the pita wraps in a grilled pan for a few minutes, turning once. Spread the tahini and tzatziki sauces over the warmed pitas and top with tuna, sundried tomatoes, and olives. Fold in half and serve immediately.

457. Herby Sauce-Grilled Sardines

Serves: 4 | Ready in about: 15 min + marinating time

12 sardines, gutted and cleaned
1 lemon, cut into wedges
2 garlic cloves, minced
2 tbsp capers, finely chopped

1 tbsp whole capers
1 shallot, diced
1 tsp anchovy paste
1 lemon, zested and juiced

2 tbsp olive oil
1 tbsp parsley, finely chopped
1 tbsp basil, finely chopped

In a bowl, blend garlic, chopped capers, shallot, anchovy paste, lemon zest, and olive oil. Add the sardines and toss to coat; let them marinate for about 30 minutes.

Preheat your grill to high. Place the sardines on the grill. Cook for 3-4 minutes per side until the skin is browned and beginning to blister. Pour the marinade into a saucepan over medium heat and add the whole capers, parsley, basil, and lemon juice. Cook for 2-3 minutes until thickens. Pour the sauce over grilled sardines. Serve with lemon wedges.

458. Zesty Lemon-Garlic Sea Bass

Serves: 2 | Ready in about: 25 minutes

2 tbsp olive oil
2 sea bass fillets

1 lemon, juiced
4 garlic cloves, minced

Salt and black pepper to taste

Preheat the oven to 380F. Line a baking sheet with parchment paper. Brush sea bass fillets with lemon juice, olive oil, garlic, salt, and pepper and arrange them on the sheet. Bake for 15 minutes. Serve with salad.

459. Home-Style Tuna Burgers

Serves: 4 | Ready in about: 20 minutes

2 tbsp olive oil
2 (5-oz) cans tuna, flaked
4 hamburger buns
3 green onions, chopped
¼ cup breadcrumbs

1 egg, beaten
2 tbsp chopped fresh parsley
1 tbsp Greek seasoning
1 lemon, zested
½ cup mayonnaise

1 tbsp chopped fresh dill
1 tbsp green olives, chopped
Sea salt to taste

Combine tuna, breadcrumbs, green onions, eggs, Greek seasoning, parsley, and lemon zest in a bowl. Shape the mixture into 6 patties. Warm olive oil in a skillet over medium heat and brown patties for 8 minutes on both sides. Mix mayonnaise, green olives, dill, and salt in a bowl. Spoon the mixture on the buns and top with the patties.

460. Tuna Medley with Pan-Fried Vegetables

Serves: 4 | Ready in about: 25 minutes

2 tbsp olive oil
4 tuna fillets, boneless
1 red bell pepper, chopped

1 onion, chopped
4 garlic cloves, minced
½ cup fish stock

½ cup cherry tomatoes, halved
½ cup black olives, halved
Salt and black pepper to taste

Warm the olive oil in a skillet over medium heat and fry tuna for 10 minutes on both sides. Divide the fish among plates. In the same skillet, cook the onion, bell pepper, garlic, and cherry tomatoes for 3 minutes. Stir in salt, pepper, fish stock, and olives and cook for another 3 minutes. Top the tuna with the mixture and serve immediately.

461. Mackerel Fillets in Herby Red Sauce

Serves: 2 | Ready in about: 15 minutes

1 tbsp butter	2 garlic cloves, minced	½ cup vegetable broth
2 mackerel fillets	½ tsp dried thyme	½ cup tomato sauce
¼ cup white wine	1 tsp dried parsley	½ tsp hot sauce
½ cup spring onions, sliced	Salt and black pepper to taste	1 tbsp fresh mint, chopped

In a pot over medium heat, melt the butter. Add in fish and cook for 6 minutes in total; set aside. Pour in the wine and scrape off any bits from the bottom. Add in spring onions and garlic; cook for 3 minutes until fragrant. Sprinkle with thyme, parsley, salt, and pepper. Stir in vegetable broth, and tomato sauce, and add back the fillets. Cook for 3-4 minutes. Stir in hot sauce and top with mint. Serve and enjoy!

462. Barramundi with Date & Hazelnut Crust

Serves: 2 | Ready in about: 25 minutes

2 tbsp olive oil	4 lemon slices	¼ cup hazelnuts, chopped
2 barramundi fillets, boneless	½ lemon, zested and juiced	4 dates, pitted and chopped
1 shallot, sliced	1 cup baby spinach	Salt and black pepper to taste

Preheat oven to 380 F. Sprinkle barramundi with salt and pepper and place on 2 parchment paper pieces. Top each fillet with lemon slices, lemon juice, shallot, lemon zest, spinach, hazelnuts, dates, and parsley. Sprinkle each fillet with 1 tbsp of oil and fold the paper around it. Place them on a baking sheet and bake for 12 minutes. Serve and enjoy!

463. Thyme Potato Hake

Serves: 4 | Ready in about: 40 minutes

1 ½ lb russet potatoes, unpeeled	½ tsp paprika	4 fresh thyme sprigs
¼ cup olive oil	Salt and black pepper to taste	1 lemon, sliced
½ tsp garlic powder	4 skinless hake fillets	

Preheat oven to 425 F. Slice the potatoes and toss them with some olive oil, salt, pepper, paprika, and garlic powder in a bowl. Microwave for 12-14 minutes until potatoes are just tender, stirring halfway through microwaving. Transfer the potatoes to a baking dish and press gently into an even layer. Season the hake with salt and pepper, and arrange it skinned side down over the potatoes. Drizzle with the remaining olive oil, then place thyme sprigs and lemon slices on top. Bake for 15-18 minutes until the hake flakes apart when gently prodded with a paring knife. Serve and enjoy!

464. Avocado Anchovy Dip

Serves: 2 | Ready in about: 5 minutes

1 avocado, peeled and pitted	¼ celery stalk, chopped	2 anchovy fillets in olive oil
1 tsp lemon juice	¼ cup chopped shallots	Salt and black pepper to taste

Combine lemon juice, avocado, celery, shallots, and anchovy fillets (with their olive oil) in a food processor. Blitz until smooth. Season with salt and black pepper. Serve.

465. Flame-Grilled Fish Fillets

Serves: 4 | Ready in about: 15 minutes

1 tbsp olive oil	4 fish fillets	2 tbsp lemon juice
1 tsp harissa seasoning	2 lemons, sliced	Salt and black pepper to taste

Preheat your grill to 400 F. In a bowl, whisk the lemon juice, olive oil, harissa seasoning, salt, and pepper. Coat both sides of the fish with the mixture. Carefully place the lemon slices on the grill, arranging 3-4 slices together in the shape of a fish fillet, and repeat with the remaining slices. Place the fish fillets directly on top of the lemon slices and grill with the lid closed. Turn the fish halfway through the cooking time only if the fillets are more than half an inch thick. The fish is done and ready to serve when it just begins to separate into chunks when pressed gently with a fork. Serve.

466. Basil Hake Fillet with Tomato Sauce

Serves: 4 | Ready in about: 30 minutes

2 tbsp olive oil
1 onion, sliced thin
1 fennel bulb, sliced

Salt and black pepper to taste
4 garlic cloves, minced
1 (14-oz) can diced tomatoes,

½ cup dry white wine
4 skinless hake fillets
2 tbsp fresh basil, chopped

Warm the oil in a skillet over medium heat. Sauté the onion and fennel for about 5 minutes until softened. Stir in garlic and cook for about 30 seconds until fragrant. Pour in tomatoes and wine and bring to a simmer. Season the hake with salt and pepper. Nestle the hake skinned side down into the tomato sauce and spoon some sauce over the top. Bring to a simmer. Cook for 10-12 minutes until the hake easily flakes with a fork. Sprinkle with basil and serve.

467. Spicy Garlic Baked Anchovies

Serves: 2 | Ready in about: 10 minutes

½ tsp red pepper flakes
16 canned anchovies

4 garlic cloves, minced
Salt and black pepper to taste

Preheat the broiler. Arrange the anchovies on a foil-lined baking dish. In a bowl, mix anchovy olive oil, garlic, salt, red flakes, and pepper and pour over anchovies. Broil for 3-4 minutes. Divide between 4 plates and drizzle with the remaining mixture from the dish. Serve and enjoy!

468. Crispy Fried Pollock Fillets

Serves: 4 | Ready in about: 25 minutes

4 pollock fillets, boneless

2 cups potato chips, crushed

2 tbsp mayonnaise

Preheat the oven to 380F. Line a baking sheet with parchment paper. Rub each fillet with mayonnaise and dip them in the potato chips. Place fillets on the sheet and bake for 12 minutes. Serve with salad.

469. Crunchy Breaded Fish Sticks

Serves: 4 | Ready in about: 15 minutes

2 eggs, lightly beaten
1 tbsp milk
1 lb skinned tilapia fillet strips

½ cup yellow cornmeal
½ cup bread crumbs
¼ tsp smoked paprika

1 hot pepper, sliced
Salt and black pepper to taste

Put a large, rimmed baking sheet in your oven. Preheat the oven to 400 F with the pan inside. In a large bowl, mix the eggs and milk. Add the fish strips to the egg mixture and stir gently to coat. Put the cornmeal, bread crumbs, smoked paprika, salt, and black pepper in a zip-top plastic bag. Transfer the fish to the bag, letting the excess egg wash drip off into the bowl before transferring. Seal the bag and shake gently to completely coat each fish stick.

Carefully remove the hot baking sheet with oven mitts from the oven and spray it with nonstick cooking spray. Remove the fish sticks from the bag and arrange them on the hot baking sheet. Top with Padrón pepper and bake for 6-8 minutes until gentle pressure with a fork causes the fish to flake.

470. Trout with Tzatziki Sauce

Serves: 4 | Ready in about: 20 minutes

1 cucumber, grated and squeezed
3 tbsp olive oil
4 trout fillets, boneless
½ lime, juiced

Salt and black pepper to taste
1 garlic clove, minced
1 tsp sweet paprika

4 garlic cloves, minced
2 cups Greek yogurt
1 tbsp dill, chopped

Warm 2 tbsp of the olive oil in a skillet over medium heat. Sprinkle the trout with salt, pepper, lime juice, garlic, and paprika and sear for 8 minutes on all sides. Remove to a paper towel–lined plate. Combine cucumber, garlic, remaining olive oil, yogurt, salt, and dill in a bowl. Share trout into plates and serve with tzatziki.

471.   Herring & Caper Deviled Eggs

Serves: 6 | Ready in about: 20 minutes

1/3 cup aioli
1 tbsp capers, drained
12 eggs

1 tbsp tarragon, chopped
2 pickled jalapenos, minced
Salt and black pepper to taste

1 (6.7-oz) can smoked herring
1 tsp paprika

Fill a pot over medium heat with water by 1 inch. Bring to a boil. Carefully add the eggs, one at a time to the pot, cover, and boil them for 10 minutes. Cool the eggs in cold water. Peel the eggs and slice them in half lengthwise; mix the yolks with the aioli, herring, paprika, capers, tarragon, jalapenos, salt, and pepper. Divide the mixture between the egg whites. Arrange the deviled eggs on a serving platter.

472.   Lemon Rice & Baked Cod

Serves: 4 | Ready in about: 45 minutes

2 tbsp olive oil
1 cup rice
1 garlic clove, minced
1 tsp red pepper, crushed
2 shallots, chopped
1 tsp anchovy paste

1 tbsp oregano, chopped
6 black olives, chopped
2 tbsp capers, drained
1 tsp paprika
15 oz canned tomatoes, diced
Salt and black pepper to taste

4 cod fillets, boneless
1 oz feta cheese, crumbled
1 tbsp parsley, chopped
2 cups chicken stock
1 lemon, zested

Preheat the oven to 360F. Warm the olive oil in a skillet over medium heat. Sauté the garlic, red pepper, and shallot for 5 minutes. Stir in anchovy paste, paprika, oregano, olives, capers, tomatoes, salt, and pepper and cook for another 5 minutes. Put in cod fillets and top with the feta cheese and parsley. Bake for 15 minutes.

In the meantime, boil chicken stock in a pot over medium heat. Add in rice and lemon zest, bring to a simmer, and cook for 15-18 minutes. When ready, fluff with a fork. Share the rice on plates and top with cod mixture. Serve.

473.   Traditional Garidomakaronada (Shrimp & Pasta)

Serves: 4 | Ready in about: 45 minutes

2 tbsp olive oil
16 shrimp, shelled and deveined
Salt and black pepper to taste
1 onion, finely chopped
3 garlic cloves, minced

4 tomatoes, puréed
½ tsp sugar
1 tbsp tomato paste
1 tbsp ouzo
1 lb whole-wheat spaghetti

½ tsp crushed red pepper
¼ tsp dried Greek oregano
2 tbsp chopped fresh parsley

Bring a large pot of salted water to a boil, add the spaghetti, and cook for 7-9 minutes until al dente. Drain the pasta and set aside. Warm the olive oil in a large skillet over medium heat. Sauté the shrimp for 2 minutes, flipping once or until pink; set aside. Add the onion and garlic to the skillet and cook for 3-5 minutes or until tender.

Add tomatoes, sugar, oregano, and tomato paste. Bring the sauce to a boil. Reduce the heat and simmer for 15–20 minutes or until thickened. Stir in ouzo and season with salt and black pepper. Add the pasta along with crushed red pepper and cooked shrimp. Remove from heat and toss to coat the pasta. Sprinkle with parsley and serve immediately.

474.   Black Olive & Shrimp Quinoa Bowl

Serves: 4 | Ready in about: 20 minutes

10 black olives, pitted and halved
¼ cup olive oil
1 cup quinoa
1 lemon, cut into wedges
1 lb shrimp, peeled and cooked

2 tomatoes, sliced
2 bell peppers, thinly sliced
1 red onion, chopped
1 tsp dried dill

1 tbsp fresh parsley, chopped
Salt and black pepper to taste

Place the quinoa in a pot and cover with 2 cups of water over medium heat. Bring to a boil, reduce the heat, and simmer for 12-15 minutes or until tender. Remove from heat and fluff it with a fork. Mix in the quinoa with olive oil, dill, parsley, salt, and black pepper. Stir in tomatoes, bell peppers, olives, and onion. Serve with shrimp and lemon wedges.

475.   Bulgur with Shrimp & Feta

Serves: 6 | Ready in about: 50 minutes

10 Kalamata olives
1 ½ lb bulgur
2 red hot peppers, minced
1 garlic clove, minced
2 whole garlic cloves
2 tbsp fresh parsley, chopped
1 ¼ cups fresh basil, sliced
½ cup extra-virgin olive oil

½ tsp honey
½ lemon, juiced and zested
¼ cup butter
1 small red onion, chopped
1 lb button mushrooms, sliced
1 tsp sweet paprika
6 ripe plum tomatoes, puréed
¼ cup dry white wine

1 oz ouzo
1 cup heavy cream
1 cup feta cheese, crumbled
24 shrimp, peeled and deveined
1 cup feta cheese, cubed
1 tsp dried Greek oregano
Salt and black pepper to taste

Bring to a boil salted water in a pot over high heat. Add the bulgur and cook for 15-20 minutes or until the bulgur is tender and the liquid is absorbed. Let it sit for 5-10 minutes before fluffing the bulgur with a fork.

Preheat your broiler. Place the hot peppers, whole garlic, parsley, ¼ cup of basil, ¼ cup of oil, honey, lemon juice, lemon zest, and salt in a food processor and blend until all the ingredients are well incorporated. Set aside.

Warm the remaining olive oil and butter in a large skillet over medium heat. Sauté the onion, minced garlic, mushrooms, and paprika for 5 minutes until tender. Pour in the tomatoes, wine, and ouzo and season with salt and pepper. Simmer for 6–7 minutes until most of the liquid evaporates, 5 minutes.

Stir in the heavy cream and crumbled feta cheese for 3 minutes until the sauce is thickened. Add in remaining basil and pasta and stir to combine. Pour the mixture into a baking dish and top with shrimp and cubed feta cheese. Broil 5 minutes or until the shrimp turn pink and the cheese melts. Drizzle with reserved parsley-basil sauce and sprinkle with oregano. Let cool for 5 minutes. Serve topped with olives.

476.   Spinach Shrimp

Serves: 4 | Ready in about: 20 minutes

1 lb fresh shrimp, shells and tails removed
1 cup baby spinach
16 oz cooked spaghetti
2 tbsp olive oil
3 anchovy fillets, chopped

3 garlic cloves, minced
½ tsp crushed red pepper
1 (14-oz) can tomatoes, diced
12 black olives, sliced

2 tbsp capers
1 tsp dried oregano

Warm the olive oil in a large skillet over medium heat. Add in the anchovies, garlic, and crushed red peppers and cook for 3 minutes, stirring frequently and mashing up the anchovies with a wooden spoon until they have melted into the oil. Pour in the tomatoes with their juices, olives, capers, and oregano. Simmer until the sauce is lightly bubbling, about 3-4 minutes. Stir in the shrimp. Cook for 6-8 minutes or until they turn pink and white, stirring occasionally. Add the baby spinach and spaghetti and stir for 2 minutes until the spinach wilts. Serve and enjoy!

477.   Celery Sticks Stuffed with Crab

Serves: 4 | Ready in about: 10 minutes

1 cup cream cheese
6 oz crab meat

1 tsp Mediterranean seasoning
2 tbsp apple cider vinegar

8 celery sticks, halved
Salt and black pepper to taste

In a mixing bowl, combine the cream cheese, crab meat, apple cider vinegar, salt, pepper, and Mediterranean seasoning. Divide the crab mixture between the celery sticks. Serve.

478.   Squid & Shrimp Medley

Serves: 4 | Ready in about: 25 minutes

2 tbsp butter
½ lb squid rings
1 lb shrimp, peeled, deveined
Salt and black pepper to taste

2 garlic cloves, minced
1 tsp rosemary, dried
1 red onion, chopped
1 cup vegetable stock

1 lemon, juiced
1 tbsp parsley, chopped

Melt butter in a skillet over medium heat and cook the onion and garlic for 4 minutes. Stir in shrimp, salt, pepper, squid rings, rosemary, vegetable stock, and lemon juice and bring to a boil. Simmer for 8 minutes. Put in parsley and serve.

479.   Spicy Tomato & Caper Squid Stew

Serves: 4 | Ready in about: 50 minutes

1 (28-oz) cans whole peeled tomatoes, diced

¼ cup olive oil	¼ tsp red pepper flakes	Salt and black pepper to taste
1 onion, chopped	1 red hot pepper, minced	⅓ cup green olives, chopped
1 celery rib, sliced	½ cup dry white wine	1 tbsp capers
3 garlic cloves, minced	2 lb squid, sliced into rings	2 tbsp fresh parsley, chopped

Warm the olive oil in a pot over medium heat. Sauté the onion, garlic, red hot pepper, and celery until softened, about 5 minutes. Stir in pepper flakes and cook for about 30 seconds. Stir in wine, scraping up any browned bits, and cook until nearly evaporated, about 1 minute. Add 1 cup of water and season with salt and pepper. Stir the squid in the pot. Reduce heat to low, cover, and simmer until squid has released its liquid, about 15 minutes. Pour in tomatoes, olives, and capers, and continue to cook until squid is very tender, 30-35 minutes. Top with parsley. Serve and enjoy!

480.   Garlic-Cilantro Calamari

Serves: 4 | Ready in about: 25 minutes

2 tbsp olive oil	4 garlic cloves, minced	2 tbsp balsamic vinegar
2 lb calamari, sliced into rings	1 lime, juiced	3 tbsp cilantro, chopped

Warm the olive oil in a skillet over medium heat and sauté garlic, lime juice, balsamic vinegar, and cilantro for 5 minutes. Stir in calamari rings and cook for 10 minutes.

481.   Mushroom Prawns

Serves: 4 | Ready in about: 25 minutes

1 lb tiger prawns, peeled and deveined

3 tbsp olive oil	½ lb white mushrooms, sliced	2 tsp garlic, minced
2 green onions, sliced	2 tbsp balsamic vinegar	

Warm the olive oil in a skillet over medium heat and cook green onions and garlic for 2 minutes. Stir in mushrooms and balsamic vinegar and cook for an additional 6 minutes. Put in prawns and cook for 4 minutes. Serve right away.

482.   Caper Prawns

Serves: 4 | Ready in about: 25 minutes

1 lb prawns, peeled, deveined	2 tomatoes, chopped	2 tbsp dill, chopped
2 tbsp olive oil	1 cup spring onions, chopped	Salt and black pepper to taste
1 lemon, zested and juiced	2 tbsp capers, chopped	

Warm the olive oil in a skillet over medium heat and cook the onions and capers for 2-3 minutes. Stir in prawns, lemon zest, tomatoes, dill, salt, and pepper and cook for another 6 minutes. Serve drizzled with lemon juice.

483.   Squid Stwe with Capers

Serves: 4 | Ready in about: 25 minutes

2 tbsp olive oil	2 red hot peppers, chopped	Salt and black pepper to taste
1 onion, chopped	2 garlic cloves, minced	2 tbsp capers, drained
1 celery stalk, chopped	14 oz canned tomatoes, diced	12 black olives, pitted and halved
1 lb calamari rings	2 tbsp tomato paste	

Warm the olive oil in a skillet over medium heat and cook the onion, celery, garlic, and hot peppers for 2 minutes. Stir in calamari rings, tomatoes, tomato paste, salt, and pepper and bring to a simmer. Cook for 20 minutes. Put in olives and capers and cook for another 5 minutes. Serve right away.

484. Tomato Sauce with Shrimp & Salmon

Serves: 4 | Ready in about: 30 minutes

1 lb shrimp, peeled and deveined

2 tbsp olive oil	1 cups tomatoes, chopped	¼ tsp red pepper flakes
1 lb salmon fillets	1 onion, chopped	1 cup fish stock
Salt and black pepper to taste	2 garlic cloves, minced	1 tbsp cilantro, chopped

Preheat the oven to 360F. Line a baking sheet with parchment paper. Season the salmon with salt and pepper, drizzle with some olive oil, and arrange them on the sheet. Bake for 15 minutes. Remove to a serving plate.

Warm the remaining olive oil in a skillet over medium heat and sauté onion and garlic for 3 minutes until tender. Pour in tomatoes, fish stock, salt, pepper, and red pepper flakes and bring to a boil. Simmer for 10 minutes. Stir in shrimp and cook for another 8 minutes. Pour the sauce over the salmon and serve sprinkled with cilantro.

485. Avocado-Enhanced Salmon Tartare

Serves: 4 | Ready in about: 10 minutes + chilling time

1 lb salmon, skinless, boneless and cubed

1 tbsp olive oil	2 tsp lemon juice	Salt and black pepper to taste
4 tbsp scallions, chopped	1 avocado, chopped	1 tbsp parsley, chopped

Mix scallions, lemon juice, olive oil, salmon, salt, pepper, and parsley in a bowl. Place in the fridge for 1 hour. Place a baking ring on a serving plate and pour in the salmon mixture. Top with avocado and gently press down. Serve.

486. Smoked Salmon & Eggplant Rolls with Dill

Serves: 4 | Ready in about: 20 minutes

2 eggplants, lengthwise cut into thin slices

2 tbsp olive oil	4 oz smoked salmon, chopped	1 small red onion, sliced
1 cup ricotta cheese, soft	2 tsp lemon zest, grated	Salt and pepper to the taste

Mix salmon, cheese, lemon zest, onion, salt, and pepper in a bowl. Grease the eggplant with olive oil and grill them on a preheated grill pan for 3-4 minutes per side. Set aside to cool. Spread the cooled eggplant slices with the salmon mixture. Roll out and secure with toothpicks and serve.

487. Delectable Salmon Stuffed Peppers

Serves: 4 | Ready in about: 25 minutes

4 bell peppers	1 red onion, finely chopped	1 cup cream cheese
10 oz canned salmon, drained	½ tsp garlic, minced	1 tsp Mediterranean seasoning
12 black olives, chopped	1/3 cup mayonnaise	Salt and pepper flakes to taste

Preheat oven to 390 F. Cut the peppers into halves and remove the seeds. In a mixing bowl, combine the salmon, onion, garlic, mayonnaise, olives, salt, red pepper, Mediterranean spice mix, and cream cheese. Divide the mixture between the peppers and bake them in the oven for 10-12 minutes or until cooked through. Serve and enjoy!

488. Tomato-Caper Roasted Salmon

Serves: 4 | Ready in about: 25 minutes

1 tbsp olive oil	½ tsp garlic powder	½ cup breadcrumbs
4 salmon steaks	2 Roma tomatoes, chopped	1 lemon, cut into wedges
Salt and black pepper to taste	¼ cup green olives, chopped	
¼ mustard powder	1 tsp capers	

Preheat oven to 375 F. Arrange the salmon fillets on a greased baking dish. Season with salt, pepper, garlic powder, and mustard powder and coat with the breadcrumbs. Drizzle with olive oil. Scatter the tomatoes, green olives, garlic, and capers around the fish fillets. Bake for 15 minutes until the salmon steaks flake easily with a fork. Serve with lemon wedges.

489.   Delicate Orange Salmon Encased in Parchment

Serves: 4 | Ready in about: 25 minutes

2 tbsp butter, melted
4 salmon fillets

Salt and black pepper to taste
1 orange, juiced and zested

4 tbsp fresh dill, chopped

Preheat oven to 375 F. Coat the salmon fillets on both sides with butter. Season with salt and pepper and divide them between 4 pieces of parchment paper. Drizzle the orange juice over each piece of fish and top with orange zest and dill. Wrap the paper around the fish to make packets. Place on a baking sheet and bake for 15-20 minutes until the cod is cooked through. Serve and enjoy!

490.   Grecian Sauce-Topped Crispy Salmon Patties

Serves: 2 | Ready in about: 30 minutes

1 cup tzatziki sauce
Salmon cakes
6 oz cooked salmon, flaked
¼ cup celery, minced
¼ cup onion, minced

2 tsp olive oil

¼ tsp hot pepper powder
½ tsp dried dill
1 tbsp fresh minced parsley

Salt and black pepper to taste
1 egg, beaten
½ cup breadcrumbs

In a large bowl, mix well all the salmon cake ingredients. Shape the mixture into balls, then press them to form patties. Warm the olive oil in a skillet over medium heat. Cook the patties for 3 minutes per side or until they're golden brown. Serve the salmon cakes topped with the tzatziki sauce.

491.   Celery Egg Bake with Salmon

Serves: 4 | Ready in about: 40 minutes

2 tbsp olive oil
2 tbsp butter, melted
4 oz smoked salmon, flaked
1 cup cheddar cheese, grated

4 eggs, whisked
¼ cup plain yogurt
1 cup cream of celery soup
1 shallot, chopped

2 garlic cloves, minced
½ cup celery, chopped
8 slices fresh toast, cubed
1 tbsp mint leaves, chopped

Preheat the oven to 360 F. In a bowl, mix eggs, yogurt, and celery soup. Warm olive oil in a skillet over medium heat and cook the shallot, garlic, and celery until tender. Place the toast cubes in a greased baking dish, top with cooked vegetables and salmon, and cover with egg mixture and butter. Bake for 22-25 minutes until it is cooked through. Scatter cheddar cheese on top and bake for another 5 minutes until the cheese melts. Serve garnished with mint leaves.

492.   Cucumber & Salmon Rolls

Serves: 4 | Ready in about: 5 minutes

8 Kalamata olives, chopped
4 oz smoked salmon strips
1 cucumber, sliced lengthwise

2 tsp lime juice
4 oz cream cheese, soft
1 tsp lemon zest, grated

Salt and black pepper to taste
2 tsp dill, chopped

Place cucumber slices on a flat surface and top each with a salmon strip. Combine olives, lime juice, cream cheese, lemon zest, salt, pepper, and dill in a bowl. Smear the cream mixture over the salmon and roll them up. Serve.

493.   Skillet Seared Scallops & Bell Peppers

Serves: 4 | Ready in about: 25 minutes

3 tbsp olive oil
2 celery stalks, sliced
2 lb sea scallops, halved
3 garlic cloves, minced

Juice of 1 lime
1 red bell pepper, chopped
1 tbsp capers, chopped
1 tbsp mayonnaise

1 tbsp rosemary, chopped
1 cup chicken stock

Warm olive oil in a skillet over medium heat. Cook celery and garlic for 2 minutes. Stir in bell pepper, lime juice, capers, rosemary, and stock and bring to a boil. Simmer for 8 minutes. Mix in scallops and mayonnaise and cook for 5 minutes.

494. Salmon Coated in Almond Crust

Serves: 4 | Ready in about: 20 minutes

1 tbsp olive oil
½ tsp lemon zest
¼ cup breadcrumbs

½ cup toasted almonds, ground
½ tsp dried thyme
Salt and black pepper to taste

4 salmon steaks
1 lemon, cut into wedges

Preheat oven to 350 F. In a shallow dish, combine the lemon zest, breadcrumbs, almonds, thyme, salt, and pepper. Coat the salmon steaks with olive oil and arrange them on a baking sheet. Cover them with the almond mixture, pressing down lightly with your fingers to create a tightly packed crust. Bake for 10-12 minutes or until the almond crust is lightly browned and the fish is cooked through. Serve garnished with lemon wedges.

495. Citrus-Infused Trout with Roasted Beets

Serves: 4 | Ready in about: 45 minutes

1 lb medium beets, peeled and sliced
3 tbsp olive oil
4 trout fillets, boneless
Salt and black pepper to taste

1 tbsp rosemary, chopped
2 spring onions, chopped
2 tbsp lemon juice

½ cup vegetable stock

Preheat oven to 390F. Line a baking sheet with parchment paper. Arrange the beets on the sheet, season with salt and pepper, and drizzle with some olive oil. Roast for 20 minutes.

Warm the remaining oil in a skillet over medium heat. Cook trout fillets for 8 minutes on all sides; reserve. Add spring onions to the skillet and sauté for 2 minutes. Stir in lemon juice and stock and cook for 5-6 minutes until the sauce thickens. Remove the beets to a plate and top with trout fillets. Pour the sauce all over and sprinkle with rosemary.

496. Trout & Farro Bowls with Creamy Avocado

Serves: 4 | Ready in about: 50 minutes

4 tbsp olive oil
8 trout fillets, boneless
1 cup farro
Juice of 2 lemons

Salt and black pepper to taste
1 avocado, chopped
¼ cup balsamic vinegar
1 garlic cloves, minced

¼ cup parsley, chopped
¼ cup mint, chopped
2 tbsp yellow mustard

Boil salted water in a pot over medium heat and stir in farro. Simmer for 30 minutes and drain. Remove to a bowl and combine with lemon juice, mustard, garlic, salt, pepper, and half olive oil. Set aside. Mash the avocado with a fork in a bowl and mix with vinegar, salt, pepper, parsley, and mint. Warm the remaining oil in a skillet over medium heat and brown trout fillets skin-side down for 10 minutes on both sides. Let cool and cut into pieces. Put over farro and stir in avocado dressing. Serve immediately.

497. Lemony Trout fillets with Horseradish Sauce

Serves: 4 | Ready in about: 35 minutes

3 tbsp olive oil
2 tbsp horseradish sauce
1 onion, sliced

2 tsp Greek seasoning
4 trout fillets, boneless
¼ cup breadcrumbs

½ cup pitted olives, and chopped
Salt and black pepper to taste
1 lemon, juiced

Preheat the oven to 380F. Line a baking sheet with parchment paper. Sprinkle trout fillets with salt and pepper and dip in breadcrumbs. Arrange them along with the onion on the sheet. Sprinkle with olive oil, Greek seasoning, and lemon juice and bake for 15-18 minutes. Transfer to a serving plate and top with horseradish sauce and olives. Serve.

498. Shrimp & White Bean Pot

Serves: 4 | Ready in about: 25 minutes

1 lb large shrimp, peeled and deveined
3 tbsp olive oil

Salt and black pepper to taste

1 red bell pepper, chopped

1 small red onion, chopped
2 garlic cloves, minced

¼ tsp red pepper flakes
2 (15-oz) cans white beans

2 tbsp lemon zest

Warm the olive oil in a skillet over medium heat. Add the shrimp and cook, without stirring, until spotty brown and edges turn pink, about 2 minutes. Remove the skillet from the heat, turn over the shrimp, and let sit until opaque throughout, about 30 seconds. Transfer shrimp to a bowl and cover with foil to keep warm.

Return the skillet to heat and reheat the olive oil. Sauté the bell pepper, garlic, and onion until softened, about 5 minutes. Stir in pepper flakes and salt for about 30 seconds. Pour in the beans and cook until heated through, 5 minutes. Add the shrimp with any accumulated juices back to the skillet cook for about 1 minute. Stir in lemon zest and serve.

499.   Roasted Vegetables with Shrimp

Serves: 4 | Ready in about: 30 minutes

2 lb shrimp, peeled and deveined
4 tbsp olive oil
2 bell peppers, cut into chunks
2 fennel bulbs, cut into wedges
2 red onions, cut into wedges

4 garlic cloves, unpeeled
8 Kalamata olives, halved
1 tsp lemon zest, grated
2 tsp oregano, dried

2 tbsp parsley, chopped
Salt and black pepper to taste

Preheat the oven to 390 F. Place bell peppers, garlic, fennel, red onions, and olives in a roasting tray. Add in the lemon zest, oregano, half of olive oil, salt, and pepper and toss to coat; roast for 15 minutes. Coat the shrimp with the remaining olive oil and pour over the veggies; roast for another 7 minutes. Serve topped with parsley.

500.   Gnocchi & Shrimp with Feta Cheese

Serves: 4 | Ready in about: 30 minutes

1 lb shrimp, shells and tails removed
1 (12-oz) jar roasted red peppers, chopped
2 tbsp olive oil
1 cup chopped fresh tomato
2 garlic cloves, minced

½ tsp dried oregano
Black pepper to taste
¼ tsp crushed red peppers

1 lb potato gnocchi
½ cup cubed feta cheese
⅓ cup fresh basil leaves, torn

Preheat oven to 425 F. In a baking dish, mix the tomatoes, olive oil, garlic, oregano, black pepper, and crushed red peppers. Roast in the oven for 10 minutes. Stir in the roasted peppers and shrimp. Roast for 10 minutes until the shrimp turn pink. Bring a saucepan of salted water to a boil and cook the gnocchi for 1-2 mins, until floating. Drain. Remove the dish from the oven. Mix in the cooked gnocchi, sprinkle with feta and basil and serve.

501.   Succulent Scallops with Basil & Tomato

Serves: 4 | Ready in about: 20 minutes

2 tbsp olive oil
1 tbsp basil, chopped
1 lb scallops, scrubbed

1 tbsp garlic, minced
1 onion, chopped
6 tomatoes, cubed

1 cup heavy cream
1 tbsp parsley, chopped

Warm the olive oil in a skillet over medium heat and cook garlic and onion for 2 minutes. Stir in scallops, basil, tomatoes, heavy cream, and parsley and cook for an additional 7 minutes. Serve immediately.

502.   Black Olive & Lemon Shrimp Dish

Serves: 4 | Ready in about: 25 minutes

1 lb peeled shrimp, deveined
3 tbsp olive oil
1 lemon, juiced

1 tbsp flour
1 cup fish stock
Salt and black pepper to taste

1 cup black olives, halved
1 tbsp rosemary, chopped

Warm the oil in a skillet over medium heat and sear shrimp for 4 minutes on both sides; set aside. In the same skillet over low heat, stir in the flour for 2-3 minutes. Gradually pour in the fish stock and lemon juice while stirring and simmer for 3-4 minutes until the sauce thickens. Adjust the seasoning with salt and pepper and mix in shrimp, olives, and rosemary.

503. Zucchini & Squid Dish

Serves: 4 | Ready in about: 25 minutes

2 tbsp olive oil
10 oz squid, cut into pieces
2 zucchini, chopped

2 tbsp cilantro, chopped
1 jalapeno pepper, chopped
3 tbsp balsamic vinegar

Salt and black pepper to taste
1 tbsp dill, chopped

Warm the olive oil in a skillet over medium heat and sauté squid for 5 minutes. Stir in zucchini, cilantro, jalapeño pepper, vinegar, salt, pepper, and dill and cook for another 10 minutes. Serve right away.

504. Tangy Lime & Orange Squid Dish

Serves: 4 | Ready in about: 30 minutes

1 lb baby squid, cleaned, body and tentacles chopped
3 tbsp olive oil
½ cup green olives, chopped
½ tsp lime zest, grated
1 tbsp lime juice

½ tsp orange zest, grated
1 tsp red pepper flakes
1 tbsp parsley, chopped
4 garlic cloves, minced

1 shallot, chopped
1 cup vegetable stock
2 tbsp red wine vinegar
Salt and black pepper to taste

Warm the olive oil in a skillet over medium heat and stir in lime zest, lime juice, orange zest, red pepper flakes, garlic, shallot, olives, stock, vinegar, salt, and pepper. Bring to a boil and simmer for 10 minutes. Mix in squid and parsley and cook for another 10 minutes. Serve hot.

505. Lemon-Butter Drunken Mussels

Serves: 4 | Ready in about: 15 minutes

4 lb mussels, cleaned
4 tbsp butter
½ cup chopped parsley

1 white onion, chopped
2 cups dry white wine
½ tsp sea salt

6 garlic cloves, minced
Juice of ½ lemon

Add wine, garlic, salt, onion, and ¼ cup of parsley in a pot over medium heat and let simmer. Put in mussels and simmer covered for 7-8 minutes. Divide mussels between four bowls. Stir butter and lemon juice into the pot and drizzle over the mussels. Top with parsley and serve.

506. Hearty Chickpea & Clam Stew with Veggies

Serves: 4 | Ready in about: 40 minutes

2 tbsp olive oil
1 yellow onion, chopped
1 fennel bulb, chopped
1 carrot, chopped

1 red bell pepper, chopped
2 garlic cloves, minced
3 tbsp tomato paste
16 oz canned s, drained

1 tsp dried thyme
¼ tsp smoked paprika
Salt and black pepper to taste
1 lb clams, scrubbed

Warm olive oil in a pot over medium heat and sauté fennel, onion, bell pepper, and carrot for 5 minutes until they're tender. Stir in garlic and tomato paste and cook for another minute. Mix in the chickpeas, thyme, paprika, salt, pepper, and 2 cups of water and bring to a boil; cook for 20 minutes.

Rinse the clams under cold, running water. Discard any clams that remain open when tapped with your fingers. Put the unopened clams into the pot and cook everything for 4-5 minutes until the shells have opened. When finished, discard any clams that haven't opened fully during the cooking process. Adjust the seasoning with salt and pepper.

507. Mussels & Spaghetti in Sauce

Serves: 4 | Ready in about: 30 minutes

2 lb cleaned mussels, beards removed
1 lb cooked spaghetti
3 tbsp butter
2 garlic cloves, minced

1 carrot, diced
1 onion, chopped
2 celery sticks, chopped
1 cup white wine

2 tbsp parsley, chopped
½ tsp red pepper flakes
1 lemon, juiced

Melt butter in a saucepan over medium heat and sauté the garlic, carrot, onion, and celery for 4-5 minutes, stirring occasionally until softened. Add the mussels, white wine, and lemon juice, cover, and bring to a boil. Reduce the heat and steam for 4-6 minutes. Discard any unopened mussels. Coat in spaghetti. Sprinkle with parsley and pepper flakes.

508. Marinara-Style Mussels with Leeks & Herbs

Serves: 4 | Ready in about: 25 minutes

2 lb mussels, cleaned and de-bearded	1 red onion, chopped	1 tbsp chives, chopped
2 tbsp olive oil	Salt and black pepper to taste	½ cup tomato sauce
2 leeks, chopped	1 tbsp parsley, chopped	

Warm the olive oil in a skillet over medium heat and cook leeks and onion for 5 minutes. Stir in mussels, salt, pepper, parsley, chives, and tomato sauce and cook for 10 minutes. Discard any unopened mussels. Serve right away.

509. Clams & Snow Peas with Scallions

Serves: 4 | Ready in about: 30 minutes

2 tbsp olive oil	4 garlic cloves, minced	1 cup snow peas, sliced
2 lb clams	Salt and black pepper to taste	½ tbsp vinegar
1 onion, chopped	½ cup vegetable stock	1 cup scallions, sliced

Warm oil in a skillet over medium heat. Sauté onion and garlic for 2 to 3 minutes until tender and fragrant, stirring often. Add in the clams, salt, pepper, vegetable stock, snow peas, and vinegar and bring to a boil. Lower the heat and simmer for 10 minutes. Remove from the heat. Discard any unopened clams. Scatter with scallions.

510. Clams in a Fragrant Sherry & Parsley Sauce

Serves: 4 | Ready in about: 20 minutes

2 tbsp olive oil	4 garlic cloves, minced	½ tsp cayenne pepper
1 cup dry sherry	4 lb littleneck clams, scrubbed	1 Lemon, cut into wedges
3 shallots, minced	2 tbsp minced fresh parsley	

Bring the sherry wine, shallots, and garlic to a simmer in a large saucepan and cook for 3 minutes. Add clams, cover, and cook, stirring twice, until clams open, about 7 minutes. With a slotted spoon, transfer clams to a serving bowl, discarding any that refuse to open. Stir in olive oil, parsley, and cayenne pepper. Pour sauce over clams. Serve with lemon wedges.

511. Steamed Clams in a White Wine

Serves: 4 | Ready in about: 30 minutes

4 lb clams, scrubbed and debearded	3 garlic cloves, minced	1 cup dry white wine
3 tbsp butter	¼ tsp red pepper flakes	3 fresh thyme sprigs

Melt the butter in a saucepan over medium heat and cook garlic and pepper flakes, stirring constantly, until fragrant, 30 seconds. Stir in wine and thyme sprigs, bring to a boil and cook until wine is slightly reduced, about 1 minute. Stir in clams. Cover the saucepan and simmer for 15-18 minutes. Remove and discard thyme sprigs and any clams that refuse to open.

512. Seafood & Vegetable Stew

Serves: 4 | Ready in about: 25 minutes

½ lb skinless trout, cubed	½ fennel bulb, chopped	1 cup fish broth
2 tbsp olive oil	2 garlic cloves, minced	1 tbsp Greek seasoning
½ lb clams	¼ cup dry white wine	⅛ tsp red pepper flakes
½ lb cod, cubed	2 tbsp chopped fresh parsley	Salt and black pepper to taste
1 onion, chopped	1 (32-oz) can tomato sauce	

Warm oil in a pot over medium heat and sauté onion and fennel for 5 minutes. Add in garlic and cook for 30 seconds. Pour in the wine and cook for 1 minute. Stir in tomato sauce, clams, broth, cod, trout, salt, Greek seasoning, red pepper flakes, and pepper. Bring just a boil and simmer for 5 minutes. Discard any unopened clams. Top with parsley.

MEATLESS RECIPES

513.   Baked Eggplant Rounds

Serves: 4 | Ready in about: 25 minutes

1 ½ lb eggplants, sliced into rounds
¼ cup olive oil
Salt and black pepper to taste

4 tsp balsamic vinegar
1 tbsp capers, minced
1 garlic clove, minced

½ tsp lemon zest
½ tsp fresh oregano, minced
3 tbsp fresh mint, minced

Preheat oven to 420 F. Arrange the eggplant rounds on a greased baking dish and drizzle with some olive oil. Sprinkle with salt and pepper. Bake for 10-12 per side until mahogany is lightly charred. Whisk remaining olive oil, balsamic vinegar, capers, garlic, lemon zest, oregano, salt, and pepper together in a bowl. Drizzle the mixture all over the eggplants and sprinkle with mint. Serve and enjoy!

514.   Halloumi & Mint Bulgur Delight

Serves: 4 | Ready in about: 35 minutes

2 tbsp olive oil
4 halloumi cheese slices
1 cup bulgur

1 cup parsley, chopped
¼ cup mint, chopped
3 tbsp lemon juice

1 red onion, sliced
Salt and black pepper to taste

Bring to a boil a pot of water over medium heat. Add in bulgur and simmer for 15 minutes. Drain and let it cool in a bowl. Stir in parsley, mint, lemon juice, onion, salt, and pepper. Warm half of olive oil in a pan over medium heat. Cook the halloumi for 4-5 minutes on both sides until golden. Arrange the fried cheese on top of the bulgur and serve.

515.   Chickpea Cakes with Zesty Cilantro-Yogurt Sauce

Serves: 4 | Ready in about: 20 minutes

¼ cup olive oil
3 garlic cloves, minced
1 cup canned garbanzo beans
2 tbsp parsley, chopped
1 onion, chopped

1 tsp ground coriander
Salt and black pepper to taste
¼ tsp cayenne pepper
¼ tsp cumin powder
1 tsp lemon juice

3 tbsp flour
¼ cup Greek yogurt
2 tbsp chopped cilantro
½ tsp garlic powder

In a blender, blitz garbanzo, parsley, onion, garlic, salt, pepper, ground coriander, cayenne pepper, cumin powder, and lemon juice until smooth. Remove to a bowl and mix in flour. Form 16 balls out of the mixture and flatten them into patties. Warm the olive oil in a skillet over medium heat and fry patties for 10 minutes on both sides. Remove them to a paper towel–lined plate to drain the excess fat. Mix Greek yogurt, cilantro, garlic powder, salt, and pepper in a bowl. Serve the patties with yogurt sauce.

516.   Plant-Based Lentil Burgers

Serves: 4 | Ready in about: 25 minutes

1 cup cremini mushrooms, finely chopped
1 cup cooked green lentils
½ cup Greek yogurt
½ lemon, zested and juiced
½ tsp garlic powder

½ tsp dried oregano
1 tbsp fresh cilantro, chopped
Salt to taste
3 tbsp extra-virgin olive oil

¼ tsp tbsp white miso
¼ tsp smoked paprika
¼ cup flour

Pour ½ cup of lentils into your blender and puree partially until smooth, but with many whole lentils still remaining. In a small bowl, mix the yogurt, lemon zest and juice, garlic powder, oregano, cilantro, and salt. Season and set aside. In a medium bowl, mix the mushrooms, 2 tablespoons of olive oil, miso, and paprika. Stir in all the lentils. Add in flour and stir until the mixture everything is well incorporated. Shape the mixture into patties about ¾-inch thick. Warm the remaining olive oil in a skillet over medium heat. Fry the patties until browned and crisp, about 3 minutes. Turn and fry on the second side. Serve with the reserved yogurt mixture.

517. Broccoli Florets with Yogurt Sauce

Serves: 4 | Ready in about: 25 minutes

2 tbsp olive oil
1 head broccoli, cut into florets

2 garlic cloves, minced
½ cup Greek yogurt

Salt and black pepper to taste
2 tsp fresh dill, chopped

Warm olive oil in a pan over medium heat and sauté broccoli, salt, and pepper for 12 minutes. Mix Greek yogurt, dill, and garlic in a small bowl. Drizzle the broccoli with the sauce.

518. Nutty Yogurt-Drizzled Steamed Beetroots

Serves: 4 | Ready in about: 30 min + chilling time

¼ cup extra virgin olive oil
1 lb beetroots, cut into wedges
1 cup Greek yogurt

3 spring onions, sliced
5 dill pickles, finely chopped
2 garlic cloves, minced

2 tbsp fresh parsley, chopped
1 oz mixed nuts, crushed
Salt to taste

In a pot over medium heat, insert a steamer basket and pour in 1 cup of water. Place in the beetroots and steam for 10-15 minutes until tender. Remove to a plate and let cool. In a bowl, combine the pickles, spring onions, garlic, salt, 3 tbsp of olive oil, Greek yogurt, and nuts and mix well. Spread the yogurt mixture on a serving plate and arrange the beetroot wedges on top. Drizzle with the remaining olive oil and top with parsley. Serve and enjoy!

519. Charred Eggplant "Steaks" with Sauce

Serves: 6 | Ready in about: 20 minutes

2 lb eggplants, sliced lengthways
6 tbsp olive oil
5 garlic cloves, minced
1 tsp dried oregano

½ tsp red pepper flakes
½ cup Greek yogurt
3 tbsp chopped fresh parsley
1 tsp grated lemon zest

2 tsp lemon juice
1 tsp ground cumin
Salt and black pepper to taste

In a bowl, whisk half of the olive oil, yogurt, parsley, lemon zest and juice, cumin, and salt; set aside until ready to serve. Preheat your grill to High. Rub the eggplant steaks with the remaining olive oil, oregano, salt, and pepper. Grill them for 4-6 minutes per side until browned and tender; transfer to a serving platter. Drizzle yogurt sauce over eggplant.

520. Timeless Pasta with Feta Cheese

Serves: 4 | Ready in about: 20 minutes

2 tbsp extra-virgin olive oil
20 Kalamata olives, chopped
¼ cup fresh oregano, chopped
4 garlic cloves, minced

2 anchovy fillets, chopped
¼ tsp red pepper flakes
3 tbsp capers
3 (14-oz) cans diced tomatoes

8 oz fettuccine pasta
2 tbsp feta cheese, grated
Salt and black pepper to taste

Cook the fettuccine pasta according to pack instructions, drain and let it cool. Warm olive oil in a skillet over medium heat and cook garlic and red flakes for 2 minutes. Add in capers, anchovies, olives, salt, and pepper and cook for another 2-3 minutes until the anchovies melt into the oil. Blend tomatoes in a food processor. Pour into the skillet and stir-fry for 5 minutes. Mix in oregano and pasta. Serve garnished with feta cheese.

521. Fiery Grilled Eggplant Discs

Serves: 4 | Ready in about: 25 minutes

1 cup roasted peppers, chopped
4 tbsp olive oil
2 eggplants, cut into rounds
12 Kalamata olives, chopped

1 tsp hot red pepper flakes, crushed
Salt and black pepper to taste
2 tbsp basil, chopped

2 tbsp Halloumi cheese, grated

Combine roasted peppers, half of the olive oil, olives, hot red pepper flakes, salt, and pepper in a bowl. Rub each eggplant slice with the remaining olive oil and salt. Grill them on the preheated grill for 14 minutes on both sides. Remove to a platter. Distribute the pepper mixture across the eggplant rounds. Top with basil and Halloumi cheese.

522.   Classic Meatless Moussaka

Serves: 4 | Ready in about: 80 minutes

2 tbsp olive oil
1 yellow onion, chopped
2 garlic cloves, chopped
2 eggplants, halved
½ cup vegetable broth

Salt and black pepper to taste
½ tsp paprika
¼ cup parsley, chopped
1 tsp basil, chopped
1 tsp hot sauce

1 tomato, chopped
2 tbsp tomato puree
6 Kalamata olives, chopped
½ cup feta cheese, crumbled

Preheat oven to 360 F. Remove the tender center part of the eggplants and chop it. Arrange the eggplant halves on a baking tray and drizzle with some olive oil. Roast for 35-40 minutes.

Warm the remaining olive oil in a skillet over medium heat and add eggplant flesh, onion, and garlic and sauté for 5 minutes until tender. Stir in the vegetable broth, salt, pepper, basil, hot sauce, paprika, tomato, and tomato puree. Lower the heat and simmer for 10-15 minutes. Once the eggplants are ready, remove them from the oven and fill them with the mixture. Top with Kalamata olives and feta cheese. Return to the oven and bake for 10-15 minutes. Sprinkle with parsley.

523.   Baked Zucchini Delight with Parsley & Olives

Serves: 6 | Ready in about: 1 hour 40 minutes

3 tbsp olive oil
1 (28-oz) can tomatoes, diced
2 lb zucchini, sliced
1 onion, chopped

Salt and black pepper to taste
3 garlic cloves, minced
¼ tsp dried oregano
¼ tsp red pepper flakes

10 Kalamata olives, chopped
2 tbsp fresh parsley, chopped

Preheat oven to 325 F. Warm the olive oil in a saucepan over medium heat. Sauté zucchini for about 3 minutes per side; transfer to a bowl. Stir-fry the onion and salt in the same saucepan for 3-5 minutes, stirring occasionally until the onion is soft and lightly golden. Stir in garlic, oregano, and pepper flakes and cook until fragrant, about 30 seconds.

Add in olives, tomatoes, salt, and pepper, bring to a simmer, and cook for about 10 minutes, stirring occasionally. Return the zucchini, cover, and transfer the pot to the oven. Bake for 10-15 minutes. Sprinkle with parsley and serve.

524.   Feta Cheese & Swiss Chard Couscous Medley

Serves: 4 | Ready in about: 20 minutes

2 tbsp olive oil
10 oz couscous

2 garlic cloves, minced
1 cup raisins

½ cup feta cheese, crumbled
1 bunch of Swiss chard, torn

In a bowl, place couscous and cover with hot water. Let sit covered for 10 minutes. Using a fork, fluff it. Warm the olive oil in a skillet over medium heat and sauté garlic for a minute. Stir in couscous, raisins, and chard. Top with feta.

525.   Couscous with Kale & Feta Cheese

Serves: 4 | Ready in about: 20 minutes

2 tbsp olive oil
1 cup couscous
1 cup kale, chopped

1 tbsp parsley, chopped
3 spring onions, chopped
1 cucumber, chopped

1 tsp allspice
½ lemon, juiced and zested
4 oz feta cheese, crumbled

In a bowl, place couscous and cover with hot water. Let sit for 10 minutes and fluff. Warm the olive oil in a skillet over medium heat and sauté onions and allspice for 3 minutes. Stir in the remaining ingredients and cook for 5-6 minutes.

526.   Tempting Stuffed Cherry Tomatoes

Serves: 4 | Ready in about: 10 minutes

2 tbsp olive oil
16 cherry tomatoes
1 tbsp lemon zest

½ cup feta cheese, crumbled
2 tbsp olive tapenade
¼ cup parsley, torn

Using a sharp knife, slice off the tops of the tomatoes and hollow out the insides. Combine olive oil, lemon zest, feta cheese, olive tapenade, and parsley in a bowl. Fill the cherry tomatoes with the feta mixture and arrange them on a plate.

527.   Feta-Stuffed Baked Zucchini Boats

Serves: 4 | Ready in about: 50 minutes

2 zucchini, halved lengthwise
2 tbsp olive oil
1 egg

2 garlic cloves, minced
2 tbsp oregano, chopped
Salt and black pepper to taste

1 cup feta cheese, crumbled

Preheat the oven to 390 F. Line a baking sheet with parchment paper. Scoop the flesh from the zucchini halves to make shells and place them on the baking sheet. In a bowl, mix egg, feta cheese, garlic, oregano, salt, pepper, and olive oil and bake for 40 minutes. Remove to a plate and serve.

528.   Feta-Topped Baked Beetroot Fries

Serves: 4 | Ready in about: 40 minutes

1 cup olive oil
1 cup feta cheese, crumbled

2 beets, sliced
Salt and black pepper to taste

1/3 cup balsamic vinegar

Preheat the oven to 340 F. Line a baking sheet with parchment paper. Arrange beet slices, salt, pepper, vinegar, and olive oil on the sheet and toss to combine. Bake for 30 minutes. Serve topped with feta cheese.

529.   Green Bean Quinoa

Serves: 4 | Ready in about: 30 minutes

2 tbsp olive oil
1 onion, chopped
2 garlic cloves, minced
1 cup quinoa, rinsed

1 lb asparagus, chopped
2 tbsp fresh parsley, chopped
2 tbsp lemon juice
1 tsp lemon zest, grated

½ lb green beans, trimmed and halved
Salt and black pepper to taste
½ lb cherry tomatoes, halved

Heat olive oil in a pot over medium heat and sauté onion and garlic for 3 minutes until soft. Stir in quinoa for 1-2 minutes. Pour in 2 cups of water and season with salt and pepper. Bring to a bowl and reduce the heat. Simmer for 5 minutes. Stir in green beans and asparagus and cook for another 10 minutes. Remove from the heat and mix in cherry tomatoes, lemon juice and lemon zest. Top with parsley and serve.

530.   Hot Collard Green Oats with Halloumi

Serves: 4 | Ready in about: 15 minutes

2 tbsp olive oil
2 cups collard greens, torn
½ cup black olives, sliced
1 cup rolled oats

2 tomatoes, diced
2 spring onions, chopped
1 tsp garlic powder
½ tsp hot paprika

A pinch of salt
2 tbsp fresh parsley, chopped
1 tbsp lemon juice
½ cup halloumi cheese, grated

Put 2 cups of water in a pot over medium heat. Bring to a boil, then lower the heat, and add the rolled oats. Cook for 4-5 minutes. Mix in tomatoes, spring onions, hot paprika, garlic powder, salt, collard greens, black olives, parsley, lemon juice, and olive oil. Cook for another 5 minutes. Ladle into bowls and top with halloumi cheese. Serve warm.

531.   Ridiculously Easy Bean with Olives

Serves: 6 | Ready in about: 15 minutes

1 lb green beans, trimmed
1 red onion, thinly sliced
2 tbsp marjoram, chopped
¼ cup black olives, chopped

½ cup canned cannellini beans
½ cup canned chickpeas
2 tbsp extra-virgin olive oil
½ cup balsamic vinegar

½ tsp dried oregano
Salt and black pepper to taste

Steam the green beans for about 2 minutes or until just tender. Drain and place them in an ice-water bath. Drain thoroughly and pat them dry with paper towels. Put them in a large bowl and toss with the remaining ingredients.

SIDES, SAUCES & SPICES

532.   Cheesy Pepper-Stuffed Tomatoes

Serves: 2 | Ready in about: 35 minutes

½ lb mixed bell peppers, chopped
1 tbsp olive oil
4 tomatoes
2 garlic cloves, minced

½ cup diced onion
1 tbsp chopped oregano
1 tbsp chopped basil

1 cup shredded halloumi
1 tbsp grated Halloumi cheese
Salt and black pepper to taste

Preheat oven to 370 F. Cut the tops of the tomatoes and scoop out the pulp. Chop the pulp and set aside. Arrange the tomatoes on a lined parchment paper baking sheet.

Warm the olive oil in a pan over medium heat. Add in garlic, onion, basil, bell peppers, and oregano, and cook for 5 minutes. Sprinkle with salt and pepper. Remove from the heat and mix in tomato pulp and halloumi cheese. Divide the mixture between the tomatoes and top with Halloumi cheese. Bake for 20 minutes or until the cheese melts.

533.   Zesty Red Pepper & Olive Spread

Serves: 6 | Ready in about: 10 minutes

¼ tsp dried thyme
1 tbsp capers
½ cup pitted green olives

1 roasted red pepper, chopped
1 tsp balsamic vinegar
2/3 cup soft bread crumbs

2 cloves garlic, minced
½ tsp red pepper flakes
1/3 cup extra-virgin olive oil

Place all the ingredients, except for the olive oil, in a food processor and blend until chunky. With the machine running, slowly pour in the olive oil until it is well combined. Refrigerate or serve at room temperature.

534.   Garlicky Broccoli Stir Fry

Serves: 4 | Ready in about: 15 minutes

1 red bell pepper, cut into chunks
3 tbsp olive oil
2 garlic cloves, minced

½ tsp red pepper flakes
½ lb broccoli florets
Salt to taste

2 tsp lemon juice
1 tbsp anchovy paste

Warm the olive oil in a skillet over medium heat. Add the broccoli, garlic, and red pepper flakes and stir briefly for 3-4 minutes until the florets turn bright green. Season with salt. Add 2 tbsp of water and let broccoli cook for another 2–3 minutes. Stir in the red bell pepper, lemon juice, and anchovy paste and cook for 1 more minute. Serve.

535.   Feta Sweet Potato Mash

Serves: 4 | Ready in about: 30 minutes

¼ cup feta cheese, grated
¼ cup olive oil

½ tsp ground nutmeg
1 ¼ lb sweet potatoes, cubed

Salt and black pepper to taste
1 tbsp fresh chives, chopped

Place the potatoes in a pot over high heat and cover with water. Bring to a boil, then lower the heat and simmer covered for 20 minutes. Drain the potatoes and back to the pot. Stir in feta cheese, olive oil, nutmeg, salt, and pepper. Mash them with a potato masher until smooth. Sprinkle with chives.

536.   Cauliflower Mash with Fragrant Cumin

Serves: 4 | Ready in about: 25 minutes

2 tbsp butter
¼ cup grated feta cheese
4 cups cauliflower florets

¼ cup milk
2 tbsp wholegrain mustard
1 tsp ground cumin

½ crushed dry, hot pepper
Salt and black pepper to taste

Boil the cauliflower in a pot of salted water for 10 minutes. Drain and place in a large bowl. Add in milk, butter, cheese, mustard, cumin, salt, and pepper. Mash until smooth with a potato masher. Top with crushed hot peppers.

537. Beloved Green Bean Stir-Fry

Serves: 4 | Ready in about: 15 minutes

1 tbsp olive oil
1 tbsp butter
1 fennel bulb, sliced

1 red onion, sliced
4 cloves garlic, pressed
1 lb green beans, steamed

½ tsp dried oregano
2 tbsp balsamic vinegar
Salt and black pepper to taste

Warm the butter and olive oil in a saucepan over medium heat. Add in the onion and garlic and sauté for 3 minutes. Stir in oregano, fennel, balsamic vinegar, salt, and pepper. Stir-fry for another 6-8 minutes and add in the green beans; cook for 2-3 minutes. Adjust the seasoning and serve.

538. Arugula & Zucchini Stuffed Mushrooms

Serves: 4 | Ready in about: 65 minutes

4 portobello mushrooms, stems removed
2 tbsp olive oil
2 cups arugula
¼ cup chopped fresh basil
1 onion, finely chopped

1 zucchini, chopped
¼ tsp dried thyme
⅛ tsp red pepper flakes
2 garlic cloves, minced

½ cup grated Halloumi cheese
Salt and black pepper to taste

Preheat oven to 350 F. Warm olive oil in a skillet over medium heat and sauté onion, arugula, zucchini, thyme, salt, pepper, and red flakes for 5 minutes. Stir in garlic and sauté for 30 seconds. Turn the heat off. Mix in basil and scoop into the mushroom caps and arrange them on a baking sheet. Top with Halloumi cheese and bake for 30-40 minutes, until mushrooms are nice and soft and the cheese is melted.

539. Cheesy Olive Tapenade Flatbread

Serves: 4 | Ready in about: 35 min + chilling time

For the flatbread
2 tbsp olive oil
2 ½ tsp dry yeast
For the tapenade
2 roasted red pepper slices, chopped
¼ cup extra-virgin olive oil
1 cup green olives, chopped
10 black olives, chopped

1 ½ cups all-purpose flour
¾ tsp salt

1 tbsp capers
1 garlic clove, minced
1 tbsp chopped basil leaves

½ cup lukewarm water
¼ tsp sugar

1 tbsp chopped fresh oregano
¼ cup goat cheese, crumbled

Combine lukewarm water, sugar, and yeast in a bowl. Set aside covered for 5 minutes. Mix the flour and salt in a bowl. Pour in the yeast mixture and mix. Knead until you obtain a ball. Place the dough onto a floured surface and knead for 5 minutes until soft. Put the dough in an oiled bowl and cover it. Leave the dough to rise until it has doubled in size, about 40 minutes.

Preheat oven to 400 F. Cut the dough into 4 balls and roll each one out to a ½ inch thickness. Bake for 5 minutes. In a blender, mix black olives, roasted pepper, green olives, capers, garlic, oregano, basil, and olive oil for 20 seconds until coarsely chopped. Spread the olive tapenade on the flatbreads and top with goat cheese to serve.

540. Broccoli & Cheese Quiche

Serves: 4 | Ready in about: 45 minutes

1 tsp Mediterranean seasoning
3 eggs
½ cup heavy cream

3 tbsp olive oil
1 red onion, chopped
2 garlic cloves, minced

2 oz halloumi, shredded
1 lb broccoli, cut into florets

Preheat oven to 320 F. Warm the oil in a pan over medium heat. Sauté the onion and garlic until just tender and fragrant. Add in the broccoli and continue to cook until crisp-tender for about 4 minutes. Spoon the mixture into a greased casserole dish. Beat the eggs with heavy cream and Mediterranean seasoning. Spoon this mixture over the broccoli layer. Bake for 18-20 minutes. Top with the shredded cheese. Broil for 5 to 6 minutes or until hot and bubbly on the top.

541. Homemade Marinara Sauce

Serves: 6 | Ready in about: 45 minutes

2 (14-oz) cans crushed tomatoes with their juices

1 tsp dried oregano	1 red bell pepper, chopped	2 tbsp chopped rosemary
2 tbsp + ¼ cup olive oil	4 garlic cloves, minced	1 tsp red pepper flakes
2 tbsp butter	Salt and black pepper to taste	
1 small onion, diced	½ cup thinly sliced basil	

Warm 2 tablespoons olive oil and butter in a large skillet over medium heat. Add the onion, garlic, and red pepper and sauté for about 5 minutes until tender. Season with salt and pepper. Reduce the heat to low and add the tomatoes and their juices, remaining olive oil, oregano, half of the basil, rosemary, and red pepper flakes. Bring to a simmer and cover. Cook for 50-60 minutes. Blitz the sauce with an immersion blender and sprinkle with the remaining basil.

542. Zucchini Pasta in Tomato-Mushroom Sauce

Serves: 4 | Ready in about: 25 minutes

1 lb oyster mushrooms, chopped	1 tsp Mediterranean sauce	2 garlic cloves, minced
2 tbsp olive oil	1 yellow onion, minced	2 zucchini, spiralized
1 cup chicken broth	1 cup pureed tomatoes	

Warm the olive oil in a saucepan over medium heat and sauté the zoodles for 1-2 minutes; reserve. Sauté the onion and garlic in the same saucepan for 2-3 minutes. Add in the mushrooms and continue to cook for 2 to 3 minutes until they release liquid. Add in the remaining ingredients and cover the pan; let it simmer for 10 minutes longer until everything is cooked through. Top the zoodles with the prepared mushroom sauce and serve.

543. Herbed Garlic Butter Spread

Serves: 4 | Ready in about: 5 minutes

½ cup butter, softened	2 tsp fresh rosemary, chopped	Salt to taste
1 garlic clove, finely minced	1 tsp marjoram, chopped	

Blend the butter, garlic, rosemary, marjoram, and salt in your food processor until the mixture is well combined, smooth, and creamy, scraping down the sides as necessary. Scrape the butter mixture with a spatula into a glass container and cover. Store in the refrigerator for up to 30 days.

544. Spicy Green Chili & Herb Sauce

Serves: 6 | Ready in about: 15 minutes

6 tbsp extra-virgin olive oil	¼ tsp ground cardamom	2 tbsp fresh parsley leaves
¼ tsp ground fennel seeds	¼ tsp salt	2 green chiles, chopped
½ tsp ground coriander	¼ tsp ground cloves	2 garlic cloves, minced
¼ tsp ground cumin	2 tbsp fresh cilantro leaves	

Place the olive oil, fennel seeds, coriander, cumin, cardamom, salt, and cloves in a microwave-safe bowl. Cover and microwave for about 30 seconds until fragrant. Leave to cool at room temperature. Blitz the oil-spice mixture, cilantro, parsley, chiles, and garlic in your food processor until coarse paste forms, scraping downside of the bowl as needed. Store in an airtight container in the refrigerator for up to 2-3 days.

545. Roasted Asparagus & Red Onion Side Dish

Serves: 4 | Ready in about: 20 minutes

2 tbsp olive oil	1 tsp garlic powder	Salt and black pepper to taste
1 ½ lb asparagus spears	1 red onion, sliced	

Preheat oven to 390 F. Brush the asparagus with olive oil. Toss with garlic powder, salt, and black pepper. Roast in the oven for about 15 minutes. Top the roasted asparagus with the red onion. Serve and enjoy!

546. Cheesy Zucchini Strips

Serves: 4 | Ready in about: 30 minutes

4 zucchini, quartered lengthwise
2 tbsp olive oil
½ cup grated halloumi cheese

1 tbsp dried dill
¼ tsp garlic powder

Salt and black pepper to taste

Preheat oven to 350 F. Combine zucchini and olive oil in a bowl. Mix cheese, salt, garlic powder, dill, and pepper in a bowl. Add in zucchini and toss to combine. Arrange the zucchini fingers on a lined baking sheet and bake for about 20 minutes until golden Set oven to broil and broil for 2 minutes until crispy. Serve and enjoy!

547. Vegetarian Cream Sauce

Serves: 6 | Ready in about: 25 minutes

3 tbsp olive oil
½ zucchini, chopped
1 celery stalk, chopped
1 red bell pepper, sliced

2 tomatoes, chopped
3 garlic cloves, minced
½ tsp dried basil
½ cup baby spinach

1 cup heavy cream
¼ cup chopped fresh parsley

Warm the olive oil in a large skillet over medium heat. Add the zucchini, celery, bell pepper, tomatoes, and garlic and sauté for 8-10 minutes until the vegetables are softened. Add the basil and cook for 1 minute. Stir in spinach and cook until wilted, about 3 minutes. Add the cream and mix well and cook for about 4 minutes. Top with parsley.

548. Classic Tahini Sauce

Serves: 4 | Ready in about: 5 minutes

¼ tsp ground cumin
½ cup tahini

¼ cup lemon juice
2 garlic cloves, minced

Salt and black pepper to taste
1 tbsp parsley, chopped

Place the tahini, lemon juice, and garlic, ½ cup of water in a bowl and whisk until combined. Season with salt and pepper to taste. Let sit for about 30 minutes until flavors meld. Refrigerate for up to 3 days. Serve topped with parsley.

549. Cherry Tomato & Fennel Roast

Serves: 4 | Ready in about: 35 minutes

¼ cup olive oil
20 cherry tomatoes, halved

2 fennel bulbs, cut into wedges
10 black olives, sliced

1 lemon, cut into wedges
Salt and black pepper to taste

Preheat oven to 425 F. Combine fennel, olive oil, tomatoes, salt, and pepper in a bowl. Place in a baking pan and roast in the oven for about 25 minutes until golden. Top with olives and serve with lemon wedges on the side.

550. Spinach Side with Pine Nuts & Raisins

Serves: 4 | Ready in about: 10 minutes

2 tbsp olive oil
4 cups fresh baby spinach

1 garlic clove, minced
2 tbsp raisins, soaked

2 tbsp toasted pine nuts
Salt and black pepper to taste

Warm olive oil in a pan over medium heat and sauté spinach and garlic for 3 minutes until the spinach wilts. Mix in raisins, pine nuts, salt, and pepper and cook for 3 minutes.

551. Fresh Herb Yogurt Sauce

Serves: 4 | Ready in about: 5 minutes

¼ tsp fresh lemon juice
1 cup plain yogurt

2 tbsp fresh cilantro, minced
2 tbsp fresh mint, minced

1 garlic clove, minced
Salt and black pepper to taste

Place the lemon juice, yogurt, cilantro, mint, and garlic together in a bowl and mix well. Season with salt and pepper. Let sit for about 30 minutes to blend the flavors. Store in an airtight container in the refrigerator for up to 2-3 days.

552. Infused Olive Oil with Rosemary & Garlic

Serves: 4 | Ready in about: 35 minutes

Salt and black pepper to taste
1 cup extra-virgin olive oil

4 large garlic cloves, smashed
4 sprigs rosemary

Warm the olive oil in a medium skillet over low heat and sauté garlic and rosemary sprigs for 30-40 minutes, until fragrant and garlic is very tender, stirring occasionally. Don't let the oil get too hot, or the garlic will burn and become bitter. Remove from the heat and leave to cool slightly. Using a slotted spoon, remove the garlic and rosemary and pour the oil into a glass container. Use cooled.

553. Velvety Mushroom Sauce

Serves: 4 | Ready in about: 15 minutes

1 cup cremini mushrooms, chopped
2 tbsp olive oil
1 small onion, chopped
2 garlic cloves, minced

3 tbsp butter
½ cup white wine
½ cup vegetable broth

1 cup heavy cream
2 tbsp parsley, chopped

Heat the olive oil in a pan over medium. Add the onion and garlic and sauté until the onion is translucent, 3 minutes. Add the butter and mushrooms and cook for 5-7 minutes until the mushrooms are tender. Pour in the wine and scrape up any browned bits from the bottom of the pan. Simmer for 3-4 minutes. Add the vegetable broth and simmer for 5 minutes until the sauce reduces by about three-quarters. Add the heavy cream and simmer for 2-3 minutes. Sprinkle with parsley. Serve and enjoy!

554. Lemony Greek Olive Oil Dressing (Ladolemono)

Serves: 4 | Ready in about: 10 minutes

3 tbsp extra-virgin olive oil
¼ tsp grated lemon zest
1 tbsp lemon juice

½ tsp Greek yogurt
½ tsp yellow mustard
Salt and black pepper to taste

¼ tsp honey

Place the lemon zest and juice, yogurt, mustard, salt, pepper, and honey in a bowl and blend until smooth. Whisking constantly, slowly drizzle in oil until emulsified. Store in an airtight container in the refrigerator for up to 2 weeks.

555. Refreshing Lemon Yogurt Sauce

Serves: 4 | Ready in about: 5 minutes

1 cup plain yogurt
1 tbsp fresh chives, chopped

½ lemon, zested and juiced
1 garlic clove, minced

Salt and black pepper to taste

Place the yogurt, lemon zest and juice, and garlic in a bowl and mix well. Season with salt and pepper. Let sit for about 30 minutes to blend the flavors. Store in an airtight container in the refrigerator for up to 2-3 days. Serve topped with chives.

556. Creamy Walnut-Cucumber Yogurt Sauce

Serves: 4 | Ready in about: 10 minutes

1 cucumber, peeled and shredded
1 tbsp walnuts, chopped
2 tbsp extra-virgin olive oil

1 cup Greek yogurt
2 tbsp minced fresh dill

1 garlic clove, minced
Salt and black pepper to taste

Place the walnuts, olive oil, yogurt, cucumber, and garlic in a bowl and mix well. Season with salt and pepper. Let sit for about 30 minutes to blend the flavors. Store in an airtight container in the refrigerator for up to 2-3 days. Top with dill.

SNACKS

557.   Peinirli (Greek Pizza)

Serves: 4 | Ready in about: 25 minutes

2 cups halloumi cheese, shredded
1 pizza crust
1 cup marinara sauce

½ tsp dried Greek oregano
1 cup feta cheese, crumbled
½ tsp garlic powder

6 Kalamata olives, sliced

Preheat oven to 400 F. Spread the pizza crust evenly with marinara sauce. Sprinkle with oregano and garlic powder. Scatter the feta cheese and olives over the sauce and top with halloumi cheese. Bake for 10–16 minutes or until the crust is golden. Serve sliced, and enjoy!

558.   Traditional Greek Potato Skins

Serves: 4 | Ready in about: 1 hour 10 minutes

2 tbsp extra-virgin olive oil
1 cup feta cheese, crumbled
1 lb potatoes
½ cup Greek yogurt

2 spring onions, chopped
3 sundried tomatoes, chopped
6 Kalamata olives, chopped
½ tsp dried dill

1 tsp Greek oregano
2 tbsp halloumi cheese, grated
Salt and black pepper to taste

Preheat oven to 400 F. Pierce the potatoes in several places with a fork. Wrap in aluminum foil and bake in the oven for 45-50 minutes until tender. Let cool. Split the cooled potatoes lengthwise and scoop out some of the flesh. Put the flesh in a bowl and mash with a fork.

Add in the spring onions, sun-dried tomatoes, olives, dill, oregano, feta cheese, and yogurt and stir. Season with salt and pepper. Fill the potato shells with the feta mixture and top with halloumi cheese. Transfer the boats to a baking sheet and place under the broiler for 5 minutes until the top is golden and crisp. Serve right away.

559.   Creamy White Bean Dip

Serves: 6 | Ready in about: 5 minutes

¼ cup extra-virgin olive oil
1 lemon, zested and juiced
1 (14-oz) can white beans

2 garlic cloves, minced
¼ tsp ground cumin
2 tbsp Greek oregano, chopped

1 tsp stone-ground mustard
Salt to taste

In a food processor, blend all the ingredients, except for the oregano, until smooth. Top with Greek oregano. Serve.

560.   Greek Yogurt Dip on Grilled Pita

Serves: 6 | Ready in about: 10 minutes

1/3 cup olive oil
2 cups Greek yogurt
2 tbsp toasted ground pistachios

Salt and white pepper to taste
2 tbsp mint, chopped
3 kalamata olives, chopped

¼ cup Greek seasoning
3 pitta bread, cut into triangles

Mix the yogurt, pistachios, salt, pepper, mint, olives, Greek spice, and olive oil in a bowl. Grill the pitta bread until golden, about 5-6 minutes. Serve with the yogurt spread.

561.   Greek Cucumber Yogurt Dip

Serves: 6 | Ready in about: 10 min + chilling time

1 large cucumber, grated
1 garlic clove, minced
1 cup Greek yogurt

1 tsp chopped fresh dill
1 tsp chopped fresh parsley
Salt and black pepper to taste

¼ cup ground walnuts

In a colander over the sink, squeeze the excess liquid out of the grated cucumber. Combine the yogurt, cucumber, garlic, salt, dill, and pepper in a bowl. Keep in the fridge covered for 2 hours. Serve topped with ground walnuts and parsley.

562.   Flavorful Greek-Style Wraps

Serves: 2 | Ready in about: 10 minutes

2 cooked chicken breasts, shredded
2 tbsp roasted peppers, chopped
1 cup baby kale

2 whole-wheat tortillas
2 oz provolone cheese, grated
1 tomato, chopped

10 Kalamata olives, sliced
1 red onion, chopped

In a bowl, mix all the ingredients except for the tortillas. Distribute the mixture across the tortillas and wrap them.

563.   Roasted Sweet Potatoes with Chickpeas

Serves: 4 | Ready in about: 30 minutes

4 sweet potatoes, halved lengthways
2 tbsp olive oil
1 tbsp butter
1 (15-oz) can s
¼ tsp dried thyme

Salt and black pepper to taste
1 tsp paprika
½ tsp garlic powder
1 cup spinach

1 cup Greek-style yogurt
2 tsp hot sauce

Preheat oven to 360 F. Drizzle the sweet potatoes with some oil. Place, cut-side down, in a lined baking tray and bake for 8-10 minutes. In a bowl, mix chickpeas with the remaining olive oil, paprika, thyme, and garlic powder. Pour them onto the other end of the baking tray and roast for 20 minutes alongside the sweet potatoes, stirring the chickpeas once.

Melt the butter in a pan over medium heat and stir-fry the spinach and 1 tbsp of water for 3-4 minutes until the spinach wilts. Stir in the roasted chickpeas. Mix the yogurt with hot sauce in a small bowl. Top the sweet potato halves with chickpeas and spinach and serve with hot yogurt on the side.

564.   Savory Roasted Butternut Squash with Tahini & Feta

Serves: 6 | Ready in about: 50 minutes

3 lb butternut squash, peeled, halved lengthwise, and seeded
3 tbsp olive oil
Salt and black pepper to taste
2 tbsp fresh thyme, chopped

1 tbsp tahini
1 ½ tsp lemon juice
1 tsp honey

1 oz feta cheese, crumbled
¼ cup pistachios, chopped

Preheat oven to 425 F. Slice the squash halves crosswise into ½-inch-thick pieces. Toss them with 2 tablespoons of olive oil, salt, and pepper and arrange them on a greased baking sheet in an even layer. Roast for 45-50 minutes or until golden and tender. Transfer squash to a serving platter. Whisk tahini, lemon juice, honey, remaining oil, and salt together in a bowl. Drizzle squash with tahini dressing and sprinkle with feta, pistachios, and thyme. Serve and enjoy!

565.   Crispy Sweet Potatoes Sheet Pan

Serves: 4 | Ready in about: 70 minutes

4 sweet potatoes, pricked with a fork
4 tbsp olive oil
1 cup arugula
1 garlic clove, minced

1 red onion, sliced
1 lemon, juiced and zested
2 tbsp dill, chopped

2 tbsp Greek yogurt
2 tbsp tahini paste
Salt and black pepper to taste

Preheat oven to 340 F. Line a baking sheet with parchment paper. Arrange potatoes on the sheet and bake for 1 hour. Peel them and slice into wedges. Remove to a bowl and combine with garlic, olive oil, onion, arugula, lemon juice, lemon zest, dill, Greek yogurt, tahini paste, salt, and pepper.

566.   Creamy Garlic-Yogurt Dip with Walnuts

Serves: 4 | Ready in about: 5 minutes

2 cups Greek yogurt
3 garlic cloves, minced

¼ cup dill, chopped
1 green onion, chopped

¼ cup walnuts, chopped
Salt and black pepper to taste

Combine garlic, yogurt, dill, walnuts, salt, and pepper in a bowl. Serve topped with green onion.

567.   Silky Trout Spread

Serves: 4 | Ready in about: 5 minutes

2 tbsp olive oil
1 cup Greek yogurt

2 oz smoked trout, flaked
1 tbsp lemon juice

2 tbsp chives, chopped
Salt and black pepper to taste

Place trout, lemon juice, yogurt, chives, salt, pepper, and olive oil in a bowl and toss to combine. Serve with crackers.

568.   Fluffy Whipped Feta Spread

Serves: 6 | Ready in about: 10 minutes

4 tbsp Greek yogurt
½ lb feta cheese, crumbled
3 cloves garlic, pressed

2 tbsp extra-virgin olive oil
2 tbsp finely chopped dill
1 tsp dried oregano

Black pepper to taste

Combine feta, yogurt, garlic, olive oil, and oregano in your food processor. Pulse until well combined. Keep in the fridge until required. To serve, spoon into a dish and sprinkle with dill and black pepper.

569.   Hummus & Tomato Filled Cucumbers

Serves: 2 | Ready in about: 5 minutes

1 cucumber, halved lengthwise
½ cup hummus

5 cherry tomatoes, halved

2 tbsp fresh basil, minced

Using a paring knife, scoop most of the seeds from the inside of each cucumber piece to make a cup, being careful not to cut all the way through. Fill each cucumber cup with about 1 tablespoon of hummus. Top with cherry tomatoes and basil.

570.   Mouthwatering Baby Artichoke Meze

Serves: 4 | Ready in about: 5 minutes

1 (14-oz) jar roasted red peppers
8 canned artichoke hearts
1 (16-oz) can garbanzo beans

1 cup whole Kalamata olives
¼ cup balsamic vinegar

Salt to taste
1 lemon, zested

Slice the peppers and put them into a large bowl. Cut the artichoke hearts into quarters, and add them to the bowl. Add the garbanzo beans, olives, balsamic vinegar, lemon zest, and salt. Toss all the ingredients together. Serve chilled.

571.   Crispy Feta & Zucchini Rosti Cakes

Serves: 4 | Ready in about: 25 minutes

5 tbsp olive oil
1 lb zucchini, shredded
4 spring onions, chopped
Salt and black pepper to taste

4 oz feta cheese, crumbled
1 egg, lightly beaten
2 tbsp minced fresh dill
1 garlic clove, minced

¼ cup flour
Lemon wedges for serving

Preheat oven to 380 F. In a large bowl, mix the zucchini, spring onions, feta cheese, egg, dill, garlic, salt, and pepper. Sprinkle flour over the mixture and stir to incorporate. Warm the oil in a skillet over medium heat. Cook the rosti mixture in small flat fritters for about 4 minutes per side until crisp and golden on both sides, pressing with a fish slice as they cook. Serve with lemon wedges.

572.   Carrot Medley with Balsamic Drizzle & Feta

Serves: 4 | Ready in about: 40 minutes

2 tbsp olive oil
1 pound baby carrots

3 tbsp balsamic vinegar
½ cup feta cheese, crumbled

½ red hot pepper, sliced
Salt and black pepper to taste

Preheat oven to 425 F. Combine carrots, salt, olive oil, and pepper in a bowl. Arrange them on a baking tray and drizzle with honey; cook for 25-30 minutes until the carrots are golden. Mix the carrots with vinegar and top with feta.

573.   Skordalia Grilled Halloumi Cheese

Serves: 2 | Ready in about: 10 minutes

1 tbsp olive oil
3 oz Halloumi cheese

2 tsp skordalia sauce
1 tomato, sliced

Cut the cheese into 2 rectangular pieces. Heat a griddle pan over medium heat. Drizzle the halloumi slices with and add to the pan. After about 2 minutes, check to see if the cheese is golden on the bottom. Flip the slices, top each with skordalia sauce, and cook for another 2 minutes or until the second side is golden. Serve with tomato slices.

574.   Garlicky Roasted Feta Cheese

Serves: 4 | Ready in about: 30 minutes

4 feta cheese slices
2 tbsp olive oil
1 Roma tomato, thinly sliced

1 bell pepper, thinly sliced
¼ tsp red pepper flakes
¼ tsp dried oregano

¼ tsp garlic powder

Preheat oven to 400 F. Brush the feta slices with some olive oil and arrange them on a small baking dish. Top with tomato and pepper slices. Drizzle with the remaining oil and sprinkle red pepper flakes, oregano, and garlic powder over vegetables. Cover the baking dish tightly with foil and bake for 20 minutes. Serve immediately.

575.   Feta-Topped Vegetable Gratin

Serves: 6 | Ready in about: 30 minutes

2 tbsp olive oil
1 medium onion, sliced
1 green bell pepper, chopped

1 red bell pepper, chopped
½ lb feta cheese slice
1 tsp dried oregano

Black pepper to taste
½ lb cherry tomatoes, halved

Preheat oven to 350 F. Warm the olive oil in a pan over medium heat. Add and sauté the onion and bell peppers for 6-8 minutes until soft. Place the feta in a small greased baking dish and top with sautéed vegetables. Top with oregano and black pepper. Arrange the cherry tomatoes around the cheese. Cover with foil and bake for 13-15 minutes.

576.   Savory Zucchini Fritters with Feta Cheese

Serves: 4 | Ready in about: 20 minutes

1 cup feta cheese, crumbled
1 cup flour
½ tsp baking powder
½ tsp dried oregano
½ tsp dried basil

½ tsp dried rosemary
Salt and black pepper to taste
1 ½ cups zucchini, grated
1 egg
½ cup rice milk

1 tsp garlic, minced
2 tbsp scallions, sliced
4 tbsp olive oil

In a bowl, thoroughly combine the flour, baking powder, and spices. In a separate bowl, combine the zucchini, egg, milk, garlic, and scallions. Add the zucchini mixture to the dry flour mixture and stir to combine well. Warm the olive oil in a pan over medium heat. Cook each pancake for 2-3 minutes per side until golden brown. Serve topped with feta cheese.

577.   Tasty Cucumber Bite Canapés

Serves: 4 | Ready in about: 10 minutes

¼ cup extra-virgin olive oil
2 cucumbers
Salt to taste

6 basil leaves, chopped
1 tbsp fresh mint, minced
1 garlic clove, minced

¼ cup walnuts, ground
¼ cup feta cheese, crumbled
½ tsp paprika

Cut cucumbers lengthwise. With a spoon, remove the seeds and hollow out a shallow trough in each piece. Lightly salt each piece and set aside on a platter. In a bowl, combine the basil, mint, garlic, walnuts, feta, and olive oil and blend until smooth. Spoon the mixture into each cucumber half and sprinkle with paprika. Cut each half into 4 pieces. Serve.

DESSERTS

578.   Peach & Walnut Cake with Caramel Drizzle

Serves: 6 | Ready in about: 50 min + cooling time

¼ cup coconut oil
¼ cup olive oil
2 peeled peaches, chopped
½ cup raisins, soaked
1 cup plain flour
3 eggs

1 tbsp dark rum
¼ tsp ground cinnamon
1 tsp vanilla extract
1 ½ tsp baking powder
4 tbsp Greek yogurt
2 tbsp honey

1 cup brown sugar
4 tbsp walnuts, chopped
¼ caramel sauce
¼ tsp salt

Preheat the oven to 350 F. In a bowl, mix the flour, cinnamon, vanilla, baking powder, and salt. In another bowl, whisk the eggs with Greek yogurt using an electric mixer. Gently add in coconut and olive oil. Combine well. Put in rum, honey and sugar; stir to combine. Mix the wet ingredients with the dry mixture. Stir in peaches, raisins, and walnuts.

Pour the mixture into a greased baking pan and bake for 30-40 minutes until a knife inserted into the middle of the cake comes out clean. Remove from the oven and let sit for 10 minutes, then invert onto a wire rack to cool completely. Warm the caramel sauce in a pan and pour it over the cooled cake to serve.

579.   Layered Strawberry Parfait

Serves: 2 | Ready in about: 10 minutes

¾ cup Greek yogurt
1 tbsp cocoa powder

¼ cup strawberries, chopped
5 drops vanilla stevia

Combine cocoa powder, strawberries, yogurt, and stevia in a bowl. Serve immediately.

580.   Peach & Pecan Parfait

Serves: 2 | Ready in about: 15 minutes

1 ½ cups Greek yogurt
½ cup pecans

½ cup whole-grain rolled oats
1 tsp honey

1 peeled and chopped peach
Mint leaves for garnish

Preheat oven to 310 F. Pour the oats and pecans into a baking sheet and spread evenly. Toast for 11-13 minutes; set aside. Microwave honey for 30 seconds. Stir in the peach. Divide some peach mixture between 2 glasses, spread some yogurt on top, and sprinkle with the oat mixture. Repeat the layering process to exhaust the ingredients, finishing with the peach mixture. Serve with mint leaves.

581.   Chia Banana Walnut Oatmeal

Serves: 2 | Ready in about: 15 minutes

½ cup walnuts, chopped
1 banana, peeled and sliced

1 cup Greek yogurt
2 dates, pitted and chopped

1 cup rolled oats
2 tbsp chia seeds

Place banana, yogurt, dates, oats, and chia seeds in a bowl and blend until smooth. Let sit for 1 hour and spoon onto a bowl. Sprinkle with walnuts and serve.

582.   Yogurt & Banana Dessert Cups

Serves: 2 | Ready in about: 5 minutes

2 bananas, sliced
2 cups Greek yogurt

1 tsp cinnamon
3 tbsp honey

2 tbsp mint leaves, chopped

Divide the yogurt between 2 cups and top with banana slices, cinnamon, honey, and mint. Serve immediately.

583.   Apple Slices with Cardamom

Serves: 2 | Ready in about: 30 minutes

1 ½ tsp cardamom
½ tsp salt

4 peeled, cored apples, sliced
2 tbsp honey

2 tbsp milk

Preheat oven to 390 F. In a bowl, combine apple slices, salt, and ½ tsp of cardamom. Arrange them on a greased baking dish and cook for 20 minutes. Remove to a serving plate.

In the meantime, place milk, honey, and remaining cardamom in a pot over medium heat. Cook until simmer. Pour the sauce over the apples and serve immediately.

584.   Bulgur Bowl with Cherries & Almonds

Serves: 6 | Ready in about: 20 minutes

1 tbsp vanilla sugar
1 ½ cups bulgur
2 cups milk

1 cup water
½ tsp ground cinnamon
2 cups cherries, pitted

8 dried figs, chopped
½ cup almonds, chopped
¼ cup fresh mint, chopped

Combine the vanilla sugar, bulgur, milk, cinnamon, and 1 cup of water in a medium pot and stir to dissolve the sugar. Bring just to a boil. Cover, reduce the heat to medium-low, and simmer for 10 minutes or until the liquid is absorbed.

Turn off the heat and stir in the cherries, figs, and almonds. Cover and let the hot bulgur thaw the cherries and partially hydrate the figs. Top with mint. Serve chilled or hot.

585.   Assorted Fresh Fruit Cups

Serves: 4 | Ready in about: 10 minutes

1 cup orange juice
½ cup watermelon cubes
1 ½ cups grapes, halved

1 cup chopped cantaloupe
½ cup cherries, chopped
1 peach, chopped

½ tsp ground cinnamon

Combine watermelon cubes, grapes, cherries, cantaloupe, and peach in a bowl. Add in the orange juice and mix well. Share into dessert cups, dust with cinnamon, and serve.

586.   Frozen Yogurt Cups with Raspberry & Pecan Topping

Serves: 4 | Ready in about: 10 minutes

2 cups fresh raspberries
4 cups vanilla frozen yogurt

1 lime, zested
¼ cup chopped praline pecans

Divide the frozen yogurt into 4 dessert glasses. Top with raspberries, lime zest, and pecans. Serve immediately.

587.   Pecan Stuffed Apples

Serves: 4 | Ready in about: 55 minutes

2 tbsp brown sugar
4 apples, cored

¼ cup chopped pecans
1 tsp ground cinnamon

¼ tsp ground nutmeg
¼ tsp ground ginger

Preheat oven to 375 F. Arrange the apples cut-side up on a baking dish. Combine pecans, ginger, cinnamon, brown sugar, and nutmeg in a bowl. Scoop the mixture into the apples and bake for 35-40 minutes until golden brown.

588.   Walnut Carrot Cake

Serves: 6 | Ready in about: 55 minutes

½ cup vegetable oil
2 tsp vanilla extract

¼ cup maple syrup
6 eggs, beaten

½ cup flour
1 tsp baking powder

| 1 tsp baking soda | 1 tsp ground cinnamon | ½ cup chopped walnuts |
| ½ tsp ground nutmeg | ½ tsp salt | 3 cups finely grated carrots |

Preheat oven to 350 F. Mix the vanilla extract, maple syrup, and oil in a large bowl. Stir to mix well. Add in the eggs and whisk to combine. Set aside.

Combine the flour, baking powder, baking soda, nutmeg, cinnamon, and salt in a separate bowl. Stir to combine. Make a well in the center of the flour mixture, then pour the egg mixture into the well and stir well. Add in the walnuts and carrots and toss to mix well. Pour the mixture into a greased baking dish. Bake for 35-45 minutes or until puffed and the cake spring back. When lightly press with your fingers. Remove the cake from the oven. Allow to cool, then serve.

589.   Pomegranate Dark Chocolate Barks

Serves: 4 | Ready in about: 20 min + freezing time

| ½ cup quinoa | 1 cup dark chocolate chips | ½ cup pomegranate seeds |
| ½ tsp sea salt | ½ tsp mint extract | |

Toast the quinoa in a greased saucepan for 2-3 minutes, stirring frequently. Remove the pan from the stove and mix in the salt. Set aside 2 tablespoons of the toasted quinoa.

Microwave the chocolate for 1 minute. Stir until the chocolate is completely melted. Mix the toasted quinoa and mint extract into the melted chocolate. Line a large, rimmed baking sheet with parchment paper. Spread the chocolate mixture onto the sheet. Sprinkle the remaining 2 tablespoons of quinoa and pomegranate seeds, pressing with a spatula. Freeze the mixture for 10-15 minutes or until set. Remove and break into about 2-inch jagged pieces. Store in the refrigerator until ready to serve.

590.   Kid-Friendly Marzipan Bites

Serves: 6 | Ready in about: 10 minutes

| ½ cup avocado oil | ½ cup sugar |
| 1 ½ cup almond flour | 2 tsp almond extract |

Add the almond flour and sugar and pulse to your food processor until the mixture is ground. Add the almond extract and pulse until combined. With the processor running, stream in oil until the mixture starts to form a large ball. Turn off the food processor. With hands, form the marzipan into six 1-inch diameter balls. Press to hold the mixture together. Store in an airtight container in the refrigerator for up to 14 days.

591.   Pear & Pecan Crisp with Cinnamon Oats

Serves: 4 | Ready in about: 30 minutes

2 tbsp butter, melted	¼ cup maple syrup	½ tsp ground cinnamon
4 fresh pears, mashed	1 cup gluten-free rolled oats	¼ tsp salt
½ lemon, juiced and zested	½ cup chopped pecans	

Preheat oven to 350 F. Combine the pears, lemon juice and zest, and maple syrup in a bowl. Stir to mix well, then spread the mixture on a greased baking dish. Combine the remaining ingredients in a small bowl. Stir to mix well. Pour the mixture over the pear mixture. Bake for 20 minutes or until the oats are golden brown.

592.   Cinnamon Spiced Hot Chocolate

Serves: 4 | Ready in about: 15 minutes

| ¼ tsp cayenne pepper powder | 4 cups milk | ½ tsp ground cinnamon |
| 4 squares chocolate | 2 tsp sugar | ½ tsp salt |

Place milk and sugar in a pot over low heat and warm until it begins to simmer. Combine chocolate, cinnamon, salt, and cayenne pepper powder in a bowl. Slowly pour in enough hot milk to cover. Return the pot to the heat and lower the temperature. Stir until the chocolate has melted, then add the remaining milk and combine. Spoon into 4 cups and serve hot.

593. Vanilla Labneh Fruit Skewers

Serves: 4 | Ready in about: 15 min + straining time

2 cups plain yogurt
2 tbsp honey

1 tsp vanilla extract
A pinch of salt

2 mangoes, cut into chunks

Place a fine sieve lined with cheesecloth over a bowl and spoon the yogurt into the sieve. Allow the liquid to drain off for 12-24 hours hours. Transfer the strained yogurt to a bowl and mix in the honey, vanilla, and salt. Set it aside.

Heat your grill to medium-high. Thread the fruit onto skewers and grill for 2 minutes on each side until the fruit is softened and has grill marks on each side. Serve with labneh.

594. Mixed Berry Sorbet

Serves: 4 | Ready in about: 10 min + freezing time

1 tsp lemon juice
¼ cup honey

1 cup fresh strawberries
1 cup fresh raspberries

1 cup fresh blueberries

Bring 1 cup of water to a boil in a pot over high heat. Stir in honey until dissolved. Remove from the heat and mix in berries and lemon juice; let cool.

Once cooled, add the mixture to a food processor and pulse until smooth. Transfer to a shallow glass and freeze for 1 hour. Stir with a fork and freeze for 30 more minutes. Repeat a couple of times. Serve in dessert dishes.

595. Dark Chocolate Avocado Mousse

Serves: 4 | Ready in about: 10 min + freezing time

2 tbsp olive oil
8 oz dark chocolate, chopped

¼ cup milk
2 ripe avocados, deseeded

¼ cup honey
1 cup strawberries

Cook the chocolate, olive oil, and milk in a saucepan over medium heat for 3 minutes or until the chocolate melt, stirring constantly. Put the avocado in a food processor, then drizzle with honey and melted chocolate. Pulse to combine until smooth. Pour the mixture into a serving bowl, then sprinkle with strawberries. Chill for 30 minutes and serve.

596. Chocolate Chia Seed Pudding

Serves: 4 | Ready in about: 10 min + chilling time

2 cups heavy cream
¼ cup cocoa powder

1 tsp vanilla extract
½ ground cinnamon

½ cup chia seeds
2 tbsp chocolate shavings

Warm the heavy cream in a saucepan over medium heat to just below a simmer. Remove from the heat and allow to cool slightly. In a large bowl, combine the warmed heavy cream, cocoa powder, vanilla extract, cinnamon, and salt.

Blend using an immersion blender until the cocoa is well incorporated. Stir in the chia seeds and let sit for 15 minutes. Divide the mixture evenly between small glass bowls and refrigerate for at least 2 hours or until set. Serve chilled.

597. Classic Vanilla Cheesecake Squares

Serves: 6 | Ready in about: 55 min + chilling time

½ cup butter, melted
1 (12-oz) box butter cake mix
3 large eggs

1 cup maple syrup
1/8 tsp cinnamon
1 cup cream cheese

1 tsp vanilla extract

Preheat oven to 350 F. In a medium bowl, blend the cake mix, butter, cinnamon, and 1 egg. Then, pour the mixture into a greased baking pan. Mix together maple syrup, cream cheese, the remaining 2 eggs, and vanilla in a separate bowl and pour this gently over the first layer. Bake for 45-50 minutes. Remove and allow to cool. Cut into squares.

598. Orange Muffins

Serves: 6 | Ready in about: 35 minutes

½ cup olive oil
1 large egg
2 tbsp powdered sugar

1 tsp orange extract
1 orange, zested and juiced
1 cup flour

¾ tsp baking powder
½ tsp salt

Preheat oven to 350 F. In a large bowl, whisk together the egg and powdered sugar. Add the olive oil, orange extract, and orange zest and whisk to combine well. In a separate bowl, mix together the flour, baking powder, and salt. Add wet ingredients along with the orange juice and stir until just combined. Divide the batter evenly between 6 greased muffin cups and bake until a toothpick inserted in the center of the cupcake comes out clean, 20-25 minutes. Remove and let sit for 5 minutes in the tin, then transfer to a wire rack to cool completely. Serve and enjoy!

599. Greek-Style Orange Mug Cake

Serves: 2 | Ready in about: 15 minutes

2 tbsp butter, melted
6 tbsp flour
2 tbsp sugar
½ tsp baking powder

¼ tsp salt
1 tsp orange zest
1 egg
2 tbsp orange juice

2 tbsp milk
½ tsp orange extract
½ tsp vanilla extract
Orange slices for garnish

In a bowl, beat the egg, butter, orange juice, milk, orange extract, and vanilla extract. In another bowl, combine the flour, sugar, baking powder, salt, and orange zest. Pour the dry ingredients into the wet ingredients and stir to combine. Spoon the mixture into 2 mugs and microwave one at a time for 1-2 minutes. Garnish with orange slices.

600. No-Bake Walnut Date Oatmeal Bars

Serves: 6 | Ready in about: 30 minutes

¼ cup butter, melted
¼ cup honey
12 dates, pitted and chopped

1 tsp vanilla extract
½ cup rolled oats
¾ cup sultanas, soaked

1 cup walnuts, chopped
¼ cup pumpkin seeds

Place dates, vanilla, honey, oats, sultanas, butter, walnuts, and pumpkin seeds in a bowl and mix to combine. Transfer to a lined with parchment paper baking sheet and freeze for 30 minutes. Slice into bars and serve.

Printed in Great Britain
by Amazon